# The Politics of Diplomacy

## Edinburgh Studies in Anglo-American Relations

Series Editors: Steve Marsh and Alan P. Dobson

## Published and forthcoming titles

euppublishing.com/series/esar

# The Politics of Diplomacy

## US Presidents and the Northern Ireland Conflict, 1967–1998

James Cooper

EDINBURGH
University Press

Edinburgh University Press is one of the leading university presses in the UK. We publish academic books and journals in our selected subject areas across the humanities and social sciences, combining cutting-edge scholarship with high editorial and production values to produce academic works of lasting importance. For more information visit our website: edinburghuniversitypress.com

© James Cooper, 2017

Edinburgh University Press Ltd
The Tun – Holyrood Road, 12(2f) Jackson's Entry, Edinburgh EH8 8PJ

Typeset in 11/13 Adobe Sabon by
IDSUK (DataConnection) Ltd

A CIP record for this book is available from the British Library

ISBN 978 1 4744 0211 8 (hardback)
ISBN 978 1 4744 0212 5 (webready PDF)
ISBN 978 1 4744 0497 6 (epub)

# Contents

*For Danielle and Macaulay*

# Acknowledgements

The completion of this monograph would not have been possible without the support and advice of friends, family and colleagues. Although any errors in this work are mine alone, I would like to take this opportunity to extend my appreciation to all those who have contributed to my study of US presidents and Northern Ireland.

I am grateful to the editors, Professor Alan Dobson and Dr Steve Marsh, for involving me in this excellent series on Anglo-American relations, and their insightful and helpful suggestions that have improved this monograph. Likewise, I thank Edinburgh University Press, especially Jen Daly and Ersev Ersoy, for all their assistance and patience. My colleagues and students at Aberystwyth University, Westminster College and Oxford Brookes University have also been generous with their advice. In particular, I would like to thank Dr Thomas Robb for his perceptive comments on the original manuscript and his camaraderie since we arrived at Brookes together.

The research for this study would not have been possible without funding from the US–UK Fulbright Commission and from Oxford Brookes University, a research grant from the Gerald R. Ford Presidential Library, and the O'Donnell Grant at the George H. Bush Presidential Library. My gratitude goes to the archivists and librarians at all the presidential libraries that I visited, and the Burns Library at Boston College, the Library of Congress, the British and Irish national archives and the Bodleian Library. My thanks also must go to Chris Collins and the Margaret Thatcher Foundation. Thank you to the interviewees who kindly gave me their time. I completed this monograph during a visiting fellowship at the Norwegian Nobel Institute in Oslo – they also have my gratitude.

The writing of this monograph coincided with new friendships after leaving Aberystwyth for Fulton and then Oxford. These new friends have helped me to maintain my sanity during the research process. I would like to thank, in particular, the Havers family (Rob, Alana, Alice and Olivia); the Landis family (Erik, Lisa, Helena and Kaspar); the Perry clan (Carolyn, Greg, Emily, Erin and Jessie); and Ken, Aiden and Jennie Petterson. I am also fortunate to have the on-going support of my parents, Bernard and Eileen, and my siblings, Mark and Michelle.

The most important thing to happen in my life during the last few years has been meeting my wife, Danielle, in February 2013. Without Danielle, nothing would be possible. This book is dedicated to my wife and to our son, Macaulay James Cooper.

James Cooper
7 May 2016

# Author Biography

James Cooper completed his PhD at Aberystwyth University in 2010 and then became Lecturer in Modern History at the same institution. In August 2012 Dr Cooper was appointed Senior Lecturer in History at Oxford Brookes University before spending the 2012–13 academic year as the twentieth Fulbright–Robertson Visiting Professor of British History at Westminster College in Fulton, Missouri, USA. In May 2016, Dr Cooper was a Visiting Fellow at the Norwegian Nobel Institute.

# Main Abbreviations and Acronyms

ACCIA      Ad Hoc Congressional Committee for Irish Affairs
ACIF       American Congress for Irish Freedom
AIA        1985 Anglo-Irish Agreement
AOH        Ancient Order of Hibernians
DSD        1993 Downing Street Declaration
FCO        Foreign and Commonwealth Office, United Kingdom
FOI        Friends of Ireland
GFA        1998 Good Friday Agreement
IFI        International Fund for Ireland
INC        Irish National Caucus
IRA        Irish Republican Army
JFD        1995 Joint Framework Document
NICC       Northern Ireland Constitutional Convention
NORAID     Irish Northern Aid Committee
NSA        National Security Adviser, United States
NSC        National Security Council, United States
RUC        Royal Ulster Constabulary
SALT       Strategic Arms Limitation Talks
SDLP       Social Democratic and Labour Party, Northern Ireland

# Introduction

If you continue your courageous path toward a permanent peace, and all the social and economic benefits that have come with it, that won't just be good for you, it will be good for this entire island. It will be good for the United Kingdom. It will be good for Europe. It will be good for the world . . . And you should know that so long as you are moving forward, America will always stand by you as you do.

President Barack Obama, Belfast Waterfront,
Northern Ireland, 17 June 2013[1]

In May 2011, President Barack Obama visited the Republic of Ireland in search of his family's 'missing apostrophe'.[2] The President was following in the tradition of many of his predecessors since John F. Kennedy, including, perhaps most notably, Bill Clinton. That US presidents have enjoyed major trips to Ireland is testament to the emotional and historical connection between the United States and Ireland, particularly with regard to migration from the old country to the new. However, this monograph is a study of connections beyond the simple photo opportunities that can be considered a cynical appeal to Irish–American votes. The relationship between US presidents and Ireland – and, more specifically, the 'Troubles' in Northern Ireland – is more complex than a president visiting the village of his ancestors for a pint of Guinness. While there is clearly an emotive visual of an American president leaving the land of his birth and returning to the land of his ancestors, a study of the United States and the Northern Ireland conflict is a case study in nuances of the American presidency and foreign policy.

Irish–American concern about Northern Ireland revolved around the 'Troubles', which was paramilitary sectarian violence that resulted from divisions caused by the constitutional relationship between Northern Ireland and the United Kingdom. From the late 1960s and arguably until the signing of the 1998 Good Friday Agreement, this was a violent period in the history of Northern Ireland and, ultimately, the rest of the UK and Republic of Ireland. The majority Protestant unionist community believed that Northern Ireland should remain part of the UK; in contrast, the minority Catholic nationalist community wanted the reunification of Ireland and the withdrawal of the British government (and related army and police). Broadly, the term 'loyalists' refers to militant unionists who engaged in paramilitary violence (such as the Ulster Volunteer Force and Ulster Defence Association) and, likewise, 'republicans' were militant and paramilitary nationalists (revolving around the Irish Republican Army). The causes of the conflict date back to the 'plantation of Ulster' during the early seventeenth century, whereby English and Scottish settlers assumed confiscated lands in the northeast of Ireland. Whereas the settlers maintained links with their previous home countries and enjoyed wealth and prosperity, the displaced Irish would fall victim to discrimination. The resulting inequality was responsible for the campaign for Catholic civil rights in Northern Ireland during the 1960s and, ultimately, for violence by paramilitary groups representing different communities and political aspirations. Violent acts by the Provisional Irish Republic Army, which viewed itself as the successor of the original Irish Republican Army (IRA), were responsible for thousands of fatalities and injuries in Northern Ireland and, after 1971, Great Britain.[3] (In this study, the Provisional IRA is referred to using the shorthand 'IRA' as per scholastic and popular convention.)

The attitude and policy of successive US presidents to the 'Troubles' is relatively unexplored in the historiography. The Clinton administration's role in the 1998 Good Friday Agreement and Clinton's interest in the peace process have unsurprisingly been afforded some attention in scholastic and journalistic accounts.[4] These works have failed, however, to contextualise Clinton's role in the Northern Ireland peace process within the broader history of US presidents' response to Irish–American interest in the Anglo-Irish process. There has been some work about Irish–America and the Northern Ireland conflict, but due to timing, these works did not include the material available in the American, British and Irish archives; instead, they relied on, for instance, oral testimony, memoirs, diaries and the American, British and Irish press.[5] This study utilises the available source material in, for instance, the British and Irish national archives, US presidential libraries and the *Foreign Relations of the United States*.[6] Thus, this monograph contributes to an emerging wave of studies that will utilise the archival material to achieve a more nuanced account of the relationship between the US and the Northern Ireland conflict.[7]

Anglo-American relations, particularly in the context of the Cold War, are a running theme throughout this monograph and are discussed in each chapter. There is much historiographical debate about the extent to which Anglo-American relations are 'special'. This debate revolves around the relationship's defining features: overlapping national interests, a shared history, common values and personal connections.[8] In contrast, Ireland has rarely featured as a leading foreign policy priority for the US government. Nevertheless, a familial relationship did endure due to Irish immigration to the US during the 1950s. The connection was therefore an emotive one, defined by a heritage and identity that Irish–Americans shared with their distant cousins across the Atlantic. The historiography about the relationship between the US and Ireland is dominated by American involvement in the Anglo-Irish process and then the peace process. There is undoubtedly further scholarship to be pursued about diplomatic relations between the two countries.[9]

Irish migration to the US has undoubtedly contributed to the American experience. In 1779–80, George Washington ordered the celebration of St Patrick's Day as a means to lift the morale of the Continental Army.[10] Between 1815 and 1845, over one million Irish migrants braved the Atlantic to settle in the US. This increased by one-and-a-half million people in the era of famine (1845–54) and settled to an average of around fifty thousand Irish immigrants arriving in America each year during the period 1860–1900. The human tragedy in Ireland was not lost on Abraham Lincoln, who in 1853 stated, 'England is perpetrating a very atrocious injustice against poor Ireland . . . . True freedom will never exist if it does not recognise for people their legitimate independence.'[11]

From the beginning of the mass movement of Irish people to the US, nationalists saw it as an opportunity to cultivate an influential diaspora. During the 1820s, the Irish political leader Daniel O'Connell enjoyed Irish–American support for his campaign for Catholic emancipation, and during the 1840s Irish–Americans demanded the dissolution of the Act of Union that bound Ireland to the UK.[12] The year 1836 saw the creation of the Ancient Order of Hibernians (AOH), the largest Irish–American group in the US, which numbers over eight thousand members at the time of writing.[13] Irish–American influence in the US was unsurprising: in the country's census in 1850, 4 million of the total 24 million citizens of the US were of Irish heritage.[14] The advantages of the diaspora continued. In 1880, Charles Stewart Parnell, an Irish nationalist politician, undertook a ten-week tour of the US, gaining Irish–American financial support for the Land League.[15] Following the 1916 Easter Rising, the Friends of Irish Freedom circulated news of British executions of the revolutionaries and, in turn, campaigned for Irish independence to be discussed at the 1919 Versailles Peace Conference. The organisation was even able to raise a million dollars in support of this cause. Woodrow Wilson, the American President (1912–21), did not share the Friends' concern, however, despite support for Irish independence within the US House of Representatives and Senate. Yet Wilson had some private sympathy for the Irish people, which reflected his worldview on national self-determination.[16] In April 1917, Wilson wrote to Walter H. Page, the US ambassador to Britain (1913–18):

> If the American people were once convinced that there was a likelihood that the Irish question would soon be settled, great enthusiasm and satisfaction would result and it would also strengthen the co-operation which we are now about to organise between the United States and Great Britain. Say this in unofficial terms to Lloyd George but impress upon him its great significance.[17]

Wilson's decision to send a private message for David Lloyd George, the British Prime Minister (1916–22), coupled with the fact that it did not become a policy objective for the Wilson administration, is indicative of the President's real diplomatic priorities and his unwillingness to undermine them by souring relations with the British government over the Irish question. During the subsequent Irish War of Independence (1919–21), the IRA received financial support from Irish–Americans, who also spread the news of British 'atrocities' in the old country. Irish–Americans broadly turned their interest away from Irish affairs following the 1921 Anglo-Irish Treaty, content that the Irish were on a path towards independence. The partition of Northern Ireland did not hold their attention. In contrast, the Republic of Ireland's neutrality during the Second World War did provoke concern amongst Irish–Americans; their long-held claims that an independent Ireland would be a reliable and strong ally for the US had been debunked. After 1945, Irish–American solidarity was further undermined by social mobility, which fractured the solidarity of old Irish–American neighbourhoods as their increasingly affluent members moved to middle-class suburbia.[18]

With regard to international affairs, during the Cold War, the US downgraded any interest in Ireland, in favour of its 'special relationship' with the UK. Ireland was viewed as being in Britain's sphere of influence and the 'Troubles' in Northern Ireland were seen as a domestic issue for the British government. During the early stages of the Cold War, Irish–Americans benefited from the baby-boomers, with their contingent doubling in size between 1940 and 1960. Coupled with a new wave of Irish immigration in the 1980s, Irish–Americans were again targeted by interested parties across the Atlantic, albeit this time over the Northern Ireland question. However, it was increasingly clear during the era of the 'Troubles' that many Americans – including some Irish–American politicians – lacked a nuanced understanding of Irish affairs and the history of Northern Ireland. Thus, parallel to pressure to involve successive US presidents in the Anglo-Irish process – and later peace process – was an attempt by some Irish–Americans, and the British and Irish governments, to educate the American people about the intricacies of Northern Ireland's 'Troubles'.[19] Such education was a means to competing objectives: to support the violence in Northern Ireland as a means to securing British withdrawal, or to combat American financial aid to paramilitaries and cultivate support for a political solution.

Given his Irish Catholic heritage, the Irish government harboured hopes that President John F. Kennedy (1961–3) would help it to foster more favourable relations with the British government.[20] In March 1963, Thomas J. Kiernan, the Irish ambassador to the US (1960–4), asked Kennedy whether he would consider urging the British government to state publicly that they sought an end to the partition of Ireland (between Northern Ireland and the Republic of Ireland).[21] In his response, the President explained that, due to the history involved, he did not believe that any British prime minister would ever make such a statement. Anticipating future developments, Kennedy suggested that circumstances for progress on the issue could improve by closer relations through membership of the European Economic Community (EEC).[22] It remained an issue that Kennedy showed little interest in directly addressing. Indeed, Kennedy's four-day expedition to Europe in the summer of 1963, which included a triumphant homecoming to Ireland, is still best remembered for his speech in Berlin in popular and scholastic memory. Favouring Anglo-American relations and a united North Atlantic Treaty Organisation (NATO), the Kennedy administration was keen to avoid any involvement in the politics of partition.[23]

When Kiernan met with Kennedy prior to his journey to Ireland, he suggested that partition would likely be a topic of conversation with Eamon de Valéra, (President of Ireland, 1959–73) and Seán Lemass, the Taoiseach (Prime Minister, 1959–66).[24] According to the ambassador's record, Kennedy 'looked as if another headache had struck him'.[25] In his meeting with the Taoiseach in Ireland on 27 June 1963, Kennedy observed that 'the attitude of a Labour Government might be more helpful' with regard to partition.[26] This was also prophetic. Kennedy shared with the Taoiseach the information that an invitation from Northern Ireland's Prime Minister, Terence O'Neill (1963–70), for him to visit Northern Ireland – which was declined – had 'embarrassed' Harold Macmillan, the British Prime Minister (1957–63).[27] This was indicative of the influence that a president of the US could have on the debate about Northern Ireland.[28] In 1963, as per his comments to the Irish ambassador, Kennedy did not raise the subject of Northern Ireland with the British government.[29]

As Clinton Rossiter, writing in 1956, observed, American presidents have a global role and, due to the US wealth and military power, they will always be able to influence questions of stability and freedom beyond American borders.[30] Therefore, the American president as a peacemaker is a component of this study. For Richard Nixon it was a public objective of his presidency, while for Bill Clinton it was a defining aspect of his foreign policy. That the Nobel Peace Prize was awarded to three serving American presidents – namely, Theodore Roosevelt, Woodrow Wilson and Barack Obama – underlines the notion of the US president serving as a peacemaker. In 2002, Jimmy Carter (US President 1977–81) was awarded the Nobel Peace Prize. George H. W. Bush's management of the ending of the Cold War earmarked him as a presidential peacemaker. Three factors determine whether a president is able to act as peacemaker: the initiative to seize an opportunity; the ability to succeed; and the matching of expectations. Indeed, given the nature of international politics, American presidents are inevitably afforded opportunities to become peacemakers. Whether a president can seize an opportunity may depend on the characteristics and qualities of an individual. It will also depend on a president's priorities and broader grand strategy. By the nature of the office, American presidents are offered the ability to succeed. In other words, presidents have at their disposal the might of the American military and the use of various diplomatic means. The American presidency therefore demands to be taken seriously by both allies and enemies. It purveys noble intentions of diplomacy but has possession of significant military power as a means, if necessary, to achieve foreign policy objectives. In terms of expectations, an American president is required to realise high expectations at home and abroad. The American electorate demand action from their president in a variety of policy areas, while presidents are also challenged to act by wider members and institutions of the US government, and by foreign leaders.[31] In the case of Northern Ireland, successive American presidents were challenged to meet the differing expectations of Irish–American groups and politicians, the people of the island of Ireland, and allies in the British and Irish governments. These expectations were countered by broader American foreign policy objectives during the Cold War, whereby the career officials in the State Department sought to offer apolitical continuity. Nonetheless, as in this study, the American president must be viewed in global terms, with a global role and global expectations.

In addition to the expectations that the American president will play a positive role beyond the US, American foreign policy is subject to other expectations, debates and institutional pressures. This project highlights the rivalry in the making of US foreign policy between the State Department and White House advisers, particularly the National Security Council (NSC), and the agenda of Congress.[32] Also under consideration is the influence of the domestic politics of foreign policy, including electioneering and ethnic lobbying.[33] Indeed, involvement in Northern Ireland increasingly became a consideration for politicians and campaign strategists in securing Irish–American votes, while a diverse Irish–American 'lobby' sought to influence successive presidents through Congress and pressure groups. In summary, the American president *shares* power with the US Congress.[34] Thus, at times, congressional pressure will influence US foreign policy, which, as this monograph demonstrates, was the case with Northern Ireland.

Any study of presidential action demands consideration of the nature of the presidency itself, in addition to external restrictions on it. As Aaron Wildavsky concluded in the 1960s, there are effectively 'two presidencies': the foreign and the domestic. In short, the American president has greater freedom to act abroad than at home.[35] Yet, as this study reveals, the president's ability to act abroad can be contingent on the relationship between the White House and Congress as regards domestic policy. Furthermore, this monograph contends that there is a third presidency: the 'campaigning president' who is attuned to electioneering concerns. In other words, just as it is important to study the nuances of the relationship between foreign and domestic policies, historians should consider a triumvirate of presidential components. In regard to Northern Ireland, foreign policy interests – namely, Anglo-American relations – influenced successive presidents, yet, increasingly, a domestic dimension to this emerged: Irish–Americans in Congress lobbied the president to act on Northern Ireland, and typically they were senior figures otherwise needed to implement the president's domestic agenda. Linked to this was the Irish–American lobby that was willing to endorse presidential candidates – and, in theory, help garner the support of millions of Irish–Americans – depending on a candidate's, or incumbent's, preparedness to take action on the 'Troubles'. Therefore, a subtle, yet potentially politically significant connection emerges between not just American domestic and foreign policy, but also with the politics of American presidential elections. For instance, foreign policy informed Irish–American campaigners, who in turn sought to convince candidates of their case, while there was also a domestic pressure from Congress for American engagement with the Anglo-Irish process. Thus, this monograph broadens out further a debate about the domestic and ethnic politics of foreign policy into one about the foreign politics of domestic policy. In short, Irish America connected the domestic, foreign and campaigning aspects of the US presidency.

This monograph covers the presidencies of Lyndon B. Johnson to Bill Clinton inclusive, with a timeframe of 1963 to 1998. Chapter 1 discusses the Johnson, Nixon and Ford administrations. In this period, the presidents followed the established State Department policy of neutrality, which favoured the UK due to Cold War concerns. Nevertheless, Nixon held a longstanding interest in Northern Ireland, and the British and Irish governments briefed both his and the Ford administrations about developments in Northern Ireland. This underlined the global role and influence of the president of the US. However, this period also witnessed an increasing realisation that the US government must act against its own citizens' involvement in the conflict, particularly through gunrunning and financial support for the IRA. Chapter 2's focus on the Carter administration underlines the power-sharing between the President and Congress. Carter was unable to control American policy towards Northern Ireland fully due to developments in Democratic Party politics and his need for congressional support for his domestic agenda. The 'divided government' of the Reagan–Bush era, as discussed in Chapter 3, contextualised congressional pressure, coupled with varying degrees of British and Irish pressure, for American involvement in the Anglo-Irish process. Chapter 4 focuses on the Clinton administration. After the ending of the Cold War, the Northern Ireland conflict was internationalised and the President had greater freedom to intervene and support the peace process, which ultimately led to the 1998 Good Friday Agreement. This study is the first to offer a nuanced and thorough examination of the history of US presidents and Northern Ireland during the 'Troubles'.

## Notes

1. 'Remarks by President Obama and Mrs. Obama in Town Hall with Youth of Northern Ireland', Belfast Waterfront, Belfast, Northern Ireland, 17 June 2013, The White House, Office of the Press Secretary, accessed via the White House, President Barack Obama, https://www.whitehouse.gov/the-press-office/2013/06/17/remarks-president-obama-and-mrs-obama-town-hall-youth-northern-ireland, 30 September 2015.

2. See, for instance, Alex Spillius, 'Obama in Ireland: president searches for "missing apostrophe"', *The Daily Telegraph*, 24 May 2011, accessed via http://www.telegraph.co.uk/news/worldnews/europe/ireland/8532091/Obama-in-Ireland-president-searches-for-missing-apostrophe.html, 7 August 2015.

3. For an introduction to the general history of Ireland, the author strongly recommends Paul Bew, *Ireland: The Politics of Enmity 1789–2006* (Oxford: Oxford University Press, 2007). For introductory texts for the 'Troubles', see Richard English, *Armed Struggle: A History of the IRA* (Oxford: Oxford University Press, 2003); David McKittrick, *Making Sense of the Troubles* (Belfast: Blackstaff Press, 2000); Jack Holland, *Hope Against History: The Ulster Conflict* (London: Coronet Books, 1999); and Sabine Wichert, *Northern Ireland Since 1945* (London: Longman, 1999). For paramilitary violence, see, for instance, Rogelio Alonso, *The IRA and Armed Struggle* (London: Routledge, 2007); Steve Bruce, *The Red Hand: Protestant Paramilitaries in Northern Ireland* (Oxford: Oxford University Press, 1992); and Peter Taylor, *Brits: The War Against the IRA* (London: Bloomsbury, 2001). For introductions to the 'peace process', see Arthur Aughey, *The Politics of Northern Ireland: Beyond the Belfast Agreement* (Oxford: Routledge, 2005); Michael Cox, Adrian Guelke and Fiona Stephen (eds), *A Farewell to Arms? From 'Long War' to Long Peace in Northern Ireland* (Manchester: Manchester University Press, 2000); and Thomas Hennessey, *The Northern Ireland Peace Process: Ending the Troubles?* (Dublin: Gill & Macmillan, 2000).

4. For examples of journalistic works, see, for instance, Conor O'Clery, *The Greening of the White House* (Dublin: Gill & Macmillan, 1996) and *Daring Diplomacy: Clinton's Secret Search for Peace in Ireland* (Boulder, CO: Roberts Rinehart Publishers, 1997); and Eamonn Mallie and David McKittrick, *Endgame in Ireland* (London: Hodder & Stoughton, 2001) and *The Fight for Peace: The Secret Story Behind the Irish Peace Process* (London: Heinemann, 1996). For examples of what is essentially an interdisciplinary scholastic field, see Roger MacGinty and John Darby, *Guns and Government: The Management of the Northern Ireland Peace Process* (New York: Palgrave Macmillan, 2001); and Paul Arthur, *Special Relationships: Britain, Ireland and the Northern Ireland Problem* (Belfast: Blackstaff Press, 2000). There are also inevitably memoirs of protagonists in the peace process. See, for instance, George J. Mitchell, *Making Peace: The Inside Story of the Making of the Good Friday Agreement* (William Heinemann: London, 1999).

5. See Seán Cronin, *Washington's Irish Policy, 1916–1986* (Dublin: Anvil Books, 1987); Andrew J. Wilson, *Irish America and the Ulster Conflict 1968–1995* (Blackstaff Press: Belfast, 1995); Ray O'Hanlon, *The New Irish Americans* (Niwot, CO: Roberts Rinehart Publishers, 1998); and Joseph E. Thompson, *American Policy and Northern Ireland: A Saga of Peacebuilding* (London: Praeger, 2001).

6. For debates about the use of archival sources, printed sources (e.g. the press) and oral testimony, see Brian Brivati, Julia Bexton and Anthony Seldon (eds), *The Contemporary History Handbook* (Manchester: Manchester University Press, 1996). For more specific work about oral history and memory studies, see, respectively, Paul Thompson, *The Voice of the Past: Oral History* (Oxford: Oxford University Press, 2000) and Geoffrey Cubitt, *History and Memory* (Manchester: Manchester University Press, 2007).

7. See, for instance, Andrew Sanders, 'The role of Northern Ireland in modern Anglo-American relations: The US Department of State and the Royal Ulster Constabulary, 1979', *Journal of Transatlantic Studies*, 12:2 (2014), 163–81; and Luke Devoy, 'The British response to American interest in Northern Ireland, 1976–79', *Irish Studies in International Affairs*, 25 (2014), 221–38.

8. There is obviously a vast historiography about the 'special relationship'. For a recent outstanding volume, see Alan Dobson and Steve Marsh (eds), *Anglo-American Relations: Contemporary Perspectives* (London: Routledge, 2012).

9. See, for instance, Troy Davis, *Dublin's American Policy: Irish American Diplomatic Relations 1945–52* (Washington, DC: Catholic University of America Press, 1998); Jack Holland, *The American Connection: U.S. Guns, Money and Influence in Northern Ireland* (New York: Viking Press, 1999); Kevin Kenny, *The American Irish: A History* (Harlow: Longman, 2000); J. J. Lee and Marion R. Casey (eds), *Making the Irish American* (London: New York University Press, 2007); Kerby A. Miller, *Ireland and Irish America: Culture, Class, and Transatlantic Migration* (Dublin: Field Day, 2008); and David Sim, *A Union Forever: The Irish Question and U.S. Foreign Relations in the Victorian Age* (Ithaca, NY: Cornell University Press, 2013).

10. Christopher Klein, 'George Washington's Revolutionary St. Patrick's Day', accessed via http://www.history.com/news/george-washingtons-revolutionary-st-patricks-day, 17 August 2015. For a history of St Patrick's Day, see Mike Cronin and Daryl Adair, *The Wearing of the Green* (New York: Routledge, 2002).

11. Cited in 'Statements on Irish freedom and partition', in National Archives of Ireland (NAI): Department of Foreign Affairs (DFA), 10/P/262/1 (hereafter NAI: DFA). I am grateful to the NAI and its director for the use of this, and similar, material. Lincoln's criticism of the British government still did not extend as far as A. J. P. Taylor's remarks in his essay on 'Genocide', in A. J. P. Taylor, *Essays in English History* (Harmondsworth: Penguin, 1976), 73–9. Mirgation statistics from Wilson, Irish America, 3–4.

12. Wilson, *Irish America*, 3–4.

13. See the organisation's official website: http://www.aoh.com/about-the-aoh/, accessed 17 August 2015.

14. Thompson, *American Policy*, 8.

15. Wilson, *Irish America*, 9. (For a transnational history about how transatlantic Irish nationalism influenced American foreign policy, particularly Anglo-American relations, in the second half of the nineteenth century, see Sim, *A Union Forever*.)

16. Ibid., 12.

17. Cited in 'Statements on Irish freedom and partition', NAI: DFA 10/P/262/1.

18. Wilson, *Irish America*, 13–16.

19. Thompson, *American Policy*, 14–15.

20. For Irish foreign policy in the period 1922–47, see Donal Lowry, 'The captive dominion: imperial realities behind Irish diplomacy, 1922–49', *Irish Historical Studies*, xxxvi:142 (Nov. 2008), 202–26.

21. Letter from T. J. Kiernan to H. J. McCann (Secretary, Department of External Affairs), 19 March 1963, NAI: DFA 10/P/262/1.
22. Ibid.
23. Thompson, *American Policy*, 14–15.
24. Letter, Embassy of Ireland to H. J. McCann, Secretary, Department of External Affairs, 17 June 1963, NAI: DFA 10/P/262/1.
25. Ibid.
26. Discussion between Taoiseach and President Kennedy at American Embassy, Thursday, 27 June, at 9:30 a.m., NAI: D/Taoiseach 17401C/63.
27. Ibid.
28. Telegram, From Foreign Office to Washington, 20 April 1963, The National Archives of the UK (hereafter TNA): PREM 11/4584, Visit of President Kennedy to UK, June 1963.
29. See memoranda of conversations in 'Visit to the United Kingdom by the President and Secretary of State of the United States, June 27–30, 1963', Volume 1 and Volume II, TNA: PREM 11/4586, Visit of President Kennedy to UK, June 1963: part 4.
30. Clinton Rossiter, 'The presidency – focus of leadership', *The New York Times*, 11 November 1956, 247.
31. J. Simon Rofe, 'George H. W. Bush and presidential peace making', in Michael Patrick Cullinane and Clare Frances Elliot (eds), *Perspectives on Presidential Leadership: An International View of the White House* (Abingdon: Routledge, 2014), 180–3 (179–95). This is an excellent essay about the American president as a peacemaker, with specific reference to George H. W. Bush.
32. The literature includes a combination of academic work and 'higher journalists'. See, for instance, John Dumbrell with David M. Barrett, *The Making of US Foreign Policy* (Manchester: Manchester University Press, 1997); Lee H. Hamilton with Jordan Tama, *A Creative Tension: The Foreign Policy Roles of the President and Congress* (Baltimore: Johns Hopkins University Press, 2002); David Mitchell, *Making Foreign Policy: Presidential Management of the Decision-Making Process* (Aldershot: Ashgate, 2005); Bob Woodward, *The War Within: A Secret White House History, 2006–2008* (London: Simon & Schuster, 2008); Steven W. Hook and Christopher M. Jones (eds), *Routledge Handbook of American Foreign Policy* (New York: Routledge, 2012); and James Bilsland, *The President, the State and the Cold War: Comparing the Foreign Policies of Truman and Reagan* (Abingdon: Routledge, 2015).
33. For the domestic politics of US foreign policy, see Thomas Alan Schwartz, '"Henry, . . . winning an election is terribly important":

Partisan politics in the history of U.S. foreign relations', *Diplomatic History*, 33:2 (2009), 173–90; Campbell Craig and Fredrik Logevall, *America's Cold War: The Politics of Insecurity* (Cambridge, MA: Harvard University Press, 2009); and Julian Zelizer, *Arsenals of Democracy: The Politics of National Security – From World War II to the War on Terrorism* (New York: Basic Books, 2010). For 'ethnic lobbying' and US foreign policy, see Alexander DeConde, *Ethnicity, Race, and American Foreign Policy* (Boston: Northeastern University Press, 1992); Tony Smith, *Foreign Attachments: The Power of Ethnic Groups in the Making of American Foreign Policy* (Cambridge, MA: Harvard University Press, 2000); Peter H. Koehn and Xiao-huang Yin (eds), *The Expanding Roles of Chinese Americans in U.S.–China Relations: Transnational Networks and Trans-Pacific Interactions* (Armonk, NY: M. E. Sharpe, 2002); John J. Mearsheimer, *The Israel Lobby and US Foreign Policy* (London: Penguin, 2008); and Kames M. McCormick (ed.), *The Domestic Sources of American Foreign Policy* (Lanham, MD: Rowman & Littlefield Publishers, 2012).

34. See Richard Neustadt, *Presidential Power and the Modern Presidents: The Politics of Leadership From Roosevelt to Reagan* (New York: Free Press Toronto, 1990).

35. Aaron Wildavsky, 'The two presidencies', *Trans-Action*, 2:4 (1996), 7–14. For further debate about this thesis, see, for instance, Brandice Canes-Wrone, William G. Howel and David E. Lewis, 'Toward a broader understanding of presidential power: A reevaluation of the two presidencies thesis', *Journal of Politics*, 70:1 (2008), 1–16.

# I The Johnson, Nixon and Ford Administrations, 1963–77

## Introduction

Between 1964 and 1976, there was increasing American interest in Northern Ireland. The outbreak of the 'Troubles' captured the imagination of the American media and support of Irish–American groups. In turn, the US government monitored developments and was lobbied by its own citizens, members of Congress and, delicately, the Irish government, to intervene in some fashion. Britain's membership of NATO, and the politics of the Cold War, ostensibly explain successive administrations' reluctance to criticise the British government's handling of the Northern Ireland question or interject itself into the Anglo-Irish process to resolve the conflict. There were precedents, however, for the US to act in similar circumstances, or certainly not to assume a stance in favour of a NATO ally. The Eisenhower and Kennedy administrations did not support France in its battle with the National Liberation Front in Algeria (1954–62) and Kennedy did not tolerate the Netherlands' attempts to justify sovereignty in Western New Guinea on the claim that its people were not related to Indonesians.[1]

During the 1960s and 1970s, tension and conflict were increasingly defining features of Anglo-American relations. John Dumbrell observes that the relationships between Lyndon Johnson and Harold Wilson, and Richard Nixon and Edward Heath, were problematised by various factors: cooler personal relations, the Vietnam War and reduced British defence spending. Institutional cooperation remained but Anglo-American relations were certainly more difficult.[2] Similarly, Alan Dobson recognises that the 1960s and 1970s saw a more problematic Anglo-American relationship due to each country's 'internal dynamics' and 'a broader based transition' in Western economic policies. The Heath government (1970–4), in particular, was 'rather barren for Anglo-American relations', with entry into the EEC dominating British foreign policy at this time.[3] British economic problems served as bookends for this period in transatlantic affairs, starting with the 1967 Sterling Crisis and ending with the bailout of the British economy by the International Monetary Fund in 1976. As Thomas Robb has identified, Anglo-American relations during the era of détente demand a more nuanced understanding, given American coercion of successive British governments. For instance, the Heath government was strongly urged to be more amenable to American interests during the infamous 1973 'Year of Europe' and Wilson was under pressure to lessen reductions in British defence spending.[4]

The position of the US government on Northern Ireland can still be attributed to an Anglo-American relationship that remained 'special' in a functional and institutional sense, based on recent history (namely, the wartime and Cold War alliance) and common security and economic interests. Nevertheless, other issues dominated both American and British agendas and international affairs, which marginalised Northern Ireland. In short, there were other points of contention and co-operation that demanded the attention of successive American presidents and British prime ministers. As this chapter will demonstrate, a reluctance to intervene in the 'Troubles' was initially due to wider considerations in the transatlantic policy of successive administrations. But this was superseded by an acknowledgement that the involvement of the Irish–American community in the Northern Ireland conflict (either through financial support for the IRA or solidarity with the campaign for Catholics' civil rights in Northern Ireland and/or a united Ireland) meant that the US government had to intervene to some degree. This intervention took the form of trying to stop the contributions of its own citizens in the conflict. Therefore, between 1963 and 1976, Northern Ireland would begin to attract the attention of all three aspects of the US presidency. In domestic policy, support for violence in Northern Ireland on the part of some Irish–American citizens required intervention. The Cold War dwarfed any concern for intervention in Northern Ireland. Similarly, electoral strategy became a factor when advising the Oval Office.

## The Johnson administration, 1963–9

It is a truism to state that Johnson's presidency became consumed by the war in Vietnam. As much as his accomplishments in policy implementation and politicking in the domestic arena have arguably been sidelined by Vietnam, Johnson's attention to other conflicts elsewhere in the world, arguably, was relatively marginal.[5] Northern Ireland is a case in point. Johnson's disinterest in Northern Ireland represented continuity in presidential policy towards the conflict but also coincided with what would be a pattern of lobbying the President on partition and Catholics' civil rights, and, in response, declarations of neutrality. Discrimination against Northern Ireland's Catholics impacted on electoral practices, public and private employment, regional policy and public housing. Policing was another area of fierce discrimination: the Royal Ulster Constabulary (RUC) was dominated by Protestants and the 1922 Northern Ireland Special Powers Act afforded the Minister of Home Affairs the ability to take any measure, effectively, in order to maintain order and preserve the peace.[6]

The Johnson administration coincided with the fiftieth anniversary of the 1916 Easter Rising and a significant upturn in tensions in Ireland and Northern Ireland. Despite Seán Lemass, the Taoiseach (1959–66), attempting to control the inevitable emotions that spiralled out of the commemorative events, at this time the IRA claimed a membership of over a thousand, while the Reverend Ian Paisley successfully utilised a Protestant backlash to begin the process of developing a strong level of support. (Paisley led the Protestant Unionist Party during its existence in the period 1966–71 until it became the Democratic Unionist Party, which Paisley would head up until 2008.) Two years later, the civil rights demonstration on 5 October 1968 in Londonderry (or Derry) saw RUC officers using batons against civil rights protestors. Footage captured by a Raidió

Teilifís Éireann (RTE) cameraman Gay O'Brien prompted wide-spread coverage.[7] Terence O'Neill, the Prime Minister of Northern Ireland (1963–9), made some attempts to improve the civil rights situation and, to great opposition from within his own party, met in 1965 with Seán Lemass. However, O'Neill's efforts were insufficient and the UK Labour government also failed to help deliver civil rights reform. Violence again emerged during a second civil rights protest in October 1968 and outraged world opinion.[8]

Éamon de Valera, the President of the Republic of Ireland (1959–73), visited the US in May 1964 and met with Johnson at the White House. Prior to the meeting, Dean Rusk, the US Secretary of State (1961–9), advised Johnson, 'There are no significant substantive issues between the United States and Ireland.'[9] This reflects Ireland's low level in the President's priorities and foreign policy concerns. Moreover, the talking points demonstrate the administration's neutrality on Northern Ireland:

> De Valera remains a firm opponent of the partition of Ireland. If he raises the issue, you should avoid comment on the central question and, instead, express approval of steps being taken to improve the economic relations between North and South.[10]

This represented continuity in the line taken by the Kennedy administration. Johnson's position in relation to that of Kennedy's was best characterised by Ambassador Kiernan's summary for the Irish government of the new president following Kennedy's assassination: 'President Johnson's attitude to Ireland and the Irish will be warm and friendly, certainly in 1964, but of course without depth of feeling.'[11] LBJ's attitude towards Ireland – including hosting de Valera – was influenced by concerns in an election year.

The Johnson administration was explicit in its view that the US should not intervene in the Northern Ireland question. Nevertheless, as with Kennedy, the President was able to grasp the geographical and political sensitivities and challenges that Northern Ireland represented for the British government, albeit much to his frustration when the British lacked empathy towards American concerns about Cuba. During a telephone conversation with McGeorge Bundy (US National Security Adviser, hereafter NSA, 1961–6) on 1 July 1964, Johnson equated the sensitivity of the two issues. After Bundy noted that the British government believed that the administration was exaggerating the Cuban threat to American national security, given that the Kennedy administration had previously agreed to sell grain to the Soviet Union, and Cuba was certainly not on the scale of the USSR as a threat, the President replied: '90 miles away from us . . . . That's where Ireland is.'[12] Johnson expected the British to support American policy towards a problematic issue so close to its borders, just as the US had done by not complicating British policy towards Northern Ireland.

The administration's neutrality was underlined by its response to lobbying attempts by both governmental and extra-governmental figures. A determination to remain neutral was accredited to Anglo-American relations. Representative James A. Burke (Democrat–Massachusetts, 1963–79; hereafter first letter of either Democratic Party or Republican Party and state's abbreviation) wrote to the President on 15 March 1965, arguing that, much like the United Irish Societies, he believed that 'the matter of the Partition of Ireland' should be placed 'on the Agenda of the United Nations'.[13] Johnson did not reply himself. It is unlikely that he ever saw Burke's letter. Douglas MacArthur II, serving as Assistant Secretary of State for Congressional Relations (1965–7), replied. He contextualised his remarks by stating that the administration wanted to maintain and strengthen its close relations with both Britain and Ireland.[14] Thus, while the administration was 'distressed by the discord' in recent Anglo-Irish relations, it was the US government's view that 'the best course of friendship' was to allow the British and Irish 'to work out their differences in their own way'. Positive developments, such as the 1965 meetings between the Taoiseach and the Northern Ireland Prime Minister, would be undermined by any 'inappropriate and ill-timed' action such as an American recommendation to the United Nations (UN) for action 'on the partition question'.[15] Harlan Cleveland (Assistant Secretary of State for International Organization Affairs, 1961–5), a colleague of MacArthur, adopted a similar stance in response to the same request from the United Irish Societies.[16] His argument was that any UN action would threaten the UK's 'territorial integrity'. The broader ramifications were also highlighted, as the precedent could 'open a Pandora's box of long dead political claims between scores of other UN members'. Again, it is unlikely that Johnson was involved in this level of correspondence: Cleveland stated that the society's letter had been directed to him, as UN affairs were his bureau's responsibility.[17] Thus, Northern Ireland was under the purview of the US State Department and did not represent a foreign policy interest for the White House. The President was unconcerned by Northern Ireland.

Discriminatory practices in Northern Ireland also prompted a reaction from the Irish–American community. The work of the Northern Ireland Civil Rights Association (NICRA), set up in Northern Ireland in 1967, inspired the establishment of a number of groups in support of its mission in the US, initially in New England. Ultimately, these smaller groups combined with larger Irish–American organisations and worked under the umbrella of the American Congress for Irish Freedom (ACIF). Led by James Heaney, a Buffalo lawyer concerned with civil rights in Northern Ireland (particularly the Special Powers Act), the ACIF became an efficient and highly organised group, determined to secure the support of the US government in pressurising Stormont to reform. However, for Heaney and much of the ACIF's membership, civil rights in Northern Ireland were a starting point: the desired endgame was a united Ireland. Heaney ensured that the ACIF staged a cogent letter-writing campaign to leading American newspapers and he even appeared on the *Alan Burke Show*, a nationally syndicated conservative talk-show that typically enjoyed a viewership of eighty million Americans.[18] Writing to Rusk, Heaney, as the ACIF chairman, argued that the British government used the Special Powers Act 'to suppress civil liberties in the north of Ireland'.[19] Heaney argued that the Johnson administration should stop 'American involvement in this matter', such as by ceasing all financial support to Britain.[20] Writing separately to the President about the Special Powers Act, Heaney stated:

> The law applies to no part of the United Kingdom except Northern Ireland. The law itself is something out of Nazi Germany. Despite these facts, our government has fully supported the British intrusion in Northern Ireland and we feel that American silence is not in the interest of this country. We urge you to take immediate action to rectify this situation.[21]

This strong indictment of British policy and alleged American collusion through silence was followed by a direct appeal to Johnson to pressure Wilson to resolve Northern Ireland's problems. But there was also a threat from the organisation: if the administration ignored the issue, they would circulate copies of the Special Powers Act amongst Congress and journalists. Heaney's frustration was further betrayed by his request that any administration reply not be the 'form letter . . . on the subject of the occupation of Ireland'.[22] In response, Edward R. Fried, serving as a member of the NSC with responsibility for Western Europe and international affairs (1967–9), replied briefly on behalf of the administration: 'The views of your organisation . . . are being taken into account.'[23] Fried clearly hoped to end the correspondence with Heaney on this issue and keep it away from the Oval Office, but Heaney's campaign did not end. Working with Conn McCluskey, an Irish civil rights activist, Heaney supported six Northern Ireland residents in taking their case of discrimination to the European Court of Human Rights (ECHR) in April 1968. The ECHR's decision that the British government should answer the charges levelled against it was embarrassing to Harold Wilson, the British Prime Minister (1964–70 and 1974–6), who, the following month, condemned the abuse of civil rights in Northern Ireland.[24]

The closing months of the Johnson administration coincided with the advent of the 'Troubles'. The British government was embarrassed by the turn of events: the British 'model' of democracy and its successful political system were shown to be nothing more than a façade for Northern Irish Catholics. Wilson told the Northern Ireland government in November 1969 that they were to make serious reforms to the status quo.[25] LBJ, understandably occupied by the Vietnam War and other international and domestic issues, clearly did not allow his administration to be distracted by what was viewed as an internal problem for the British government.

## The Nixon administration, 1969–74

Nixon comfortably defeated Hubert Humphrey (US Vice-President, 1965–9) for the American presidency on 5 November 1968. The

Vietnam War was a key factor in the campaign: Nixon promised to end the draft and secure 'peace with honour'. He also campaigned on a 'law and order' ticket, speaking out against the violent protests, such as those on college campuses, that had been a feature of the previous few years. Even the 1968 Democratic National Convention in Chicago is remembered for the violent clashes between anti-war protestors and the police. Nixon's foreign policy was defined by détente – an easing of tensions between the US and Soviet Union – in order to further American interests. Similarly, the Nixon Doctrine sought a less interventionist US foreign policy, with America's allies taking more responsibility for their own security, albeit within the context of a US security umbrella. A signature policy of the Nixon administration (1969–74) was 'triangular diplomacy', which utilised China as a counterweight to the Soviet Union in the international system. Working with Henry Kissinger, the NSA (1969–75) and US Secretary of State (1973–7), Nixon sought to manage the Cold War through summitry and arms agreements.[26] In his 1969 inaugural address, Nixon was clear in his mission:

> The greatest honor history can bestow is the title of peacemaker. This honor now beckons America – the chance to help lead the world at last out of the valley of turmoil and onto that high ground of peace that man has dreamed of since the dawn of civilization.[27]

It was through this framework that Irish–American groups attempted to persuade the Nixon administration to intervene in Northern Ireland.

The ACIF sought to use Nixon's determination to end the war in Vietnam by jeopardising Anglo-American relations, and in turn American foreign policy, in favour of their campaign for civil rights in Northern Ireland and, ultimately, a united Ireland. In letters to American newspapers, the ACIF claimed that North Vietnam was receiving military supplies from British merchant ships, meaning that the British were assisting the killing of American soldiers. Heaney and Robert McCann (an ACIF colleague) met with Elliot Richardson, an undersecretary at the State Department, on 22 April 1969, to discuss these allegations. Richardson simply explained that the British ships carried medicine and food, and this was not justification for the US government to act on ACIF's suggestion of economic sanctions against Britain without an improved situation in Northern Ireland. Nevertheless, Heaney was able to convince Rep. Thomas P. 'Tip' O'Neill (D-MA) and one hundred other Congressmen to write to Nixon about their concern for what amounted to legalised discrimination in Northern Ireland. The administration subsequently asked for further information from the US consul-general in Belfast, although it made no difference to the State Department's position that Northern Ireland was an internal matter for the British government.[28]

The Nixon administration coincided with key changes in Northern Ireland's politics. Wilson's concerns about the British government placing too much pressure for reform on Terence O'Neill proved justified on 3 February 1969, when a dozen unionist backbenchers called for his resignation. In response, O'Neill called an election. The plan almost backfired when O'Neill himself only barely defeated the Reverend Ian Paisley's challenge for his constituency. Following violence from the Ulster Volunteer Force (UVF), O'Neill resigned as prime minister in April 1969. The new Prime Minister, James Chichester-Clark (1969–71), saw British troops deployed to guard key installations, such as electricity and water, following further violence in Derry. Riots during the Marching Season resulted in the British Army being further deployed in August 1969 and utilised by Stormont in an attempt to maintain the peace so that there would be sufficient time to implement the necessary reforms (in housing, public sector employment and community relations). With regard to any political process, the Downing Street communiqué of that same month maintained that the border was not in question as long as the people of Northern Ireland wished to remain part of the UK. Thus, August 1969 saw the beginnings of 'Ulsterisation': in short, the British Army was deployed in Northern Ireland following the breakdown of law and order, although the priority was to strengthen local security so that the soldiers could withdraw as early as possible.[29]

In this context of discrimination, rioting, violence and troop deployment, members of the US House of Representatives lobbied the Nixon administration about Northern Ireland. For instance, on 18 August 1969, Rep. John M. Murphy (D-NY) asked Nixon to instruct the US representative at the UN Security Council to 'seek ways and means of preserving the human rights of the Catholic people of Northern Ireland' and warned that he would also introduce a congressional resolution for this to happen.[30] A few weeks later, Kissinger replied to Murphy on behalf of the President. The NSA agreed on 'the need to protect the rights of all citizens in a free society to vote and to seek employment and housing without discrimination on the grounds of religion, race, or colour' and assured the Congressman that the administration had made this known to the governments of Northern Ireland and Britain.[31] On UN action, however, Kissinger argued that such a course would be 'inappropriate', as it was a British 'internal domestic situation', and the British government would respond to American intervention 'in the same way as we would react to foreign intervention in our efforts to resolve problems of civil rights and equality of opportunity in the United States'.[32]

Around this time, Patrick Hillery, the Irish Minister for External Affairs (Foreign Minister, 1968–73), met with William Rogers, US Secretary of State (1969–73). According to the American record, Hillery delivered a 'low-key presentation on Northern Ireland', arguing that the British government could not continue to exclude the Irish government, as 'the problem cannot be solved by treating it simply as a domestic political problem; it is one tragic aspect of several hundred years of Irish history'.[33] Rogers enquired as to the Irish government's plans for Northern Ireland, to which the Foreign Minister responded: 'To keep trying to get the British to talk on this matter.' Subsequently, Rogers explained that the Nixon administration 'did not wish to interfere in problems between our good friends' and that any advice would be 'presumptuous', given America's 'unsolved problems'. Nonetheless, Rogers stressed that the British government knew that the administration 'hope[d] this problem will be dealt with' and that Hillery 'should feel free' to contact John D. J. Moore, the US ambassador to Ireland (1969–75), about 'any specific matters he might wish to raise with the U.S. Government'. The Nixon administration was therefore privately willing to receive updates about the Anglo-Irish process and had told the British government that the 'Troubles' should end, albeit with the caveat of neutrality. Hillery concluded the discussion by suggesting that 'the time may come' when Rogers would need to offer 'a little encouragement' to the British government to answer the Northern Ireland question, but in the meantime declared, 'I have got all from you that I could have asked.'[34] Hillery was content that the US government was willing to listen to Irish views and diplomatically alert British counterparts to American hopes for a solution.

Less than a year after this meeting, some Irish–Americans decided to become much more involved in the Northern Ireland question, albeit through the funding of violence. Following the division within the IRA in December 1969 between the leftist faction that sought the political achievement of a socialist republic and the 'provisional' faction who believed in militant tactics in order to end the British presence in Northern Ireland, the Irish Northern Aid Committee (NORAID) was established in April 1970, under the leadership of Michael Flannery, as a means to raise money for the families of members of the Provisional IRA who were in prison; the money would be distributed in Northern Ireland by the Northern Aid Committee Belfast. The American, British and Irish governments noted that most of the money was actually used to finance gunrunning and violence.[35] The context of this new American money in support of violence was an escalation of the 'Troubles'. In October 1969, Victor Arbuckle became the first police officer to be killed by the Ulster Volunteer Force (UVF) and two nights of violence on Belfast's Shankill Road also saw three other fatalities and sixty-six injuries. It was clear that, despite the implementation of Northern Ireland's reform agenda, violence continued. In April 1970, the British Army clashed with Irish Catholic civilians at Ballymurphy, a Belfast housing estate. The divisions within the community were further underlined by two Protestant unionist by-election victories later that month, including a victory for Ian Paisley. The tensions and violence saw General Officer Commanding Ian Freeland announce that the army was prepared to shoot anyone who carried or threw a petrol bomb. Following the election of a Conservative government in Westminster, the introduction of the Falls Road Curfew on 3–5 July 1970 saw a significant amount of arms recovered by the army, albeit at a cost: five civilians were killed, sixty civilians were injured, and the operation alienated Catholics from the army and only assisted IRA recruitment. The result was that, early the following year, the IRA was undertaking operations against the British Army and in February 1971 they succeeded in murdering the first British soldier (Robin Curtis) in Northern Ireland.[36] Nixon did not comment on these events. His St Patrick's Day statements, issued in 1969 and 1971, preferred to focus on celebrating Irish contributions to the world.[37] Likewise, Nixon did not comment on the 'Troubles' on other opportune occasions, such as in his remarks at the State Luncheon in Dublin to mark his visit to Ireland in October 1970.[38]

This period also saw Irish–American politicians continue to issue statements on Northern Ireland and raise the subject on Capitol Hill. In March 1970, Tip O'Neill, along with Rep. Edward Boland (D-MA) and Rep. Allard Lowenstein (D-NY), vehemently criticised the Special Powers Act. On 20 October 1971, Senator Edward Kennedy (D-MA) – working with Senator Abraham Ribicoff (D-CT) and Rep. Hugh Carey (D-NY) – introduced a congressional resolution demanding the dissolution of Stormont, temporary direct rule from London, the piecemeal withdrawal of British soldiers, and an all-party convention to resolve the Northern Ireland question with a unified Ireland at the heart of any solution. Kennedy was widely criticised by British and unionist politicians; the State Department and the American Embassy in London quickly asserted that Kennedy's resolution was not the policy of the US government.[39]

Between 27 September and 8 October 1970, Nixon undertook a European tour, visiting Ireland, the UK, Spain, Yugoslavia and Italy. Nixon's visit to Ireland prompted the Irish Embassy in the US to unearth a letter and article, dated June 1952 and September 1952, respectively, which demonstrated Nixon's views towards Northern Ireland while serving as a US senator and campaigning to be Eisenhower's vice-president. Nixon wrote to Reverend D. Manning on 17 June 1952, stating that he shared his opposition to the Irish partition.[40] In an interview with *The Boston Daily Globe* in September 1952, Nixon acknowledged that while partition could not be ended immediately, the US government could pressure the British government to do so as a condition for any American financial aid.[41] Nixon then politicised the issue, arguing that the

Republican Party – and, in particular, an Eisenhower administration – would be better placed to resolve the Northern Ireland issue by means favourable to Irish–Americans, rather than a complacent Democratic Party who had long discussed the issue and took the Irish–American votes for granted. Nixon had been campaigning with Rep. Patrick J. Hillings (R-CA) in Maine. Hillings added that Congress should adopt the Fogarty resolution and condemn the partition of Ireland. The resolution demanded a united Ireland and the cancellation of American financial aid (Mutual Security Aid) if Britain refused to concede. Hillings even connected this policy to the Cold War, claiming that a Republican Congress would support measures against partition, as the Irish (especially Catholics) were among the staunchest anti-Communists in the US.[42]

Nixon's past statement on Northern Ireland was forgotten in his administration's preparation for his visit to Ireland. In Kissinger's briefings for Nixon prior to his visit to Ireland in October 1970, the NSA explained that the President's 'central objectives will be to demonstrate that our bilateral relationship continues warm and non-partisan, and that we have a sympathetic interest in Ireland's extensive involvement in world affairs'.[43] On the 'Troubles', Kissinger added, 'Without becoming involved in the debate over Irish partition, you should delicately demonstrate tacit support for Prime Minister Lynch's moderate policy toward Northern Ireland.'[44] (Jack Lynch was first Taoiseach between 1966 and 1973.) Thus, the President was advised to remember that Northern Ireland would be 'in the background' of discussions. While the administration had 'made clear repeatedly' that the US considered it an internal British matter, the President 'should express hope that the conciliatory Irish policy together with the efforts of the British and Northern Ireland governments will continue to help reduce tensions'.[45] Thus, beyond polite encouragement for the Anglo-Irish process to succeed, Nixon was strongly advised not to intervene in the issue. On 5 October 1970, Nixon met with the Taoiseach at Dublin Castle. The American record of the meeting stated, 'Participants did not refer to Northern Ireland . . . but it is possible that these matters could have been touched upon at private session.'[46]

The President acted on his advisers' suggestions and briefings, and chose not to interject his administration into the Anglo-Irish process at this time in any formal fashion. However, the reference to the private talks suggests that Nixon is likely to have discussed the issue in a less formal capacity. Regardless, the visit to Ireland receives only a passing reference in Kissinger's memoir and none at all in Nixon's.[47] Away from the high politics of summitry, in 1970 there was surveillance activity and even infiltrations by the Federal Bureau of Investigation (FBI) of Irish–American groups who were helping to fund violence across the Atlantic. Such activity and pressure from the US Justice Department ensured that on 14 January 1971 NORAID registered under the Foreign Agents Registration Act. This ensured that NORAID was required to give details about its relationship with its foreign agent, Northern Aid Committee Belfast, and was subject to the relevant authorities examining its correspondence and financial records.[48]

On 5 February 1971, James Heaney (on behalf of ACIF) wrote to Nixon following reports of a planned visit by Chichester-Clark to the White House. Heaney promised the President that, 'while we have no intention to embarrass you or your administration, Irish American pickets will picket the White House in the event that you do recognise Mr. Chichester-Clark or invite him into the White House'.[49] Heaney stressed that, given 'Chichester-Clark's sordid record in Northern Ireland . . . it would be an insult to the Irish American community for you to meet him in the White House or extend any official recognition to him on his American visit'.[50] A few weeks later, Helmut Sonnenfeldt (NSC staff, 1969–74) replied to Heaney on behalf of the President.[51] He explained that 'speculation' about Chichester-Clark's visit was 'overtaken by events' as he 'cancelled his proposed visit'. Seemingly in an attempt to placate Heaney, Sonnenfeldt added, 'there had been no plans for Mr. Chichester-Clark to be received at the White House'.[52] Following further violence in Northern Ireland, including the killing of the first British soldier, and Heath's refusal of his request for further repressive measures to bolster the unionists in Northern Ireland, Chichester-Clark resigned his office on 20 March 1971. Brian Faulkner (1971–2) succeeded Chichester-Clark.

Although Chichester-Clark did not visit the White House, Nixon met with Lynch on 17 March 1971 to mark St Patrick's

Day. Prior to what Kissinger described as Lynch's 'private and unofficial visit', Nixon was warned that the Taoiseach would want to discuss Northern Ireland.[53] Kissinger added that, although Lynch 'fully understands that we are unable to become involved in this problem', the President could express 'appreciation' for his conciliatory approach and ask for his opinion on 'the prospects for a resolution'.[54] According to the Irish record, the conversation was scheduled to last half an hour, but the Taoiseach and President spoke for an hour and twenty minutes.[55] Before discussing other issues, such as the EEC, Vietnam and the internal economy, the first topic was Northern Ireland. Lynch explained that any suggestion that he was seeking Nixon's support for his approach to Northern Ireland 'was exaggerated'. The record also states that Lynch 'got the impression' that Nixon 'was not completely well informed about the true facts of Northern Ireland'. Thus, Lynch 'gave the President a resumé of the situation there'.[56] This probably was in accordance with a 'secret' briefing that was presented to the Taoiseach the previous day.[57] The document was blunt in its description of the Northern Ireland situation:

> As we see it a relatively small community . . . continues to be able to hold Britain to ransom in terms of military and economic support while refusing to give effective justice to a half million people within their jurisdiction; they continue also to hold Ireland to ransom by their refusal to concede any respect to the sizeable minority within Northern Ireland in terms of their political and cultural aspirations.

The Irish government – in their view – sought to be reasonable and pragmatic, but the endgame was clear:

> We are not seeking the reunification of Ireland overnight. We do not think it wise or possible to obtain this. What we do seek is a decision by Britain – let it be a tacit understanding – that between London and Dublin we should gradually begin to thaw out the situation in the North so that peaceful co-existence of the communities in the North can be guaranteed and made effective. That is our sole political aim at present. We reserve, of course, our right to aspire to Irish unification by peaceful means but have no intention of ramming this down anyone's throat.

As for the community divisions in Northern Ireland, the Irish government's view was that the Protestant majority would – piecemeal – accept 'the idea of justice within the Northern community' and then 'will gradually begin to see the sense of an Irish arrangement about which Dublin is perfectly prepared to be large-minded'. In order to achieve his government's long-term objective of a united Ireland, Lynch appealed to Nixon to intervene quietly:

> I am hopeful, Mr. President, that you will use your good offices with Mr. Heath in this direction. I know that you may not be in a position to do as much as Irish–Americans might expect you to do. I am not myself asking you to take a public view, either official or personal, on the question of the unification of Ireland. I am asking you simply to use your influence with Mr. Heath in the interest of preventing a return to the status quo ante in the North – that is to say a Unionist hegemony which has shown itself to be unacceptable to the minority, incapable of good government and fraught with danger to the peace in Ireland.[58]

The Taoiseach clearly wanted to convince the President of the Irish government's view of the Northern Ireland situation so that Nixon would privately steer Heath towards a solution along those lines. As discussed below, Lynch was unsuccessful.

A month later, the President met with Harold Wilson, now the leader of Her Majesty's Opposition (1970–4), on 30 April 1971, while he was visiting the US to give lectures about education and labour relations in public employment, and to visit Lyndon Johnson in Texas.[59] Prior to the meeting, the President was advised that, amongst other topics such as Britain's entry to the EEC and the British economy, this was an opportunity to seek Wilson's opinion about the Northern Ireland situation amid concerns that a worsening situation would test Westminster's bipartisan approach.[60] Meetings with opposition leaders were typically a cordial formality for US presidents.[61] However, given Wilson's experience as prime minister, the meeting had the potential to be one of greater depth and immediate utility for the White House. This advice, for Nixon to ask for Wilson's opinion about Northern Ireland, is indicative of his administration's increasing interest in the issue.

In August 1971, internment without trial was introduced in Northern Ireland. Although it was widely viewed in Britain to be a reasonable response to the ever-increasing IRA activity, it made a deteriorating situation worse. Any hopes of a political accommodation between the unionists and the nationalists at Stormont were dashed with the significant intensification of violence. In 1971, before the advent of internment, 28 people died in the 'Troubles', compared to 146 during the rest of the year after internment was introduced. It also provoked outrage amongst the Catholic community, which viewed it as a discriminatory policy.[62] Using the British Embassy's chargé, Heath wrote to Nixon to explain this new development.[63] Kissinger informed Nixon that the British government understood 'that we cannot be drawn into the substances of this issue'.[64] The Prime Minister hoped that Nixon would empathise with the situation and was clearly hoping to convince the President of the merits of the policy and pre-empt any complaints from the Irish government. Heath claimed that internment would be more effective if the Irish government were to introduce it 'south of the border at the same time', although he acknowledged there would be no such 'parallel action south of the border'. The Prime Minister added that he had sent a message to his Irish counterpart in the hope that he would 'react with understanding, even if with regret', and accept the British hope 'that these measures can be strictly temporary' and would not 'prejudice' the Anglo-Irish process. Heath also invited Lynch for talks in London in October to discuss a 'whole range of matters of interest to us both'.[65]

Heath's decision to inform Nixon of these developments is illustrative of the administration's concern for Northern Ireland and, due to the acceptance of the President's global role, Nixon's de facto position as a neutral intermediary in the Anglo-Irish process. For such correspondence to have taken place suggests that the two men had discussed the issue and that Heath was aware that internment was something that Irish–Americans and the Irish government might complain about to the Nixon administration. Kissinger advised the President to 'express your appreciation for the thoughtfulness' of Heath's confidential letter when he met with

Sir Alec Douglas-Home, the British Foreign Secretary (1970–4), on 30 September 1971.[66] According to the American record of this meeting, however, Northern Ireland was not discussed, with South Africa being the topic of discussion.[67] *The New York Times*, however, criticised internment, as it would worsen the situation.[68] Internment was also discussed in a wide-ranging conversation about Northern Ireland between senior British civil servants and American representatives from the State Department in London on 22 November 1971.[69] Martin Hillenbrand (a career diplomat who served as Assistant Secretary of State for European and Canadian Affairs in the Nixon administration) requested the meeting with British officials before offering any testimony to the Irish caucus in the US House of Representatives on 1 December 1971. In addition to internment, the discussion covered the use of the British Army in Northern Ireland, the direction of British policy, the economic situation in the province, and the activities of the IRA and Protestant paramilitary groups. Closing the meeting, Hillenbrand remarked to the British that he 'hoped to be able to leave the problems of Northern Ireland to them'.[70] The American officials viewed the meetings as a briefing session, and not an opportunity to influence British policy. British officials had met with their American counterparts in acknowledgement of Irish–American interest and America's global role in international affairs, and in order to ensure that the US Congress heard the British account of the situation in Northern Ireland.

Nixon continued to be unsuccessfully lobbied by Irish–American groups. On 15 November 1971, Joseph C. Clark, who served as Chairman for Peace and Justice in Ireland, telegrammed Rosemary Woods, the President's secretary, asking the President to 'intercede for Peace and Justice for Ireland', and to see 'a box full of petitions' that underlined 'the genuineness of some people who would hold them for him to see'.[71] Clark received a reply from Scott George, who served as Nixon's Country Director for Ireland, Malta and the UK. The familiar administration position was the basis of the letter he wrote on behalf of the President and on Woods' instructions. Clark was informed that the US government was aware of the situation and of Irish–American concern, but that 'any intervention on our part would only exacerbate and not help to resolve this situation.'[72]

Woods also received a letter from Timothy B. Driscoll, a concerned Irish–American, on 29 December 1971, asking her to arrange for Nixon to meet with Irish–Americans travelling to Washington, DC, on 26 January 1972 in support of the Kennedy–Ribicoff–Carey Resolution (which called for temporary direct rule of Northern Ireland from London).[73] Playing on Woods' background, Driscoll ended with: 'The President seems to think a lot of you – unless he is using you to gain the Catholic Vote. But I think you have an obligation to help.'[74] On 25 January 1972, David N. Parker (staff assistant to the President) turned down the request but significantly added,

> During his recent meeting with the British Prime Minister in Bermuda, the President told Mr. Heath of the concern of the American people over this tragic situation and assured the British Prime Minister of our support for any efforts to put Northern Ireland on the road to peace with justice.[75]

The American and British records suggest that other topics dominated the formal meetings between members of the American and British governments in Bermuda on 20–1 December 1971 (for instance, China, Britain's relationship with the EEC, relations between India and Pakistan, strategic arms limitation talks, and Japan).[76] The only occasion that Northern Ireland was formally discussed is when Douglas-Home briefed Rogers and 'spoke briefly of the hopes for discussion with the various parties in Northern Ireland, saying that it might still be possible to persuade the SDLP to take part'.[77] (The SDLP, or the Social Democratic Labour Party, is a nationalist party established in Northern Ireland in 1970.) However, Parker's letter suggests that Nixon discussed Northern Ireland on an informal basis, as he had with Lynch. Five days after Parker's letter, the British Army killed thirteen Catholic civilians on 'Bloody Sunday'.

Although the Nixon administration maintained neutrality, other American politicians condemned British policy in light of this tragic event. Between 28 February and 1 March 1972, the US Foreign Affairs Subcommittee on Europe initiated hearings about Kennedy's resolution. Kennedy and thirteen other members of Congress spoke out against the British government while another twenty-two submitted written testimony.[78] These hearings prompted members of Congress, including Kennedy, to undertake many visits to Northern Ireland. Later that year, Kennedy would meet John Hume, a leading figure in the Northern Ireland civil rights campaign and one of the founders of the SDLP, to discuss Northern Ireland. Hume fostered a more nuanced understanding of the situation in Northern Ireland. Subsequently, the Kennedy–Ribicoff–Carey Resolution was revised to state that any American action should be in consultation with the Irish government, and the demand for British soldiers to leave Northern Ireland immediately became a request for a piecemeal departure.[79]

On 17 March 1972, Nixon met with the Irish ambassador, William Warnock (1970–3), so that the President could receive a shamrock to celebrate St Patrick's Day. In advance of the meeting, Kissinger briefed the President that, although 'substantive issues' were not typically discussed at such occasions, it was possible that Warnock might raise Northern Ireland.[80] The NSA explained that while the Irish government had 'publicly and privately asked us to weigh in with the British and convince them their policy is wrong and should be changed', the administration refused to take sides as it 'would do no good'. He added that this was in line with Canada and all other European countries that the Irish had approached about this situation.[81] In his meeting with Warnock, Nixon expressed some sympathy for the Irish position on Northern Ireland.[82] The ambassador 'told President Nixon that he regretted that this St. Patrick's Day was marked by violence in his country, and raised the hope that by this time next year the situation would have been resolved in the interests of peace'. In reply, Nixon, perhaps betraying his 1952 comments on partition, observed 'that the British had been somewhat negligent in the past on the issue of Northern Ireland, but . . . the current British Leadership was doing all that it could to resolve the issue in a thoughtful and just way'.[83] Yet a resolution was not found. By the end of March 1972, the British government transferred security powers back to Westminster. Unwilling to be prime minister without those powers, Faulkner resigned and Stormont was prorogued. The British government undertook direct rule for Northern Ireland and Heath appointed William ('Willie') Whitelaw as Secretary of State for Northern Ireland (1972–3). Utilising direct rule, Whitelaw implemented a 'hearts and minds' policy in order to develop better relations with the Catholic community without antagonising the Protestant community. This policy revolved around the British Army taking a 'low profile', a decision not to reoccupy republican 'no-go' areas, the release of detainees and, in what would prove a hostage to fortune, 'special category' status for republican prisoners who would be afforded political status.[84]

These developments in Northern Ireland, coupled with the Nixon administration's broader foreign policy priorities, contextualised the President's dispatching of Ronald Reagan across the Atlantic. Between 1969 and 1973, Reagan, while serving as governor of California (1967–75), made four trips abroad on behalf of the Nixon administration in both a ceremonial and a Goodwill capacity.[85] In July 1972, Reagan travelled to Denmark, Belgium, France, Spain, Italy, Britain and Ireland.[86] The broader context of Reagan's expedition was the 1969 Nixon Doctrine, which advocated a more equitable partnership and the sharing of an increased military burden with Europe.[87] Reagan's European mission was therefore one of reassurance of America's allies. Similarly, the tour coincided with the Nixon administration's desire for a rapprochement with Western Europe as the President sought to end the war in Vietnam.[88] Yet Northern Ireland was factored into Reagan's tour.

Northern Ireland was a potential topic of conversation between Reagan and Edward Heath. Although there is no available record of conversation, the issue was the first listed on the Prime Minister's briefing, thus underlining Nixon's interest.[89] It was noted that 'Reagan has not made extreme public statements about British policy in Ireland, despite his Irish ancestry' and the Irish–American lobby in California was 'not as strong as in many of the older states on the east coast'. Nonetheless, the briefing advised that Heath might 'wish to explain HMG's policy' so as to 'help him in dealing with any of the wilder accusations put up by the American–Irish community'.[90] Reagan was welcomed to Ireland by picket lines of protestors, who were angered by his dismissal of Kennedy's call for the US government to assume a mediatory role in the Northern Ireland conflict as 'unseemingly' [sic], and his status as a representative of the Nixon administration and its 'anti-Irish position'.[91]

Beyond diplomatic pleasantries between Nixon and de Valera, there is little archival material available about this particular visit. In a letter to de Valera, Nixon presented Reagan as the embodiment of Irish–American success: 'Reagan exemplifies the best of the traditions that our nations share. He is both an American and a son of Ireland.'[92] De Valera echoed Nixon's sentiments in his remarks at a dinner in Reagan's honour. The Irish President expressed the hope that 'the warm welcome which Irishmen and women have always received in the hospitable State of California and elsewhere throughout the United States', and hoped that the Governor would share the 'pride we in Ireland take in the important contribution made by Irishmen and women to the greatness of the State of California and to the United States'.[93] The Irish government identified Reagan's potential. A senior civil servant at the Irish Foreign Office had strongly urged that the Taoiseach agree to meet Reagan, as he was potentially 'a possible candidate for the Vice-Presidency or for some other high office, such as that of Secretary of State'.[94]

The introduction of direct rule was partly influenced by the critique in the US, particularly the moves by Kennedy and other Irish–American politicians.[95] But that was not the endgame for interested parties on Capitol Hill, who continued to express concern on behalf of themselves and their constituents about the 'Troubles'. In turn, Senators Alan Bible (D-NV) and Milton R. Young (R-ND), for instance, were told by Tom C. Korologos, Deputy Assistant to the President, that the administration shared this concern and again confirmed that the President discussed Northern Ireland with Heath in Bermuda.[96] Korologos added that, in January 1973, William Rogers also discussed it with Patrick Hillery and Lord Cromer, the British ambassador to the US (1971–4). According to Korologos, Rogers expressed deep concern and stated that 'if we can play a useful role, and the parties concerned feel it is possible for us to play a useful role, then we could naturally consider it'.[97] The administration's stance on Northern Ireland had evolved to a stated willingness to become involved if invited to do so. That the 'Troubles' had continued for five years was clearly of interest and concern to the US government. Young wrote to the administration on behalf of his constituent, the Right Reverend Monsignor William McNamee, who had read a newspaper article that claimed Nixon 'had something to do with the sending of British troops into Northern Ireland in connection with the turmoil in that country'.[98] Korologos clarified that the withdrawal of British troops from elsewhere and redeployment to Northern Ireland, and their replacement by other NATO countries, including American soldiers, was standard procedure and did not represent Nixon's support for the British government in Northern Ireland.[99]

Yet Nixon's line of non-intervention did not convince Irish–Americans or Democrats who were long predisposed to be critical of the President. For instance, Rep. Michael J. Harrington (D-MA) wrote to the President,

> As reports from Ulster continue to paint a picture of incipient civil war ... I cannot in good conscience accept the proposition that Ulster is the sole affair of the British, and not a matter of international concern, appropriate for U.N. cognizance.[100]

Harrington argued that the central problem of Nixon's position was that 'because we risk the certain displeasure of the Heath government, and the possible veto of any U.N. action, we, as a nation, should stand by and observe the tragedy unfold'. He believed that the administration's view was inconsistent with American policy towards conflicts elsewhere, and argued that the US 'should not be paralysed by a fear of offending the British government while the needless suffering, bloodshed and death continues'.[101] A few months later, Nixon received a letter from the AOH, rebuking his administration's position on Northern Ireland.[102] The President was told:

> You will not 'con' us by your visits to Ireland, or your empty pledges of support for parochial schools ... we demand that you put American pressure on the English government to end an unjust partition of a small nation, and the discriminatory tactics employed there.[103]

Nixon had discussed the issue with the British and Irish governments during the preceding two years, but unconcerned by the nuances of diplomacy, the AOH sought public and speedier action from the President.

During the summer of 1972, there was some discussion within the NSC about whether the US could intervene in the Northern Ireland conflict. An NSC memorandum shows that 'The President has expressed an interest in learning what, if anything responsible, might be done by the US in helping achieve a solution to the Ulster problem.'[104] Thus, Nixon wanted to explore options for American involvement. In turn, Robert Gerald Livingston (NSC staff, 1972–3) informed Alexander Haig, the Deputy NSA, that the province was 'in a state of civil war' and that any intervention would be viewed as a 'partisan move' by one of the involved governments or religious communities, even 'a reference in a Presidential speech'.[105] He argued that 'the situation is not driving us to act,' given that the British government had 'dampened down the violence' and the British and Irish public had 'become used to our non-intervention policy'. Nevertheless, Livingston advised that if the situation deteriorated to the extent that 'we believe we should act', then it would be best 'to go for outright mediation', but support from other external parties could be vital, such as the Vatican, and the Nixon administration would need assurance that 'the British and Irish governments would not oppose us.'[106] Livingston was clearly aware that American intervention required political cover. Haig's reply was pure realpolitik:

> I can conceive of no more self-defeating initiative than to move one inch beyond our current policy. Thus far, we have avoided a hornets' nest by confining ourselves to saying that we are concerned about the Ulster tragedy, welcome all responsible efforts to stop the violence, and would consider playing a 'useful role' if asked, at the same time emphasizing that it would be 'inappropriate and counter-productive' to intervene in any way.[107]

This position still amounted to a reluctance to intervene. Turning to domestic political concerns, Haig observed that the 'fact that U.S. Catholics are heartened by our domestic policies on abortion, busing and aid to parochial schools should more than compensate for a lack of do-goodism on the Ulster problem'. Haig noted that 'there is no way that we can "out-Kennedy" Kennedy on this issue and before the campaign goes very long, McGovern will be way out in left'. Moreover, in terms of the forthcoming 1972 presidential election, he added that 'our best posture in the post-Vietnam climate is the overriding need to keep out from the foreign policy point of view'.[108] In short, there was no electoral benefit and it was viewed as an inevitable foreign policy failure, which could jeopardise relations with the British and Irish governments – in other words, a 'no-win' scenario for the President. Haig was thus determined to dissuade Nixon from intervention; that these briefing materials never included Kissinger or Nixon underlines the fact that presidential aides did not want Northern Ireland to become an issue for the Oval Office.

The potential political dimension of Northern Ireland during the 1972 presidential election campaign was also not lost on Nixon. Acknowledging a letter from Heath, dated 29 July 1972, about security developments in Northern Ireland, Nixon explained that he had followed developments 'with the closest interest', and 'greatly appreciated' both the 'advance notification' of the British Army's operations in Belfast and Londonderry 'against the terrorists' and Heath's 'thoughtfulness in laying out in such detail the situation'.[109] The President assured Heath that he would 'continue to resist' domestic pressure on him to intervene and that he had his 'full support' in efforts to resolve the issue peacefully. In a handwritten addition, the President wrote, 'You can be sure that despite the pressure of a political campaign, I shall not add to your problems on this issue.'[110] This Heath–Nixon correspondence probably referred to 'Operation Motorman', in which 12,000 British soldiers – the most mobilised since the Suez Crisis – cleared republican 'no-go' areas in a successful move to undermine IRA activities severely. Nevertheless, loyalists remained unconvinced by British policy. Unionist oratory became increasingly militant and the Ulster Defence Association (UDA) subsequently – albeit briefly – directed their violence towards the British Army in October 1972.[111]

Irish–American attitudes towards Northern Ireland were the principal reason for Nixon's decision to meet with Patrick Hillery, still the Irish Foreign Minister, in October 1972. Hillery was attending the UN General Assembly, and the Irish Embassy called the State Department about whether 'there might be an opportunity for Hillery to meet with the President'.[112] Sonnenfeldt advised Kissinger that Nixon might wish to meet Hillery due to 'the intensity of Irish–American concern over the problems of Northern Ireland'. While the meeting would not influence policy, it 'would be a clear demonstration of the President's concern'.[113] In other words, the White House was concerned about the difficulties between two allies but would continue to remain neutral. Indeed, as an aside, Sonnenfeldt noted that such a meeting would 'balance the President's meeting with Sir Alec' (Douglas-Home) as far as the Irish–American community was concerned.[114] Given the power and influence of the US presidency, Nixon had to be seen as adopting a balanced approach to the 'Troubles' so as not to suggest any favoured protagonists. Prior to his meeting with Hillery on 6 October 1972, Nixon was briefed by Kissinger.[115] Kissinger cautioned, 'While expressing your deep concern, you should tell Hillery that you continue to believe that a solution to the problems of Ulster can only be worked out by the parties involved.'[116] This was exactly the line taken by Nixon during his meeting with Hillery. According to the American record of the conversation, Nixon 'expressed his profound sadness at the continuing bitterness and strife in Northern Ireland' and 'said that he had a keen interest in finding a peaceful solution'.[117] Hillery explained that 'he had been encouraged by the British Government's recent actions in Northern Ireland . . . the British have seemed to be seeking a political solution rather than a military solution which has the approval of the Irish Government'. The President cautioned that his administration was 'not in a position to openly or publicly intervene in Northern Ireland' but he appreciated the Taoiseach's 'constructive attitude in cooperating with the British to find a peaceful solution'. In response, Hillery told the President that the Irish government 'did not seek open or public declarations by the United States Government', although he 'hoped' that, in 'private discussions with the British', the administration would make its views 'known'. Nixon assured Hillery 'that in all of our high level discussions with the British our views on Northern Ireland are expressed'.[118] Thus, in private Nixon remained keen for a solution to be agreed and encouraged all parties to do this. Yet the public position of the US remained one of neutrality.

On 31 October 1972, the British government published its Green (or discussion) Paper about the future of Northern Ireland.

Published in the context of loyalist and republican violence, the Green Paper outlined proposals for a power-sharing agreement across the communities and acknowledged that the Irish government had a legitimate interest in Northern Irish affairs.[119] On 3 December 1972, the NSA wrote a detailed memorandum for the President about 'Northern Ireland – Recent Moves by London and Dublin'.[120] Kissinger noted, 'While bombings and killings continue in Northern Ireland, the Irish have joined the British in meaningful moves against the Irish Republican Army, as well as political moves that may possibly point toward a solution to Ulster's seemingly intractable problems.' The Green Paper was explained to Nixon, including the fact that the British had acknowledged the 'Irish dimension' to the conflict:

> Northern Ireland is a part of Ireland; no solution to its problems can be found without taking the interests of the Irish Republic into account: and this, in turn, includes obligations on the part of the Republic to reciprocate, taking interests of Great Britain and Northern Ireland into account.

According to Kissinger, the Green Paper emphasised 'that there will be no change in Northern Ireland's status without the consent of its people, coupling this pledge with a statement of the UK's conditions for continuing support'. Thus, Jack Lynch, the Taoiseach, was 'earnestly trying to come to grips with the social and political problems that are fundamental to any lasting solution to the trouble in Ulster – with moves against the IRA and toward Constitutional reform in Ireland'. Kissinger believed that these developments offered 'cause for cautious optimism'. However, his concluding remarks to the President are unsurprising: 'The purpose of this memorandum is to advise you of recent developments in Northern Ireland. There is no need for any action on your part at this time.'[121]

Later that month, Sonnenfeldt suggested to Kissinger that Nixon should meet with Lynch during the Taoiseach's informal visit to the US.[122] Although Lynch would be promoting American investment in Ireland, Sonnenfeldt believed that a meeting 'would be very useful' because Nixon would have 'the opportunity to receive Lynch's views on the Northern Ireland crisis', particularly as the Taoiseach had 'recently toughened his stand against the IRA'.[123] While the administration was prepared for Nixon to discuss Northern Ireland with the Taoiseach, there was a clear unwillingness to raise it with the British Prime Minister. On 16 January 1973, over cocktails, Kissinger and Sonnenfeldt met with Sir Burke Trend (Secretary to the British Cabinet), Cromer, Richard Sykes (British Minister to the US) and Brian Norbury (Trend's secretary). After arranging in detail the content and topics for Heath's forthcoming visit to the US, Northern Ireland was the final issue discussed, and briefly too. Kissinger was clear that the administration was happy for it not to be discussed:

> Sikes [sic]: There is one other topic, Ireland.
> Trend:     Yes, the Prime Minister may want to discuss how things are going.
> Kissinger: We will not raise it.
> Trend:     The Prime Minister may want to fill him in.[124]

Kissinger clearly did not want Northern Ireland to be a priority for Nixon (who was more concerned with, for instance, Vietnam, China, the recent Strategic Arms Limitation Treaty, or SALT, and nuclear policy), but it was obvious that Heath would continue his practice of consulting with the President. The briefing documents for the Prime Minister suggested that, in his meeting with Nixon, he 'may wish to say that the British Government have been grateful for the helpful attitude of the US Administration, particularly in the action they have taken against the smuggling of arms destined for Northern Ireland'.[125] Moreover, Heath was advised to emphasise the government's acceptance 'that there is no purely military solution in Northern Ireland, but that success against terrorists, from whatever quarter, is necessary to achieve a political settlement' and satisfaction with Irish measures 'against the IRA'. The Prime Minister was informed that Northern Ireland was not politicised in the recent presidential election, 'although had the two candidates been more evenly matched the temptation to make a play for the Irish vote might have been irresistible'. On the concerns of the US government on Northern Ireland, Heath was briefed: 'The United States authorities have been helpful in refusing visas to IRA members and sympathisers, and . . . in dealing with arms smuggling.'[126]

Somewhat foreshadowing President Jimmy Carter's 1977 statement on Northern Ireland, Heath was also briefed that, in a meeting with Nixon on 6 October 1972, Hillery, the Irish Foreign Minister, raised the possibility of economic development.[127] Subsequently, the State Department proposed discussions with the Irish and British governments about potential American investment in Northern Ireland and the Republic. The British government was cautious:

> An American proposal in the economic sphere might appear to Dublin as a nudge to HMG to accept Dublin's proposals for discussions about a political solution to Northern Ireland's problems. The Irish have on other occasions sought to bring international and especially American pressure to bear on us.[128]

Irish efforts to involve the US in Northern Ireland were equalled by British resistance to the possibility.

During his visit to the US in early 1973, Edward Heath, in addition to meeting with Nixon, also spent time with members of Congress. In a meeting with the Senate Foreign Relations Committee, Heath explained the situation in Northern Ireland from his government's perspective, stressing that the British were 'dealing with a formidable urban guerrilla movement'.[129] Heath added that during an event at the National Press Club, he was asked 'to compare the situation in Ireland to Vietnam: but any such comparison was quite false, as Ulster was part of the United Kingdom'. He explained British policy within the context of the politics and demographics of Northern Ireland:

> people were inclined to think of the population of Ireland merely as Irish. But the basic fact was the sectarian division, flowing from the injection of a largely Scottish Protestant population into an Irish Catholic native population. The politics of the last 50 years had been based on this division . . . No British Government was going to try to keep Northern Ireland from joining the Republic if the majority of the population wanted that.[130]

In a private meeting with Senator Kennedy, Heath also discussed Northern Ireland. Crucially, as the British record shows, Heath wanted to ensure that the Senator supported the British and Irish governments' efforts to reduce American funding for violence in Northern Ireland in favour of support for organisations such as the Red Cross. Kennedy said that he would do so.[131] This meeting underlines the importance of the congressional dimension to American interest in, and policy towards, Northern Ireland, as in any other foreign policy agenda. Indeed, when Heath met Nixon, Kennedy's interest in Northern Ireland was the particular focus of their discussion about the issue, before turning to other geopolitical concerns.[132] The Nixon administration's concern for action on Northern Ireland was dwarfed by broader international worries. This is demonstrated in a conversation between Nixon and Kissinger two days after the President's meeting with Heath:

Nixon:      With Heath now we'll want to play to get him and we've got to play with him. See, what I think he appreciates, Henry, is that we didn't bug him on Northern Ireland.

Kissinger:  No way.

Nixon:      He knows that. He appreciates the fact that we didn't bug him on Rhodesia. He appreciates the fact that we didn't bug him on other things –

Kissinger:  But then you did it in such a delicate way when you said, 'All right, now, we've talked about Northern Ireland.'

Nixon:      Yeah. We're God, now, and – But now, therefore, on a much bigger thing he didn't give us hell, and as a matter of fact made all the right noises.[133]

The publication of the British government's White Paper, *Northern Ireland Constitutional Proposals*, in March 1973 confirmed its acknowledgement of the Irish dimension to Northern Ireland. The British government accepted the need for co-operation and consultation with its Irish counterparts in security concerns and North–South relations. That the British and Irish governments had reached an understanding on the situation is perhaps best demonstrated by the acknowledgement of Liam Cosgrave (the new Taoiseach, 1973–7) to Conservative MPs in July 1973 that, even though he ultimately sought Irish reunification, the contemporaneous climate made it impossible under the threat of loyalist unrest and potential escalation of tensions.[134] In December 1973, the Sunningdale Agreement promised the introduction of a cross-border Council of Ireland and a power-sharing National Executive. However, the agreement collapsed at the end of May 1974 following a general strike called by the loyalist Ulster Workers Council and the murder of thirty-three civilians in Dublin and Monaghan on 17 May. Wilson, at this point again British Prime Minister (1974–6), publicly criticised the strikes' organisers as 'thugs dependent on the generosity of the British taxpayer' and even considered withdrawal altogether.[135] The Labour government ultimately decided that withdrawal would be a disaster for Britain and Ireland.[136]

Upon the collapse of the Sunningdale Agreement, the British government moved towards a Northern Ireland Constitutional Convention (NICC). Following the release of the *Northern Ireland Constitution* White Paper in July 1974, Kissinger informed Nixon that it 'tells the Northern Ireland Protestants that they must devise their own political rules, that these rules must include some form of power sharing with the minority Catholic community'.[137] The non-intervention stance continued: 'This memorandum is to advise you of recent British steps in Ulster; no action is required on your part.'[138] The State Department also advocated a similar position to the Executive Branch: 'U.S. interests are still best served by our policy of strict non-intervention.'[139] The subsequent elections to the NICC resulted in a unionist majority, which undermined any attempt to achieve a power-sharing agreement. It was dissolved on 4 March 1976.

Nixon certainly held sufficient interest in Northern Ireland to identify the potential political gain from the issue and discuss it with the Irish and British prime ministers. Since the 1950s he had been concerned by the politics and policies of the issue. In 1952, Nixon argued that the Republican Party offered renewed hope for ending partition. This was clearly politicking, but it also demonstrated his awareness of a controversial issue across the Atlantic.

As president, Nixon's understanding of the politicisation of Northern Ireland extended to the British fears of Irish–Americans utilising the issue in presidential elections. The realities of foreign policy priorities, concurrent with the neutral stance of the State Department, shaped the concerns of his administration. However, the Irish government – coupled with Irish–Americans – sought to convince Nixon to intervene on their behalf. In response, the British government consulted with the Nixon administration in order to offer a counter-narrative of the 'Troubles'. Both the British and the Irish recognised the power of the US President and the potential influence that Nixon could wield on the issue. Thus, aware of the significance attached to any presidential action on any issue, Nixon was essentially an informal intermediary, who discussed Northern Ireland with the British and Irish governments and encouraged a resolution. In an attempt to underline his peace-making credentials, the President briefly considered intervention but was persuaded otherwise, and the issue was not important enough to override his advisers and intervene in the Anglo-Irish process. Ultimately, the events of Watergate propelled Nixon's career in an unforeseen direction.

## The Ford administration, 1974–7

Nixon's resignation amid the Watergate Scandal on 9 August 1974 saw the advent of President Gerald Ford and, at least in the immediate term, no change in policy towards Northern Ireland. Ford's contribution to the American dimension of the Anglo-Irish process is widely ignored in the historiography of both the Ford administration and Irish–American activity.[140] The remainder of this chapter therefore explores Ford's policy towards Northern Ireland.

Ford's presidency coincided with the abortive NICC, the IRA's 1975–6 ceasefire, and a fear that Britain would withdraw from Northern Ireland and usher in a civil war. In November 1975, special category status was removed, meaning that, from 1 March 1976, convicted republicans would again be criminalised and would no longer be considered as political prisoners. In January 1976, Wilson announced that a united Ireland was unlikely to be imposed by any British political party and a series of new security measures were introduced. Later that month, the ceasefire between the British government and IRA ended, with their respective representatives meeting for the last time on 10 February 1976. Subsequently, the IRA abandoned its hopes that a 'truce' would lead to British withdrawal. The organisation adopted a new strategy for the 'Long War' and implemented a cellular structure to minimise the intelligence opportunities available to British security forces.[141] Given the inevitable lobbying from Irish–Americans, it is unsurprising that Kissinger wrote a four-page memorandum for Ford, explaining the causes and history – in his view – of the conflict and potential outcomes.[142] He advised:

> Religious differences and resulting hatred between Protestants and Catholics in Northern Ireland are so deep-rooted that the prospects of a settlement remain very slim . . . In the event of a civil war, it would be difficult to prevent outsiders, such as the Dublin government and elements of the Irish–American community in the U.S., from supporting the Ulster Catholics. UN intercession is another possibility.[143]

The President was briefed on what was essentially a potentially important, albeit immediately peripheral, issue. As per Kissinger's briefing, Northern Ireland could potentially have an impact on the Ford administration in terms of domestic politics and foreign policy.

Shortly after his inauguration, Ford received a letter from John Bownes, who served as public relations chairman for the AOH.[144] Bownes asked Ford to reverse Nixon's policy towards Ireland. Whereas had Nixon 'refused' to intervene in what his administration viewed as 'an internal problem', the former President angered the AOH by allowing American 'troops to take the place of British soldiers in NATO to enable them to buttress a military regime in Northern Ireland'. Bownes appealed to the new President on the grounds that life is equally important in Northern Ireland, Asia and the Middle East: 'The American people have sacrificed a lot to bring peace to people all over the world. We ask you to help bring peace to the minority in Northern Ireland.'[145] Writing on behalf of Ford, Roland L. Elliot (Director of Correspondence in the White

House, 1971–7) offered the standard reply since the Johnson and Nixon administrations:

> The United States has avoided direct involvement, our position being that if the parties directly involved agreed there is anything the US could usefully do, we would consider it, but that in the absence of such a request any involvement on our part would be inappropriate and counterproductive.[146]

The NSC considered Bownes's letter and drafted the reply to Elliot.[147] The issue was clearly one that the administration sought to handle carefully.

In September 1974, the AOH agreed its support for the creation of the Irish National Caucus (INC), under the leadership of Father Seán McManus, a Roman Catholic priest and republican activist who had moved from Northern Ireland to the US two years earlier. As an umbrella organisation for all other Irish–American organisations, the INC sought to be the only Irish–American lobbyists of the US government and, likewise, be the sole information source for American media on the Northern Ireland conflict, while promoting its republican view of its Northern Irish history, challenges and solutions. This development ensured that Irish–Americans were therefore presented with two contrasting analyses of the situation in Northern Ireland: that of the republican INC and their reports of human rights abuses in Northern Ireland, and that of the US government's position of neutrality and de facto defence of the British government. Links between the INC and NORAID (and the connection between NORAID and the IRA) meant that the INC was subject to surveillance in the US. However, the INC ceased to support NORAID actively at around the same time that McManus's attention shifted to investigating and reporting claims of human rights abuses in Northern Ireland in 1975.[148]

Yet the AOH wished to go further than simply writing to the President. Seán W. Walsh IV, Executive Director of the AOH, wrote to Ford on 14 November, requesting that, 'in the interest of justice', the President would 'meet with us so that we may offer you our expertise and our support to assist a struggling people'.[149] The AOH even attempted to contextualise its ambitions within

Ford's intention 'to improve relations with Britain' and, in order to do so, added that 'we urge you to include Northern Ireland in your discussions'. The NSC flatly denied the AOH's request. Brent Scowcroft (Deputy NSA, 1973–5, and NSA, 1975–7) argued that such a meeting with the President or any other senior White House figure 'would be inadvisable from the standpoint of foreign policy'.[150] Broader foreign policy concerns therefore triumphed. Walsh was subsequently told that his offer was 'being considered together with the many other suggestions which compete for his personal time and attention'.[151] The NSC distanced the issue from the Oval Office.

The continuation of Nixon's settled policy towards Northern Ireland was clear when Ford met with Wilson. Prior to Wilson's departure for the US in January 1975, the Northern Ireland Office briefed him that the administration 'wishes to remain uninvolved' and that Kissinger was 'especially understanding and helpful'.[152] It was noted that Senator Kennedy continued to advocate a 'satisfactory role by the United States, but this has raised no response from the Administration'.[153] It is clear from Kissinger's briefing of Ford in advance of Wilson's visit that he advocated American neutrality:

> We trust that both the British and the Irish Governments are doing all they can to avoid a civil war. The fact that both Governments share a common view and are able to arrive at common policies greatly lessens domestic political pressure on the USG to get involved.[154]

Kissinger's briefing for the President was much more concerned with issues such as the international economy, East–West security and defence policy.[155] Ultimately, Northern Ireland was not discussed when Wilson met Ford on 30–1 January 1975.[156] Wide-ranging conversations covered, for instance, the Middle East, nuclear matters, economic policy and energy cooperation.[157] Despite the administration's concern about IRA gunrunning, this was not raised.[158] This was the case in other meetings between Wilson and Ford.[159] Unlike Nixon, Ford lacked interest in the issue; there is no suggestion that it was even discussed informally. Ford followed Kissinger's advice. However, the administration's concern about gunrunning remained. In February 1976, Edward

Levi, the Attorney General (1975–7), wrote to Scowcroft with advice for the President regarding 'the illegal exportation of weapons from the United States to Northern Ireland'.[160] Levi advised Ford to take the line that, in addition to neutrality on Northern Ireland, his administration was opposed to the violence there and would 'vigorously enforce all applicable criminal statutes in our effort to deter the smuggling of weapons and explosives from the United States'.[161] The associated American criminal activity captured Ford's attention.

Gunrunning was a potential topic of discussion when Kissinger met with Garret FitzGerald, the Irish Foreign Minister (1973–7), in January 1975. The State Department reminded Kissinger to emphasise that the US government was determined to quash American gunrunning and fund-raising for the IRA.[162] Similarly, he was advised to inform FitzGerald of American concern about the issue, yet 'stress our non-involvement and urge him to work to avoid civil war'.[163] The State Department believed that Liam Cosgrave's Irish government (1973–7) sought 'reunification through peaceful means, but has moved slowly in Northern Ireland to create the type of society and the climate where Protestants would forego their present determination to fight to avoid joining the Republic'. The State Department believed that the inability of the Irish government to influence 'the situation in the North' meant that 'The drift into civil war continues.' Kissinger was briefed that the Irish government could adopt a variety of policies to help further the Anglo-Irish process, such as a willingness to extradite fugitives back to Northern Ireland, firmer security cooperation with the British, and the implementation of a secular state, which would better enable the integration of one million Protestants. Nonetheless, he was advised against raising any such policy with FitzGerald. Instead, Kissinger was urged to 'at least show a studied scepticism' that the Irish government was exhausting all efforts 'to avoid civil war'. With regard to gunrunning, it was noted that FitzGerald had 'repeatedly condemned Americans who contribute money to the IRA', but, despite American successes in limiting Irish–American financial support for the IRA, the efforts were undermined by the Irish government's unwillingness to share intelligence, probably because they feared it would become known to 'IRA sympathizers' in the American government.[164] (There is ostensibly no record available of this meeting.)

On 23 April 1975, Ford was informed in his presidential daily briefing about the Irish government's pessimism and fear that 'hardline Protestants' would dominate Northern Ireland's elections for a constitutional convention and cause it to collapse.[165] Such an outcome would mean that direct rule would continue amid fears in the Irish government that the British would withdraw 'before a stable political solution can be achieved'.[166] FitzGerald expressed these fears to Kissinger when they met again in October 1975. Towards the end of their conversation, FitzGerald stated that he would 'take only a moment to mention Northern Ireland'. Commenting on the NICC, FitzGerald candidly admitted that the Irish government had been 'alarmed' that it 'might decide on majority rule which the UK would reject and thus bring on more violence and perhaps civil war'. However, the subsequent compromise meant that 'the danger of an explosion has been postponed until January or February.' The Foreign Minister believed that further clarification of British policy was needed: 'If they opt out, there will be anarchy.' Fearing violence, he shared the knowledge that the Irish government was 'building up our army but for the foreseeable future it will be smaller than the RUC and the Protestant paramilitaries'. For FitzGerald, the next actions of the British government were vital:

> The departure of the British would create a disaster, but they seem to be seeing more hope. The Ulster strike damaged their credibility, but direct rule could stabilize the situation and restore their credibility. We are more hopeful in the shortrun [sic]. What could have a bad effect would be an IRA bombing campaign in the UK.[167]

Kissinger noted that 'In the fading days of empire, people want the British troops to stay,' to which FitzGerald agreed: 'We want them to stay until a solution is reached.' Both men discussed how the solution had to be found from inside the British Isles. FitzGerald explained, 'The Protestants must realize that they have no other alternative but to accept power-sharing.' He told Kissinger that it was possible 'if the British are determined enough'. Kissinger was less than optimistic, noting that his wife (who had Irish heritage) 'says that is not possible'. FitzGerald concluded this part of the conversation with 'I hope she doesn't convince you.'[168] Northern Ireland was on the agenda, but not a priority.

Wilson raised the issue of Irish–American support for the IRA publicly to American correspondents in a speech to the association's annual dinner in London on 17 December 1975. As much as the Irish government feared British withdrawal from Northern Ireland, the British government was tired of Irish–American support for violence in the province.[169] Less than a month later, Stanley Orme, Minister of State for Northern Ireland (1974–6), met Robert Ingersoll, the US Deputy Secretary of State (1974–6), at the State Department.[170] Orme briefed Ingersoll – 'on a confidential basis' – about the NICC. Also discussed were Irish–American financial support for the IRA and gunrunning.[171] The British and Irish governments recognised American interest in Northern Ireland.

After consultation with the British Foreign and Commonwealth Office (FCO), the American Embassy reported to the administration on 12 January 1976 that British strategy towards Northern Ireland had at best a forty per cent chance of success.[172] The strengthening of British armed forces in South Armagh was designed to 'prevent a possible Protestant paramilitary offensive' in the region. Politically, the British government accepted a 'partial acceptance of the constitutional convention report, rejection of other parts of the report, and recall of the convention to seek consensus as to the future form of devolved government for Northern Ireland'. While the British government did not wish to use phrases such as 'power-sharing' and 'Irish dimension', as they were 'anathema to Loyalists', it argued 'that failure to reach agreement with the minority (Catholic) community will mean an indefinite period of continued direct rule from Westminster'.[173] Seán Donlon, in his capacity as a key adviser to FitzGerald about Northern Ireland affairs, briefed the American Embassy in Dublin about the situation in Northern Ireland on 15 January 1976.[174] According to the report, the British government consulted with their Irish counterparts prior to its army's deployment in South Armagh. As for the NICC, FitzGerald had 'little hope' that it would succeed and feared that, within a couple of months, its collapse would result 'in institutionalized direct rule from Westminster'. This echoed his comments to Kissinger a few months earlier. Interestingly, Donlon revealed that the Irish government was cooperating with the British in terms of security and acknowledged that 'it needs to erase its image . . . that it is lackadaisical about security'.[175] That Northern Ireland was included in presidential daily briefings suggests that it was at least of some interest to the White House.

The Ford administration continued to acknowledge Irish–American support for violence in Northern Ireland and was prepared to do so publicly when the President met with the Taoiseach in March 1976. Briefing the President, Scowcroft explained that successful prosecutions by the Justice Department had seen a decline in American gunrunning; however, there was still a strong level of Irish–American financial support for the IRA, which enabled weapons to be purchased (albeit outside of the US).[176] Unlike the British government, its Irish counterparts raised the topic of Northern Ireland in talks with Ford, and such financial support was at the heart of their conversations. This was anticipated by the Ford administration. In advance of the President's meeting with Cosgrave in March 1976, Scowcroft typically briefed that American policy was 'to avoid involvement, despite pressure by Irish–American groups', including attempts to secure congressional hearings by the House International Relations Subcommittee. He added that the administration's stance was that 'a solution can only be arrived at by the parties directly concerned – the UK, Ulster, and Ireland – and that unsolicited outside efforts could impact unfavourably on the situation'.[177] The talking points recognised that Irish–American financial support for the IRA might be raised in the meeting and Ford should explain that, whenever this is identified, the administration 'vigorously' enforces American laws against it.[178] The Ford administration's focus was therefore on the involvement of American citizens in aiding and abetting violence in Northern Ireland.

Cosgrave's visit proved to be controversial within the Irish–American community, given that he was due to ask them not to support the IRA financially. Bernadette O'Reilly, writing to Ford on behalf of the INC, objected to the prospect of Cosgrave's apparent intention to 'instruct' Irish–Americans 'where – and where not – to send their monies for Irish relief'.[179] In turn, she argued that such a prospect was 'unconscionable' and the administration should not enable Cosgrave to 'criticize or belittle hundreds of thousands of American citizens of Irish descent'. The INC objected to Cosgrave's opportunity to address a joint session of Congress on 17 March as 'we – American citizens – have been denied the right to testify before hearings in the Congress'.[180] Denis Clift (NSC) briefed Scowcroft on the INC's objections, albeit after the Ford–Cosgrave meeting. Clift believed that O'Reilly and her colleagues were determined 'to continue supporting "the Irish people" – i.e., the IRA'.[181] At Clift's suggestion, Elliot, a month later, wrote to O'Reilly and enclosed the agreed communiqué between Cosgrave and Ford.[182] This communiqué is discussed below.

Prior to his departure for America, Cosgrave was briefed that, three years earlier, Patrick Hillery (then the Irish Foreign Minister) had appealed to Secretary of State Rogers 'to use his good offices with the British authorities to improve their security policies in Northern Ireland'; Rogers, in turn, 'agreed to consult the British authorities but would not agree that the U.S. should play a prominent role in the situation'.[183] Rogers' assurance had revolved around Nixon's de facto position as an intermediary in the Anglo-Irish process. He agreed to discuss the issue with the British but not to intervene – and it was Rogers, not Nixon, who agreed to it. Cosgrave's visit coincided with the American presidential election campaign, particularly the nomination process. He was advised that it was unlikely to be an issue, as Ford would adhere to the State Department's neutrality and Ronald Reagan (the former Republican Governor of California, 1967–75) was unlikely to 'take a more forward position on the issue'. However, it was deemed possible that it would be 'invoked' by candidates for the Democratic Party's presidential nomination. For instance, Senator Henry M. Jackson (D-WA) 'sent a message to the last annual dinner of the NORAID'. While the Irish government did not object to the statement – it marked 'a departure in current U.S. policy in envisaging a more active role for the U.S. Government in attempting to conciliate the conflicting factions in Ireland' – the Irish did object to a statement being delivered to a NORAID event. In a far-fetched scenario, Cosgrave was advised that at a brokered Democratic convention:

> Governor Hugh Carey . . . might emerge as an agreed candidate and might even be nominated by Senator Kennedy in such circumstances. . . . In a recent speech at the American Irish Historical Society he

advocated the unification of Ireland as a solution. He can confidently be counted upon not to support violence.[184]

Cosgrave met Ford on St Patrick's Day, 17 March 1976. The final topic of conversation was Northern Ireland. According to the Irish record, Cosgrave offered a summary of the Northern Ireland situation and his government's policy towards it.[185] Ford acknowledged 'that the flow of arms and money from America had apparently created many difficulties'. Garret FitzGerald interjected, saying 'they would like a reference to this, if possible, in some joint statement or communiqué'. The President moved the conversation on with the response, 'let me talk to the Secretary of State about this'.[186] The American record is more detailed. For instance, Cosgrave's account of the situation in Northern Ireland included the collapse of the constitutional convention and concern about aid funding for violence from outside the province.[187] FitzGerald's comment on this was clearly designed to stress the importance of Ford's position: 'If we put something in the communiqué about not sending money to Ireland, it would help coming from you.' Interestingly, rather than refer to Kissinger, the American record simply notes the President's response as: 'There is a brief inconclusive look at the communiqué.' Thus, the Irish record is indicative of either Ford's reliance on Kissinger's advice or an attempt by the President to use the Secretary of State in order to avoid addressing the issue politely and immediately himself. Cosgrave tried to be diplomatic about the request: 'It might be counterproductive to make much of it.' The meeting closed with the Taoiseach inviting Ford to visit Ireland, which the President was happy to do after the presidential election.[188] The subsequent communiqué marked a gradual, piecemeal change in the position of the American executive branch towards Northern Ireland. The statement read:

> The President and the Prime Minister noted with regret the continued violence arising from the Northern Ireland situation. They deplored all support for organizations involved directly or indirectly in campaigns of violence and reiterated in particular their determination to continue and to intensify their cooperation in the prosecution of illegal activities. They appealed to the American and Irish people to refrain from supporting, with financial or other aid, this violence.[189]

Again, the focus of the statement was on American involvement in the conflict, not the conflict itself. Nevertheless, the communiqué was subject to debate between the State Department and the NSC.[190] Given Cosgrave's determination to release a communiqué condemning Irish–American support for violence, the department 'recommend[ed] that his wishes be acceded to', although 'the draft Irish text should be modified in several respects'.[191] Any suggestion of Irish–American – or American involvement – in the Anglo-Irish process was deleted from the final draft.

The coverage of the communiqué in the American, British and Irish press was mixed. This is surprising, given that it was the first time that a US president had issued such a statement on the 'Troubles'. Alternatively, that such an intervention was ignored underlines that it was unexpected, in light of the previous American refusal to intervene. In the British case, for instance, *The Guardian* focused on Cosgrave's appeal to Irish–Americans to cease any financial support for the IRA during his address to a joint session of Congress and did not refer to the communiqué in subsequent reports or editorials.[192] *The Times* only reported on Cosgrave's announcement that American companies would be investing $105 million in Ireland.[193] In the US, *The New York Times* reported on Cosgrave's speech while an editorial the following day noted that the speech was significant as it explained that violence was not a means to achieve a united Ireland, which could only happen through consent.[194] *The Boston Globe* reported that Ford joined with Cosgrave in calling for Americans to stop funding the IRA and an end to the violence in Northern Ireland.[195] Inevitably, in Ireland, Cosgrave's message about support for the IRA and the communiqué were headline news: for instance, in *The Irish Times*.[196] *The Irish Press* reported that Cosgrave received a standing ovation for his speech to Congress.[197] The relative lack of press attention to the Ford–Cosgrave communiqué is parallel to the complete sidelining of its existence within the historiography of the American contribution to the Anglo-Irish process. Nevertheless, it should not be ignored. The Ford administration was the first to make a statement that clarified the US government view about Northern Ireland, specifically in regard to the activities of some American citizens. This was a key development in the recognition that, even though the

US was reluctant to intervene in the issue, it could not ignore it or stand by, while some of its citizens were doing just that.

## Conclusion

The Nixon–Ford epoch saw the executive branch of the US government become more interested in Northern Ireland. Both the British and Irish governments kept the Nixon administration informed and, with the advent of the Ford administration, the President was subject to further briefings on Northern Ireland and its impact in the US, especially gunrunning and NORAID. Whereas the Johnson administration's neutrality was one of disinterest, the Nixon–Ford era coupled neutrality with expressions of interest when liaising with interested parties. Nevertheless, US foreign policy had higher priorities. Nixon was undoubtedly interested in the Anglo-Irish process but he was advised to maintain his focus elsewhere. Nixon would not be a peacemaker in Northern Ireland. By the end of Ford's presidency, however, there was a change in the American response to the Anglo-Irish process. A reluctance to become embroiled in Northern Ireland was countered by a realisation that the US President had to do something in response to the related activities of American citizens. Irish–American citizens were involved in Northern Ireland; subsequently, so was the American government. This domestic politicisation of Northern Ireland in the US was underlined during the 1976 presidential election.

## Notes

1. Graeme Mount with Mark Gauthier, *895 Days That Changed The World: The Presidency of Gerald R. Ford* (London: Black Rose Books, 2006), 10. See also, for instance, Martin Evans, *Algeria: France's Undeclared War* (Oxford: Oxford University Press, 2012); and Christian Lambert Maria Penders, *The West New Guinea Debacle: Dutch Decolonisation and Indonesia, 1945–1962* (Honolulu: University of Hawai'i Press, 2002).

2. John Dumbrell, *A Special Relationship: Anglo-American Relations from the Cold War to Iraq* (Basingstoke: Palgrave, 2006), 75. It is important to note, however, that there is some recent scholarship that challenges the notion of a decline in the 'specialness' of Anglo-American relations in this period. See, for instance, Niklas Rossbach, *Heath, Nixon and the Rebirth of the Special Relationship: Britain, the US and the EC, 1969–74* (Basingstoke: Palgrave, 2009).

3. Alan P. Dobson, *Anglo-American Relations in the Twentieth Century: Of Friendship, Conflict and the Rise and Decline of Superpowers* (London: Routledge, 1995), 140–1. For a wider discussion of 1961–79, see Dobson, *Anglo-American Relations*, 124–47. For other recent examples of the historiography of Anglo-American relations in the period covered by this chapter, see, for instance, Jonathan Colman, *A 'Special Relationship'? Harold Wilson, Lyndon B. Johnson and Anglo-American Relations 'at the Summit', 1964–68* (Manchester: Manchester University Press, 2004); Catherine Hynes, *The Year That Never Was: Heath, the Nixon Administration and the Year of Europe* (Dublin: University College Dublin Press, 2009); and Andrew Scott, *Allies Apart: Heath, Nixon and the Anglo-American Relationship* (Basingstoke: Palgrave, 2011).

4. Thomas Robb, *A Strained Partnership? US–UK Relations in the Era of Détente, 1969–77* (Manchester: Manchester University Press, 2013), 88–92, 144–50. It should be noted that American coercion was not unique to this period. For the 1946 Anglo-American loan, see, for instance, Richard Wevill, *Britain and America After World War II: Bilateral Relations and the Beginnings of the Cold War* (London: I. B. Tauris, 2010), 53–108; and Philip A. Grant, Jr, 'President Harry S. Truman and the British Loan Act of 1946', *Presidential Studies Quarterly*, 25:3 (summer 1995), 489–96. For the 1956–7 Suez Crisis, see, for instance, Diane B. Kunz, *The Economic Diplomacy of the Suez Crisis* (Chapel Hill: University of North Carolina Press, 1991).

5. See, for instance, Jonathan Colman, *The Foreign Policy of Lyndon B. Johnson: The United States and the World, 1963–69* (Edinburgh: Edinburgh University Press, 2010); and Francis J. Gavin and Mark Atwood Lawrence (eds), *Beyond the Cold War: Lyndon Johnson and the New Global Challenge of the 1960s* (Oxford: Oxford University Press, 2014).

6. Paul Dixon, *Northern Ireland: The Politics of War and Peace* (Basingstoke: Palgrave Macmillan, 2008), 66–7.

7. Bew, *Ireland*, 488–9.

8. Dixon, *Northern Ireland*, 76–80.

9. Memorandum, Dean Rusk to the President, Visit of President de Valera, 22 May 1964, National Security File: Country File, Ireland, De Valera Visit, 5/27-30/64 [1 of 2], National Security File: Country File, Box 195, Lyndon Baines Johnson Library (hereafter LBJ Library).

10. Ibid.

11. Kiernan to McCann (Secretary, Department of Foreign Affairs), 4 December 1963, NAI: D/Foreign Affairs 313/2J.

12. Telephone conversation, Lyndon B. Johnson Presidential Recordings, Johnson Conservation with McGeorge Bundy, 7 January 1964, Tape: WH6401.07, conversation 1226, accessed via the Miller Center, http://millercenter.org/presidentialrecordings/lbj-wh6401.07–1226, 16 October 2014.

13. Letter, James A. Burke to President Johnson, 16 March 1965, CO 125 Ireland, EX CO 125 6/7/66, Box 42, LBJ Library.

14. Letter, Douglas MacArthur II to the Honorable James A. Burke, 22 March 1965, CO 125 Ireland, EX CO 125 6/7/66, White House Central Files (hereafter WHCF), Box 42, LBJ Library.

15. Ibid.

16. Letter, Harlan Cleveland to Andrew A. McKenna, 10 March 1965, CO 125 Ireland, EX CO 125 6/7/66, WHCF, Box 42, LBJ Library.

17. Ibid.

18. Wilson, *Irish America*, 17–25.

19. Letter, James C. Heaney to Dean Rusk, 8 February 1968, CO 125 Ireland, EX CO 125 6/7/66, WHCF, Box 42, LBJ Library.

20. Ibid.

21. Letter, James C. Heaney to President Lyndon B. Johnson, 8 February 1968, CO 125 Ireland, EX CO 125 6/7/66, WHCF, Box 42, LBJ Library.

22. Ibid.

23. Letter, Edward R. Fried to James C. Heaney, 23 February 1968, CO 125 Ireland, EX CO 125 6/7/66, WHCF, Box 42, LBJ Library.

24. Wilson, *Irish America*, 26.

25. Bew, *Ireland*, 487–91. For the first Wilson government's approach to Northern Ireland (and a discussion of its mistakes), see, for instance, Peter Rose, *How the Troubles Came to Northern Ireland* (Basingstoke: Palgrave, 2001).

26. For détente, see, for instance, Melvyn P. Leffler and Odd Arne Westad (eds), *The Cambridge History of the Cold War, Volume II: Crises and Détente* (Cambridge: Cambridge University Press, 2010). Examples of the historiography related to Nixon's foreign

policy are Robert Dallek, *Nixon and Kissinger* (New York: HarperCollins, 2007); and Barbara Zanchetta, *The Transformation of American International Power in the 1970s* (New York: Cambridge University Press, 2014). For the domestic politics and policies of the Nixon era, see, for instance, Robert Mason, *Richard Nixon and the Quest for a New Majority* (Chapel Hill: University of North Carolina Press, 2004); and Sarah Katherine Mergel, *Conservative Intellectuals and Richard Nixon: Rethinking the Rise of the Right* (New York: Palgrave, 2010). Nixon's approach to transatlantic relations is discussed in Luke A. Nichter, *Richard Nixon and Europe: The Reshaping of the Postwar Atlantic World* (New York: Cambridge University Press, 2015). For Anglo-American relations and Vietnam, see Sylvia Ellis, *Britain, America and the Vietnam War* (London: Praeger, 2004).

27. Richard Nixon, 'Inaugural address', 20 January 1969. Online by Gerhard Peters and John T. Woolley, *The American Presidency Project*, http://www.presidency.ucsb.edu/ws/?pid=1941, accessed 24 June 2015.

28. Wilson, *Irish America*, 28–9.

29. Dixon, *Northern Ireland*, 100–5.

30. Letter, Rep. John M. Murphy to President Richard Nixon, 18 August 1969; folder [GEN] CO 160 8/20/69-12/30/69; Box 82; White House Central Files: Subject Files, CO (Countries); Richard Nixon Presidential Library and Museum, Yorba Linda, CA (hereafter Nixon Library).

31. Letter, Henry A. Kissinger to Honorable John M. Murphy, House of Representatives, Washington, D.C.; 29 September 1969; folder [GEN] CO 160 8/20/69-12/30/69; Box 82, White House Central Files: Subject Files, CO (Countries); Nixon Library.

32. Ibid.

33. Memorandum of Conversation, The Secretary's Bilateral Talk with Minister for External Affairs Hillery – Northern Ireland, New York, 22 September 1969, 5:30 p.m., *Foreign Relations of the United States* (hereafter *FRUS*), 1969–1976, Volume XLI, Western Europe; NATO, 1969–1972, ed. James E. Miller and Laurie Van Hook, Washington, DC, United States Government Printing Office, 2012, document 164, accessed via https://history.state.gov/historicaldocuments/frus1969–76v41/d164, 15 June 2014.

34. Ibid.

35. Jack Holland, *The American Connection* (Poolbeg: Dublin, 1989), 27–62.

36. Dixon, *Northern Ireland*, 106–11.
37. See Richard Nixon, 'Statement on St. Patrick's Day', 17 March 1969. Online by Gerhard Peters and John T. Woolley, *The American Presidency Project*, http://www.presidency.ucsb.edu/ws/?pid=1956; and Richard Nixon, 'St. Patrick's Day Statement', 16 March 1971. Online by Gerhard Peters and John T. Woolley, *The American Presidency Project*, http://www.presidency.ucsb.edu/ws/?pid=2938. Both accessed 15 September 2015.
38. Richard Nixon, 'Toasts of the President and Prime Minister John M. Lynch of Ireland at a state luncheon in Dublin', 5 October 1970. Online by Gerhard Peters and John T. Woolley, *The American Presidency Project*, http://www.presidency.ucsb.edu/ws/?pid=2699, accessed 15 September 2015.
39. Wilson, *Irish America*, 57–60.
40. Senator Richard Nixon to Reverend D. Manning, 17 June 1952, enclosed with Letter, Roinn Gnothai Eachtracha from Ambasadora, 28 Mean Fomhair, 1970, An Runai, Richard M. Nixon President of the USA, Visit to Ireland, Oct. 1970, NAI: D/Taoiseach, 2001/6/490.
41. Brendan Malis, 'Nixon opposed to partition of Ireland', *The Boston Daily Globe*, Tuesday, 9 September 1952, enclosed with Letter, Roinn Gnothai Eachtracha from Ambasadora, 28 Mean Fomhair, 1970, An Runai, Richard M. Nixon President of the USA, Visit to Ireland, Oct. 1970, NAI: D/Taoiseach, 2001/6/490.
42. Ibid. The resolution was sponsored by Rep. John F. Fogarty (D-RI); see, for instance, John T. McNay, *Acheson and Empire: The British Accent in American Foreign Policy* (University of Missouri Press: Columbia, 2001), 92–3.
43. Memorandum, Henry A. Kissinger to the President, re: Your Visit to Ireland, 3–5 October 1970; date unknown; folder President's Trip Files [Oct 70] [2]; Box 469; National Security Council (NSC): Files President's Trip Files; Nixon Library.
44. Ibid.
45. Ibid.
46. Department of State telegram, From American Embassy Dublin to Secretary of State Washington D.C. re: Telcon requesting report on exchange of views between the President and the Taoiseach at Dublin Castle; 8 October 1970; folder Presidential European Trip 27 September to 3 October 1970, Memorandum of Conversations; Box 467; National Security Council (NSC) Files President's Trip Files; Nixon Library.

47. See Richard Nixon, *The Memoirs of Richard Nixon* (London: Arrow Books, 1978); and Henry Kissinger, *The White House Years* (London: Weidenfeld & Nicolson, 1979), 935–6. Kissinger argues that the Irish visit 'was frankly a political one', which 'enabled Nixon to bring his claim to Irish ancestry to the attention of Irish–American voters and to pay off an obligation to a wealthy American contributor at whose extravagant castle we stayed'. An advance man's proposal for Nixon to lead a St Patrick's Day parade was ignored.

48. Wilson, *Irish America*, 85.

49. Letter, James C. Heaney (President and Chairman, American Congress for Irish Freedom) to President Richard M. Nixon; 5 February 1971; folder [GEN] CO 160 United Kingdom 1/1/71- [1 of 2]; Box 82; White House Central Files: Subject Files, CO (Countries); Nixon Library.

50. Ibid.

51. Letter, Helmut Sonnenfeldt to James C. Heaney; 24 February 1971; folder [GEN] CO 160 United Kingdom 1/1/71- [1 of 2]; Box 82; White House Central Files: Subject Files, CO (Countries); Nixon Library.

52. Ibid.

53. Memorandum from the President's Assistant for National Security Affairs (Kissinger) to President Nixon, Washington, 15 March 1971, FRUS, 1969–1976, Volume XLI, Western Europe; NATO, 1969–1972, ed. James E. Miller and Laurie Van Hook, Washington, DC, United States Government Printing Office, 2012, document 166, accessed via https://history.state.gov/historicaldocuments/frus1969-76v41/d166, 14 June 2014.

54. Ibid.

55. Draft notes on conversation of the Taoiseach with President Nixon, 17 March 1971, NAI: D/Taoiseach, 2002/8/435.

56. Ibid.

57. SECRET, Taoiseach's meeting with President Nixon at Washington – 16 March 1971, NAI: D/Taoiseach, 2002/8/435.

58. Ibid.

59. Memorandum, Henry A. Kissinger to the President re Your Breakfast Meeting with Harold Wilson (April 30 at 8:00 a.m.); 29 April 1971; folder National Security Council Files, Country Files Europe, United Kingdom Vol. VI, 31 April to August 1971 [2 of 4]; Box 728; National Security Council (NSC) Files, Country Files – Europe; Nixon Library.

60. Ibid.

61. See, for instance, James Cooper, 'The foreign politics of opposition: Margaret Thatcher and the transatlantic relationship before power', *Contemporary British History*, 24:1 (March 2010), 23–42.

62. Paul Arthur, *Special Relationships: Britain, Ireland and the Northern Ireland Problem* (Belfast: Blackstaff Press, 2001), 113–14.
63. Memorandum, Henry A. Kissinger to the President re Heath informs you on Northern Ireland situation; 13 August 1971; folder National Security Council Files, Country File, United Kingdom Vol. VI, 1 Apr to 31 Aug 71, Europe, [1 of 4] 2; Box 728; National Security Council (NSC) Files, Country Files – Europe; Nixon Library.
64. Ibid.
65. Ibid.
66. Memorandum, Henry A. Kissinger to the President re Your Meeting with Sir Alec Douglas-Home, September 30 at 4:00 p.m.; 29 September 1971; folder National Security Council Files Country Files Europe, United Kingdom Vol. VIII, Sept. 1971 to Sept. 1972 [2 of 4]; Box 729; National Security Council (NSC) Files Country Files – Europe; Nixon Library.
67. Conversation Among President Nixon, British Foreign Secretary Douglas-Home, the President's Assistant for National Security Affairs (Kissinger) and the White House Press Secretary (Ziegler), Washington, 30 September 1971, *FRUS*, 1969–76 Volume XXVIII, Southern Africa, ed. Myra Burton, Washington, DC, United States Government Printing Office, 2011, Document 58, accessed via http://history.state.gov/historicaldocuments/frus1969-76v28/d58, 8 January 2015. (For an introduction to apartheid in South Africa, see, for instance, Adrian Guelke, *Rethinking the Rise and Fall of Apartheid* (Basingstoke: Palgrave, 2004).)
68. See, for instance, Anthony Lewis, 'Terror in Ulster: Security measures that may worsen the problem', *The New York Times*, 11 August 1971, 3; Anthony Lewis, 'Tet in Belfast', *The New York Times*, 11 October 1971, 35; and Anthony Lewis, 'Internment doesn't work, say the dead', *The New York Times*, 2 January 1972, E3.
69. Memorandum of Conversation, London, November 22, 1971, Subject: Northern Ireland, Participations: Sir Stewart Crawford (FCO Deputy Under Secretary), Philip Woodfield (Home Office Asst. Under Secretary), Kelvin White (FCO Asst. Head Western European Dept.), Hon. Martin Hillenbrand (Department of State), Hon. Earl Sohm (Minister of American Embassy), Robert M. Scott (American Embassy), Grover Penberthy (Consul General Belfast), Jack Sulser (American Embassy), ed. James E. Miller and Laurie Van Hook, Washington, DC, United States Government Printing Office, 2012, Document 347, *FRUS*, 1969–1976, Volume XLI, Western Europe; NATO, 1969–1972, accessed via http://static.history.state.gov/frus/frus1969-76v41/pdf/frus1969-76v41.pdf, 25 June 2015.

70. Ibid.
71. Telegram, Joseph C. Clark (Chairman, Peace and Justice for Ireland) to Miss Rosemary Woodes [sic] (Secretary to the President); 15 November 1971; folder [GEN] CO 160 United Kingdom 1/1/71- [1 of 2]; Box 82; White House Central Files: Subject Files, CO (Countries); Nixon Library.
72. Letter, Scott George (Country Director for Ireland, Malta and the United Kingdom) to Joseph C. Clark (Chairman, Peace and Justice for Ireland); 7 December 1971; folder [GEN] CO 160 United Kingdom 1/1/71- [1 of 2]; Box 82; White House Central Files: Subject Files, CO (Countries); Nixon Library.
73. Letter; Timothy B. Driscoll to Miss Woods; 29 December 1971; folder [GEN] CO 160 United Kingdom 1/1/71- [1 of 2]; Box 82; White House Central Files: Subject Files, CO (Countries); Nixon Library.
74. Ibid.
75. Letter, David N. Parker (Staff Assistant to the President) to Timothy B. Driscoll; 25 January 1972; folder [GEN] CO 160 United Kingdom 1/1/71- [1 of 2]; Box 82; White House Central Files: Subject Files, CO (Countries); Nixon Library.
76. For records of the Bermuda discussions, see TNA: FCO 82/71: Discussion between Mr Richard Nixon, President of USA and Mr Edward Heath, Prime Minister of UK in Bermuda – and other Ministers.
77. Record of a conversation between the Foreign and Commonwealth Secretary and Mr. William Rogers, United States Secretary of State, at the Princess Hotel, Bermuda, on 21 December, 1971, at 10.30 a.m., Talks between the Prime Minister and the President of the United States at Bermuda, 20–1 December 1971, TNA: PREM 15/1268: Meeting between Prime Minister and President Nixon, Bermuda, Dec 1971, part 3.
78. Wilson, *Irish America*, 64–5.
79. Thompson, *American Policy*, 39.
80. Memorandum, Mr. Henry A. Kissinger to the President re Meeting with Irish Ambassador and Mrs. William Warnock for Presentation of Shamrocks on St. Patrick's Day, Friday, March 17, 1972, 12:00 Noon, Oval Office; 16 March 1972; folder Ireland Vol. 1; Box 694; National Security Council (NSC) Files, Country Files – Europe; Nixon Library.
81. Ibid.
82. Memorandum, General A. M. Haig, Jr. to The President's Files re Meeting between The President, Irish Ambassador Warnock and

Mrs. Warnock and General Haig on St. Patrick's Day, Date & Time: March 17, 1972 at 12 Noon; 17 March 1972; folder Ireland Vol. 1; Box 694; National Security Council (NSC) Files, Country Files – Europe; Nixon Library.

83. Ibid.
84. Dixon, *Northern Ireland*, 116.
85. Lou Cannon, *President Reagan: The Role of a Lifetime* (New York: Public Affairs, 2000), 405.
86. Note, Research File, Foreign Travel (RR), Europe/NATO, 7/3-22/72 (1/2), Box GO 178, Governor's Mansion Reports, Ronald Reagan Governor's Papers, Ronald Reagan Library.
87. Dobson, *Anglo-American Relations*, 139–41.
88. See Robb, *A Strained Partnership?*, 73–90.
89. 'Points for Prime Minister to raise', TNA: PREM 15/1267: Visit of Governor Reagan.
90. Ibid.
91. News report, *The New York Times*, 21 July 1972, 29.
92. Letter, Richard Nixon to Eamon De Valera, 30 June 1972, NAI: Office of Secretary to the President, 2003/18/62.
93. Speech, Eamon De Valera, 'Dinner by the Taoiseach and Mrs. Lynch in honour of the personal representative of the President of the University, the Honourable Ronald Reagan, Governor of California, and Mrs. Reagan, at Iveagh House on 18 July 1972', NAI: D/Taoiseach, 2003/16/564.
94. Letter from unknown civil servant (Department of Foreign Affairs) To N.S. Ó Nualláin (Roinn an Taoisigh), 22 Bealtaine 1972, NAI: Office of Secretary to the President, 2003/18/62.
95. Adrian Guelke, 'The American connection to the Northern Ireland conflict', *Irish Studies in International Affairs*, 1:4 (1984), 29.
96. Letter, Tom C. Korologos (Deputy Assistant to the President) to Senator Alan Bible; 4 April 1972; folder [GEN] CO 160 United Kingdom 1/1/71- [1 of 2]; Box 82; White House Central Files: Subject Files, CO (Countries); Nixon Library.
97. Ibid.
98. Letter, Milton R. Young to Tom C. Korologos; 24 August 1972; folder [GEN] CO 160 United Kingdom 1/1/71- [1 of 2]; Box 82; White House Central Files: Subject Files, CO (Countries); Nixon Library.
99. Letter, Tom C. Korologos (Deputy Assistant to the President) to Senator Milton R. Young; 25 September 1972; folder [GEN] CO 160 United Kingdom 1/1/71- [1 of 2]; Box 82; White House Central Files: Subject Files, CO (Countries); Nixon Library.

100. Letter, Rep. Michael J. Harrington to President Richard Nixon; 15 March 1972; folder [GEN] CO 160 United Kingdom 1/1/71-; Box 82; White House Central Files: Subject Files, CO (Countries); Nixon Library.
101. Ibid.
102. Letter, Ancient Order of Hibernians in America to President Richard Nixon; 10 July 1972; folder Ireland Vol. 1; Box 694; National Security Council (NSC) Files: Country Files – Europe; Nixon Library.
103. Ibid.
104. Memorandum, Les Janka to Jerry Livingston re Ulster; 26 July 1972; folder Ireland Vol. 1; Box 694; National Security Council (NSC) Files, Country Files – Europe; Nixon Library.
105. Memorandum, Robert Gerald Livingston to General Haig re Options for Ulster; 28 July 1972; folder Ireland Vol. 1; Box 694; National Security Council (NSC) Files: Country Files – Europe; Nixon Library.
106. Ibid.
107. Memorandum, Al Haig to Bruce Kehrli re Ulster; 31 July 1972; folder Ireland Vol. 1; Box 694; National Security Council (NSC) Files, Country Files – Europe; Nixon Library.
108. Ibid.
109. Letter, Richard Nixon to Edward Heath, 17 August 1972, PRO, PREM 15/1038, 1972 Ireland.
110. Ibid.
111. Dixon, *Northern Ireland*, 118.
112. Memorandum, Helmut Sonnenfeldt to Mr. Kissinger re Irish Feeler on Hillery Meeting with President; 2 September 1972; folder Ireland Vol. 1; Box 694; National Security Council Files: Country Files – Europe; Nixon Library.
113. Ibid.
114. Ibid.
115. Memorandum; Henry A. Kissinger to the President, re Meeting with Irish Foreign Minister Patrick Hillery, Friday, October 6, 1972, 11:30 a.m. (fifteen minutes), The Oval Office; 5 October 1972; folder [CF] CO 70 Ireland (1971–74); Box 7; White House Special Files: Subject Files: Confidential Files, 1969–1974; Nixon Library.
116. Ibid.
117. Memorandum of Conversation; President's Meeting with Irish Foreign Minister; 6 October 1972; folder Ireland Vol. 1; Box 694; National Security Council Files: Country Files – Europe; Nixon Library.
118. Ibid.

119. Dixon, *Northern Ireland*, 129–30.
120. Memorandum; Henry A. Kissinger to The President re Northern Ireland – Recent Moves by London and Dublin; 3 December 1972; folder [CF] CO 70 Ireland (1971–74); Box 7; White House Special Files: Subject Files: Confidential Files, 1969–1974; Nixon Library.
121. Ibid.
122. Memorandum; Helmut Sonnenfeldt to Mr. Kissinger re Proposed Presidential Meeting with Irish Prime Minister Lynch; 21 December 1972; folder [CF] CO 70 Ireland (1971–74); Box 7; White House Special Files: Subject Files: Confidential Files, 1969–1974; Nixon Library.
123. Ibid.
124. Memorandum of Conversation; Sir Burke Trend, Secretary to the British Cabinet, Earl of Cromer, UK Ambassador to the US, Richard Sikes, UK Minister to US, Brian Norbury, Secretary to Sir Burke Trend, Dr. Henry A. Kissinger, Helmut Sonnenfeldt, Place: The Ambassador's Office, The British Embassy Residence, Washington, DC; Tuesday, January 16, 1973, 1:30 p.m. – 4:55 p.m.; folder U.K. Memcons 1973 Jan.–April (originals) [2 of 2]; Box 62; National Security Council Files: Henry A. Kissinger Office Files: Country Files – Europe; Nixon Library.
125. Prime Minister's Meeting with President Nixon, Brief on Item 12 – Northern Ireland, Northern Ireland Office, 17 January 1973, TNA: CJ 4/350: Prime Ministers [sic] Visit to President Nixon.
126. Ibid.
127. Ibid.
128. Ibid.
129. Record of a meeting between the Prime Minister and the Senate Foreign Relations Committee at the Capitol, Washington, DC, at 3 pm on Thursday 1 February 1973, TNA: CJ 4/350.
130. Ibid.
131. Note for the record, Senator Edward Kennedy called on the Prime Minister and the Foreign and Commonwealth Secretary in the British Embassy at Washington on Friday 2 February 1973 at 10.00 a.m. The Ambassador and Mr. Armstrong were present, TNA: CJ 4/350.
132. Memorandum for the President's File by the President's Assistant for National Security Affairs (Kissinger), Washington, February 1, 1973, Meeting with British Prime Minister Heath and Sir Burke Trend, Thursday, February 1, 1973, 10:43 a.m.–12:25 p.m., The Oval Office, The White House, document 216, *FRUS*, 1969–1976, Volume E-15, Part 2, Documents on Western Europe, 1973–1976.

133. Conversation Between President Nixon and the President's Assistant for National Security Affairs (Kissinger), Washington, 3 February 1973, *FRUS*, 1969–1976, Volume E-15, Part 2, Documents on Western Europe, 1973–1976, ed. Kathleen B. Rasmussen, Washington, DC, United States Government Printing Office, 2014, document 6. (Accessed via e-book: http://history.state.gov/historicaldocuments/frus1969-76ve15p2, 16 October 2015.)

134. Dixon, *Northern Ireland*, 130–5.

135. Bew, *Ireland*, 512–16. For the Sunningdale Agreement, see, for instance, Cillian McGrattan, 'Dublin, the SDLP and the Sunningdale Agreement: Maximalist nationalism and path dependency', *Contemporary British History*, 23:1 (March 2009), 61–78; and Gordon Gillespie, 'The Sunningdale Agreement: Lost opportunity or an agreement too far?', *Irish Political Studies*, 13 (1998), 100–14.

136. Dixon, *Northern Ireland*, 153.

137. Memorandum, Henry A. Kissinger to the President re New UK White Paper on Northern Ireland; date unknown; folder Ireland Vol. 1; Box 694; National Security Council Files: Country Files – Europe; Nixon Library.

138. Ibid.

139. Memorandum, George S. Springsteen (Executive Secretary, Department of State) to Major General Brent Scowcroft re New British White Paper on Northern Ireland; 8 July 1974; folder Ireland Vol. 1; Box 694; National Security Council Files: Country Files – Europe; Nixon Library.

140. See, for instance, Mount, *894 Days*, 8–11; and Thompson, *American Policy*, 49–70.

141. See Richard English, *Armed Struggle: The History of the IRA* (Oxford: Oxford University Press, 2003), 187–262.

142. Memorandum from the President's Assistant for National Security Affairs (Kissinger) to President Ford, Washington, undated, Subject: Crisis in Ulster, *FRUS*, 1969–1976, Volume E-15, Part 2, Documents on Western Europe, 1973–1976, ed. Kathleen B. Rasmussen, Washington, DC, United States Government Printing Office, 2014, document 237.

143. Ibid.

144. Letter John Bownes to Honorable Gerald R. Ford, 28 August 1974, folder: Wars/United Kingdom (Northern Ireland) 8/9/74-12/25/74, Box 35, White House Central Files, Gerald R. Ford Library (hereafter Ford Library).

145. Ibid.

146. Letter, Roland L. Elliot to John Bownes, 24 September 1974, folder: Wars/United Kingdom (Northern Ireland) 8/9/74-12/25/74, Box 35, White House Central Files, Ford Library.

147. Memorandum, Jeanne W. Davis to Roland L. Elliot, 18 September 1974, folder: Wars/United Kingdom (Northern Ireland) 8/9/74-12/25/74, Box 35, White House Central Files, Ford Library.

148. Thompson, *American Policy*, 50–6.

149. Letter, Seán W. Walsh IV to Honorable Gerald R. Ford, 14 November 1974, folder: Wars/United Kingdom (Northern Ireland) 8/9/74-12/25/74, Box 35, White House Central Files, Ford Library.

150. Memorandum, Brent Scowcroft to Theodore C. Marrs, date unknown, folder: Wars/United Kingdom (Northern Ireland) 8/9/74-12/25/74, Box 35, White House Central Files, Ford Library.

151. Letter, Theodore C. Marrs (Special Assistant to the President) to Seán W. Walsh IV, 10,December 1974, folder: Wars/United Kingdom (Northern Ireland) 8/9/74-12/25/74, Box 35, White House Central Files, Ford Library.

152. Visit of the Prime Minister to Washington, 29 to 31 January 1975, Northern Ireland, Brief by the Northern Ireland Office, 23 January 1975, TNA: CJ 4/743 United States interest in Northern Ireland.

153. Ibid.

154. Memorandum, Henry A. Kissinger to The President, date unknown, folder: 1/29-2/1/75 – United Kingdom – Prime Minister Wilson (1), Box 5, National Security Adviser, Presidential Briefing, Material for VIP Visits, 1974–1976, Ford Library.

155. Ibid.

156. Memorandum of Conversation, Prime Minister Harold Wilson and President Ford, Thursday, January 30, 1975, The Oval Office, The White House, accessed via http://www.fordlibrarymuseum. gov/library/document/0314/1552934.pdf, 23 July 2014; Memorandum of Conversation, Prime Minister Harold Wilson and President Ford, Friday, January 31, 1975, The Oval Office, The White House, accessed via http://www.fordlibrarymuseum.gov/library/ document/0314/1552937.pdf, 23 July 2014. (Digital files from http://www.fordlibrarymuseum.gov/library/ are scanned from the National Security Adviser's Memoranda of Conversation Collection at the Gerald R. Ford Presidential Library.)

157. Ibid.

158. Memorandum, Henry A. Kissinger to the President, Subject: Wilson Visit – U.S. Crackdown on IRA Gunrunning, date unknown, folder:

Ireland (1), Box 7, National Security Adviser: Presidential Country Files for Europe and Canada, Ford Library.

159. See Memorandum of Conversation, Harold Wilson and Gerald Ford, The Oval Office, The White House, 7 May 1975, accessed via http://www.fordlibrarymuseum.gov/library/document/0314/1553063.pdf; Memorandum of Conversation, Harold Wilson and Gerald Ford, Brussels, 30 May 1975, accessed via http://www.fordlibrarymuseum.gov/library/document/0314/1553097.pdf; Memorandum of Conversation, Harold Wilson and Gerald Ford, Helsinki, 30 July 1975, accessed via http://www.fordlibrarymuseum.gov/library/document/0314/1553188.pdf, 23 July 2014.

160. Letter, Edward H. Levi to Brent Scowcroft, 27 February 1976, folder: Ireland (2), Box 7, National Security Adviser: Presidential Country Files for Europe and Canada, Ford Library.

161. Ibid.

162. Briefing Memorandum, Arthur A. Hartman to The Secretary of State through Mr. Sonnenfeldt, Your Meeting with Irish Foreign Minister Fitzgerald, Wednesday, January 8, 3:00 p.m., 3 January 1975, folder: Ireland, 1975 (1) WH, Box 12, National Security Adviser: NSC Europe, Canada, and Ocean Affairs Staff: Files, 1974–1977, Ford Library.

163. Ibid.

164. Ibid.

165. Memorandum, Henry A. Kissinger to The President, 23 April 1975, folder: Presidential Daily Briefing 4/23/75, Box 6, National Security Adviser, White House Situation Room Presidential Daily Briefings 1974–77, Ford Library.

166. Ibid.

167. Memorandum of Conversation, Secretary's Meeting with Irish Foreign Minister, 7 October 1975, folder: Ireland, 1975 (4) WH, Box 12, National Security Adviser, NSC Europe, Canada, and Ocean Affairs Staff: Files, 1974–1977, Ford Library

168. Ibid.

169. Extract from a speech by the prime minister, the Rt. Hon. Harold Wilson, OBE, FRS, MP, at the annual dinner of the Association of American Correspondents in London, Savoy Hotel, Wednesday, 17 December 1975, TNA: CJ 4/1412: Visits by British Politicians to the United States of America Visits Foreign and Commonwealth.

170. Record of meeting between Minister of State for Northern Ireland and Deputy Secretary of States, Thursday 8 January 1976, at 4PM in the State Department, TNA: CJ 4/1412.

171. Ibid.
172. Memorandum, The Situation Room to General Scowcroft, Additional Information Items, Northern Ireland – British Strategy, 12 January 1976, folder: Presidential Daily Briefings, 3 April 1975, Box 6, National Security Adviser: White House Situation Room Presidential Daily Briefings 1974–77, Ford Library.
173. Ibid.
174. Memorandum, Brent Scowcroft to the President, 20 January 1976, folder: Presidential Daily Briefing, 1/20/76, Box 12, National Security Adviser: White House Situation Room, Presidential Daily Briefings, 1974–77, Ford Library.
175. Ibid.
176. Memorandum from the President's Assistant for National Security Affairs (Scowcroft) to President Ford, Washington, March 11, 1976, Subject: Northern Ireland – Gun-Running and Other Foreign Support for the IRA, *FRUS*, 1969–1976, Volume E-15, Part 2, Documents on Western Europe, 1973–1976, ed. Kathleen B. Rasmussen, Washington, DC, United States Government Printing Office, 2014, document 240.
177. Brent Scowcroft to President Ford, Meeting with Liam Cosgrave, Prime Minister of the Republic of Ireland (Wednesday, March 17, 1976), 15 March 1976, folder: CO 70 Ireland, 3/1/76 – 3/15/76, Box 25, White House Central Files, Ford Library.
178. Ibid.
179. Letter, Bernadette O'Reilly to the Honorable Gerald R. Ford, 16 March 1976, folder: CO 70 Ireland, 3/1/76 – 3/15/76, Box 25, White House Central Files, Ford Library.
180. Ibid.
181. Memorandum, Mr Clift to Brent Scowcroft, Correspondence on Northern Ireland and Cosgrave Visit, 29 March 1976, folder: CO 70 Ireland, 3/18/76–1/20/77, Box 26, White House Central Files, Ford Library.
182. Letter, Roland L. Elliot to Bernadette O'Reilly, 7 April 1976, folder: CO 70 Ireland, 3/18/76–1/20/77, Box 26, White House Central Files, Ford Library.
183. Visit of Taoiseach to the United States, 16–22 March 1976, Briefing Material, The United States and Northern Ireland, NAI: D/Taoiseach, 2006/133/435.
184. Ibid.
185. Meeting with President Ford – 17th March, Roinn an Taoisigh, Official Visit by Taoiseach to United States, 16th March – 23rd March, 1976, NAI: D/Taoiseach, 2006/133/434.

186. Ibid.
187. Memorandum of Conversation, President Ford and Liam Cosgrave, Prime Minister of the Republic of Ireland, Wednesday, March 17, 1976, The Oval Office, accessed via http://www.fordlibrarymuseum. gov/library/document/0314/1553398.pdf, 23 July 2014.
188. Ibid.
189. Gerald R. Ford, 'Joint communique, following discussions with Prime Minister Cosgrave of Ireland', 18 March 1976. Online by Gerhard Peters and John T. Woolley, *The American Presidency Project*, http://www.presidency.ucsb.edu/ws/?pid=5718, accessed 15 January 2015.
190. Memorandum, George S. Springsteen (Executive Secretary, Department of State) to Mr. Brent Scowcroft, Visit of Irish Prime Minister Cosgrave: Possible Communique, 15 March 1976, folder: Ireland, 1976 (4) WH, Box 12, National Security Adviser: NSC Europe, Canada, and Ocean Affairs Staff: Files, 1974–1977, Ford Library.
191. Ibid.
192. From our own correspondent, 'Appeal to stop aid for IRA', Thursday, 18 March 1976, *The Guardian*, 2.
193. News, 'Americans will invest $105m in Irish factories', Tuesday, 23 March 1976, *The Times*, 17.
194. Richard D. Lyons, 'Cosgrave asks halting of aid from U.S. to Irish extremists', 18 March 1976, *New York Times*, 6; Editorial, 'The Cosgrave Message', Friday, 19 March 1976, *The New York Times*, 32.
195. News, 'Ford joins Cosgrave against IRA', Friday, 19 March 1976, *The Boston Globe*, 2.
196. News, 'Cosgrave urges curb to US funds for IRA', Thursday, 18 March 1975, *The Irish Times*, 1; News, 'Cosgrave and Ford draft a message', Friday, 19 March 1976, *The Irish Times*, 1.
197. News, 'Cosgrave attacks IRA aid in US', 18 March 1976, *The Irish Press*, 1.

# 2 The Carter Administration, 1977–81

## Introduction

Jimmy Carter's presidency (1977–81) was defined by the collapse of détente, 'oil shocks' that weakened a troubled Western economy, and humiliation during the Iranian hostage crisis (1979–81). A concern for human rights was a significant feature of Carter's agenda. This was articulated in his inaugural address and in his speech at the University of Notre Dame a few months later.[1] While this commitment is subject to debate in the historiography, it certainly afforded an opportunity to Irish–American politicians and lobbyists.[2] Anglo-American relations saw an upturn in fortunes, Carter enjoying a cordial relationship with James Callaghan, the British Prime Minister (1976–9). Although there was some disappointment with the later advent of a Conservative British government, the administration made efforts to welcome the new Prime Minister, Margaret Thatcher (1979–90), to ensure that this sentiment was not obvious or damaging.[3] The Carter epoch showed continuing close ties between the US and the UK. This was evident, for example, when the British acquired Trident as a successor to the Polaris programme in 1980.[4] Notably, Carter only references Ireland once in his diary, and then only tongue-in-cheek: 'Mother called me from Ireland. She's really having a good time and would like to stay longer. She said if she could stay an extra month she could resolve the problem between the Catholics and Protestants.'[5] Similarly, the issue is also ignored in the recollections of key figures in his administration.[6]

As the previous chapter demonstrated, the American executive branch had placed little pressure on the British government in relation to Northern Ireland. In contrast, as a candidate for the US presidency, Carter made statements about Northern Ireland that irritated the British government and gave hope to Irish–Americans, with Carter casting the British as the villain of the piece. For instance, as a presidential candidate, he walked down Fifth Avenue in New York City on St Patrick's Day in 1976 wearing a lapel badge bearing the slogan 'Get Britain out of Ireland.'[7] As President, Carter made a 1977 statement on the issue that promised American investment if the British and Irish governments were able to achieve a power-sharing agreement. But he also infuriated the British government with his deference to Congress over the suspension of the sale of arms to the RUC.

During the Carter epoch, a new strategy emerged amongst Irish–American politicians. They sought to influence the political process in Washington, DC, and in turn shape Anglo-American relations, in an attempt to resolve the Northern Ireland conflict. The 'Four Horsemen' – Speaker Thomas P. 'Tip' O'Neill (D-MA), Senator Ted Kennedy (D-MA), Governor Hugh Carey (D-NY) and Senator Daniel Patrick Moynihan (D-NY), under the guidance of John Hume (a leading nationalist and civil rights activist in Northern Ireland), were key protagonists in this process. This reflected the reality of the political process in the US. As Richard Neustadt observes, it is clear that the US presidency may be separate institutions, but they share power in the development and implementation of domestic *and* foreign policy.[8] While this may often be complicated when different parties occupy different branches of government, Carter's presidency coincided with Democratic control of both houses of Congress. Nevertheless, Carter still needed to have a strong relationship with his fellow Democrats on Capitol Hill, particularly Tip O'Neill, who served as Speaker of the US House of Representatives (1977–87).[9]

Having a Democratic Speaker did not guarantee Carter's domestic agenda. The implementation of policies and action on agendas was complicated by the fact that congressional politics underwent a transformation during the 1970s. Internal power structures and procedures, which favoured seniority and saw greater fluidity in the voting patterns of moderate Republicans and conservative Democrats, was challenged by an increasing number of younger

Democrats, who Matthew Green describes as 'activist, liberal, and more independent'.[10] These junior representatives, supported by reforming Republicans, campaigned for a redistribution of authority over policies, committees and agendas. Subsequently, more members of Congress were granted more powers, including wider powers for the subcommittees, party caucuses, party leaders and the Speaker.[11] This further complicated Carter's domestic agenda, which, according to Neustadt, from the beginning suffered from its complexity.[12] In addition, the nature of Carter's meteoric rise, from winning the governorship of Georgia in 1972 to president of the US, added fuel to this fire: Carter suffered from his 'newness *in* office, also with newness *to* it'.[13] The relationship between Carter and Congress, particularly Speaker O'Neill, was therefore vital to the President's ambitions. The White House would need to consider issues important to key figures in Congress, which included Northern Ireland.

All speakers are constitutionally obliged to ensure the passing of legislation but, overall, Democratic speakers have historically been more inclined to support the legislative agenda of their party's president than their Republican counterparts. O'Neill was no exception to this.[14] Unfortunately, Carter's administration was a period of frustration for Democrats and of difficulties between President and Speaker. For instance, the passing of the President's energy programme in 1977 served only to enhance O'Neill's reputation and further undermine Carter – the final outcome was a shadow of Carter's initial ambitions but its passage through the House was credited to O'Neill's legislative prowess. Despite the Speaker's attempts to be a loyal supporter of the President's ambitions, the Carter–O'Neill relationship was undermined by two factors: the Carter administration struggled to work effectively with Congress and O'Neill was to the left of the President.[15] Problems in policy development and implementation were matched by divisions within the Democratic Party over Northern Ireland. The battle for political influence between the Four Horsemen and Rep. Mario Biaggi (D-NY) and his congressional Ad Hoc Congressional Committee for Irish Affairs (ACCIA) essentially was a division between Democrats over how best to answer the Northern Ireland question. This chapter reveals how Carter's response to Northern Ireland was shaped by this conflict within the Democratic Party and how Irish–Americans utilised the constitutional reality constraining the President's agenda.

## Carter's 1976 presidential campaign

The Irish government closely monitored the 1976 American presidential election campaign, with a particular concern that candidates should not be influenced by Irish–American groups who sympathised with violence in Northern Ireland. In March 1976, FitzGerald wrote to all the leading presidential candidates, aside from Ford, warning that 'they might come under pressure from IRA support groups, specifically NORAID and the Irish National Caucus, to issue statements of support.'[16] Ireland's worst fears were confirmed during the Democratic primaries when Senator Henry M. Jackson (D-WA), while campaigning in the Eastern States, 'received the endorsement of NORAID and the Caucus'. After Carter secured his party's nomination in July, the Irish government noted that he was subject to supporters of the IRA involving 'themselves heavily in his campaign in some Eastern and Mid-Western States'. Thus, representatives in various American offices of the Irish government established connections with campaign leaders at national and local levels.[17] The British Embassy in Washington, DC, also monitored any apparent connections between the Carter campaign and the Irish–American lobby. On 4 May, Jonathan Davidson, working at the British Embassy, wrote to his colleague, Michael Hodge, at the Republic of Ireland Department in the FCO that Carter's campaign staff claimed to be 'completely puzzled' about how Carter came to wear an 'England out of Ireland' button while campaigning in New York and Chicago. (It would easy to be cynical of that claim, given the potential electioneering advantages.) In May 1976, as far as the FCO was concerned, the Carter campaign was not aware of its candidate issuing 'any statements about Northern Ireland in the course' or even 'any questions having been asked him'.[18]

With regard to Carter's rivals for the presidency, Gerald Ford's position was already established in the communiqué that he issued with Liam Cosgrave (Taoiseach, 1973–7). For Reagan, who was still a serious presidential candidate until the 1976 Republican convention, Northern Ireland was not expected to be a topic of interest. Senator (and former US Vice-President, 1965–9) Hubert Humphrey (D-MN) reportedly had 'no need to court the Irish American vote', and Jackson's campaign was effectively finished in May 1976, although he had ostensibly courted pro-IRA forces during his campaigns in Massachusetts and New York.[19] The Embassy also monitored developments at the Democratic National Convention, noting that at the Drafting Subcommittee there was an attempt to insert 'the United States should work for a united Ireland' into the party platform.[20] The extra sentence was proposed again in the Full Committee but was rejected. Ultimately, according to Davidson's report, the platform included a passage about Ireland, which was 'reasonably innocuous as far as we are concerned'.[21] The Democratic Party's platform passage on Ireland called for an acknowledgement of American interest in the Northern Ireland question:

> The voice of the United States should be heard in Northern Ireland against violence and terror, against the discrimination, repression and deprivation which brought about that civil strife, and for the efforts of the parties toward a peaceful resolution of the future of Northern Ireland. Pertinent alliances such as NATO and international organizations such as the United Nations should be fully appraised of the interests of the United States with respect to the status of Ireland in the international community of nations.[22]

While the presidential candidate was not bound to the platform, the British Embassy and FCO understood that Carter's representatives were involved in its drafting and it subsequently secured his overall approval.[23] The British were admittedly perplexed about the meaning and purpose of the second sentence in the passage, viewing it as 'an unwelcome attempt to internationalize the Northern Ireland situation'.[24] But none the less, the Embassy expected that the platform was so 'broad and all embracing' that references to Northern Ireland would 'simply get lost in the wash'.[25]

This optimistic British reading of Democratic politics was not shared in other quarters. Recalling the inclusion of Northern Ireland in the Democrats' platform, Senator Kennedy argued that it was an extremely significant development in the internationalisation of the Northern Ireland conflict. He argued that:

> It was recognition that this was not going to be a local problem. It wasn't just a British problem; it was going to be an international problem and an international issue, and the United States was going to be involved . . . . It was the first time any political party platform had recognized that this was going to happen, that the United States as a country was going to have an interest in Ireland.[26]

Kennedy and Rep. Bruce Morrison (D-CT) worked with Carter's staff to ensure that it was included and the Governor himself 'was aware of what we were doing'.[27]

Even as late as 16 September, the British Embassy was still unaware of either Carter or Ford, or even their respective running mates, Senators Walter Mondale (D-MN) and Bob Dole (R-KS), having issued any statements about Northern Ireland during the campaign.[28] However, Carter did court the Irish–American electorate. On 10 August 1976, Carter wrote a letter to John Michael Keane, National President of the AOH.[29] In a message to the seventy-eighth AOH convention, Carter offered unsurprising praise for the contribution of Irish–Americans to the American saga:

> Hibernians can take pride in these accomplishments. It was not by accident that nearly one half of George Washington's army was Irish, nor was it simply coincidental that Lafayette arrived with troops of the Irish Brigade who had fled to France to escape annihilation in their native land.

Thus, Carter was 'pleased' that the Democrats' 1976 platform supported 'a just and humane approach to the difficulties now facing the people of Ireland'. The issue certainly had not been sidelined amid the platform's competing priorities. Carter told the AOH that he ordered the inclusion of Northern Ireland in his party's platform. He explained that he was 'sympathetic with those who seek to promote a stable and free Ireland with full civil and human rights for all of the citizens'.[30] On 8 September, Carter included a reference to the 'Troubles' in his speech about foreign policy and human rights to B'nai B'rith, a Jewish fraternal organisation, in Washington, DC: 'Denials of human rights occur in many places and many ways. In Ireland, for example, violence has bred more violence, and caused untold human suffering which brings sorrow to the entire civilized world.'[31] Carter was therefore speaking on the issue, albeit not on a national platform. However, occasional political platitudes were insufficient for the AOH. The New York State Board's president, Thomas D. McNabb, wrote to Carter and simply demanded, 'What will you do?'[32] McNabb's efforts to influence Carter must be viewed within political reality: Nixon had won New York in the 1972 presidential election, but in the three presidential elections beforehand the state had supported the Democratic candidate and Ford had essentially allowed New York City to become bankrupt in 1975 amid the city's fiscal crisis. Thus, it was likely that Carter was confident of securing New York's Electoral College votes without the support of the AOH.

The hope – if not, expectation – that Carter would respond favourably to Irish–American concerns culminated in the Governor's first presidential debate with Ford in October 1976. Carter failed to mention Northern Ireland at all during the first two presidential debates and the AOH responded angrily to this. John F. Finucane, writing on their behalf, explained:

> I would like to let you know that our membership was greatly let down by your failure to even mention the trouble in Northern Ireland. There was ample opportunity to do so. We hope that you will make up for this in your final debate with Mr. Ford. Just a small mention of a unified Ireland would bring many many votes into your camp.[33]

Finucane noted that, after a recent meeting between representatives of the AOH and the Carter campaign, the AOH had hoped that Carter 'would speak publicly on the Irish Question'. Finucane simply asked, 'What happened?'[34] Clearly disgruntled, he enclosed a profile on the presidential candidates. Carter was warned that the AOH profiles had been distributed throughout the US and a letter would likewise be dispatched after the final debate: 'We want it to be favourable to you.'[35] Adding a cautionary note, Carter was warned that Daniel Moynihan was enjoying a substantial lead in the polls over the incumbent senator from New York, James L. Buckley (Conservative Party, 1971–7) because the Senator had 'failed the Irish people'. Thus, Carter was encouraged 'to be more positive in reference to the Irish Question' and even told that 'A reply would be in order.'[36]

Despite the protests of the AOH, Carter failed to mention Northern Ireland during his third and final debate with Ford on 22 October 1976.[37] However, Carter did comment on the Northern Ireland question just days before the general election, albeit to an audience that had republican sympathies. On 27 October 1976, Carter met with over fifty members of the INC. In his remarks, he discussed civil rights in Northern Ireland, advocated a united Ireland, and promised that, as president, he would support American economic aid should the Northern Ireland conflict come to an end during his administration. Subsequently, the INC endorsed his candidacy.[38] Carter's comments surprised the Irish government. On the day that he made his remarks to the INC, the Irish Embassy in Washington, DC, had received assurances from Paul Sullivan, the coordinator of Carter's campaign in Chicago, 'that to the best of his knowledge' Carter would not make any statement on Northern Ireland.[39] Sullivan confirmed that the issue was 'discussed fully' by the campaign's leaders in a meeting at Carter's house in Georgia before the Democratic Convention. The decision was made that Carter 'would not adopt a position which appeared sympathetic to the IRA' as he understood 'the complexities of the Northern Ireland situation'. Sullivan told the Irish that although 'he was not personally in close touch with Governor Carter . . . he had direct access to some of his "issues people" and was certain that he would have been made aware of any change of policy in regard to Northern Ireland'.[40] Carter's comments contradicted this intelligence. Irish officials attributed Carter's Pittsburgh remarks to poor communication with their contacts in Pennsylvania (in contrast to their experience with their Chicago operatives), as they had been unable to prevent the 'surprise meeting' between Carter and leading INC figures.[41] The key concern for the Irish government was that the meeting 'was of course heralded by IRA supporters as a triumph and an augury of political support from a Carter administration'.[42] As far as the Irish government was concerned, until

Carter had surprisingly met with the INC, Northern Ireland was 'a relatively unimportant issue in Carter's set of populist foreign policy issues'.[43] That these comments were deemed so surprising suggests that a Carter administration was hitherto expected to be consistent with its predecessors on the Northern Ireland question.

On 28 October, the Irish shared with their British counterparts the content of Carter's message to FitzGerald following reports of his meeting with the INC. The Governor clarified his remarks, explaining that they had been 'misrepresented':

> The facts of the matter are simple and have been stated many times before. I do not favour violence as part of a solution to the Irish question. I favour negotiations and peaceful means for finding a just solution which involves the two communities of Northern Ireland and protects human rights which have been threatened. My position has always been the responsible one adopted by the Democratic Party in its platform.[44]

Carter's message was to be made public. Likewise, his campaign issued a press statement in order to clarify the candidate's position:

> Governor Carter has never advocated violence as a part of the solution to the tragic problems of Northern Ireland. He has never endorsed the tactics of organisations which either implicitly or explicitly advocate such a solution. Governor Carter has expressed his concern for the just and peaceful resolution of these problems through negotiations which involve the two communities of Northern Ireland. His statement . . . in Pittsburgh reaffirmed these commitments . . . .[45]

The Carter campaign also contacted the British Embassy on 29 October. Jerry Doolittle, who served as a press adviser on the campaign, called the Embassy 'in a nervous state', in order to stress that, contrary to a forthcoming *Daily Express* story, the Governor had not worn an 'England out of Ireland' badge during the meeting at Pittsburgh (and, again, the one he was photographed wearing in New York City had been pinned to Carter's lapel without his knowledge and the photograph taken before he could remove it).[46] Doolittle told the Embassy that, even though 'there was no record' of Carter's remarks at Pittsburgh, he emphasised that the Governor did not support the IRA. He betrayed the campaign's naiveté by their 'surprise that the affair should have caused such a stir in Britain when there had been no reaction in the United States'.[47] John Biggs-Davison, MP, a Conservative Party front-bench spokesman on Northern Ireland, issued a press statement following Carter's remarks: 'Foreigners should not interfere in United States elections. Nor should American politicians intervene in internal affairs of the United Kingdom.'[48] He turned the issue back on the Governor: 'he would do well to follow the example of other US leaders, of Irish Ministers and of the Women's Peace Movement in urging Irish Americans to put a stop to the subsidising of murder through bogus funds for Irish relief'.[49]

Carter marginally defeated Ford on 2 November 1976. Following the US election, Roy Mason, the Northern Ireland Secretary (1976–7), met with Sir Peter Ramsbotham, British ambassador to the US (1974–7), in London.[50] On Carter's Pittsburgh remarks, Ramsbotham said that he believed that while Carter 'had demonstrated poor judgment', the President-Elect's 'lapse had perhaps been salutary', as it now 'disposed him more favourably to listen to what the British Embassy had to say'.[51] Even so, there was still apprehension about the direction of Irish–Americans interested in the situation. John Hume (also a founding member of the SDLP) informed Mason about 'a struggle' within the AOH 'involving an attempt by those sympathetic to the Provisional IRA to take the organisation over'.[52] Hume advised that representatives of the Irish government 'were fighting the battle and it was a battle best left to them'.[53]

The extent of Irish–American support for Carter and any consequent influence Irish–Americans would enjoy over his administration were debated within the FCO. One civil servant suggested that Carter's success was based on support in southern and north-eastern states, which meant that the Democratic Party's political machine in the New York area was key to his victory. That particular component of the party was to be 'heavily influenced by Irish–Americans'.[54] Subsequently, it was observed that Carter had 'incurred a considerable political debt'.[55] In contrast, the FCO's research department offered an alternative hypothesis. Carter owed 'a considerable political debt of gratitude' to the American labour movement, African–Americans, Jewish–Americans, and Democratic voters generally.[56] Irish–Americans formed part of the Democratic machine, but that was not necessarily 'particularly important' as Irish–Americans, like other supporters of the Democratic Party, were motivated by 'party loyalty' and 'pocketbook issues', meaning that the Northern Ireland issue was not 'the determinant of the voting pattern for Irish Americans'. Furthermore, whereas Carter and Ford attempted to 'outbid the other in their support for Israel' to secure 'Jewish votes', presidential candidates of either party typically 'do not engage in propaganda about Northern Ireland aimed largely at obtaining the Irish American vote'. Northern Ireland was viewed to be 'of little importance'. It was not anticipated that Carter would 'make any significant moves' with regard to Northern Ireland and 'certainly not within the next year'. The FCO believed that, even though Carter would 'assert his moralistic theme in foreign policy', there were many international issues where he could do this and therefore avoid 'antagonising one of America's major allies'.[57] A settled FCO view emerged in the New Year. Despite the unknown of America's first Democratic President during the 'Troubles', Carter was unlikely to act on Northern Ireland, as he 'must realise that he stirred up a hornet's nest at Pittsburgh'.[58] The FCO would be proven wrong before the end of Carter's first year as president.

## The Carter administration and Northern Ireland

In contrast to the FCO's observations, Northern Ireland was an emerging factor in American politics and the Carter campaign certainly sought to capture the Irish–American vote. However, campaign politics soon gave way to the formulation of policy. Initially, the Carter administration was keen to continue their predecessors' policy of neutrality towards the Anglo-Irish process and focus on tackling Irish–American support for the IRA. The Irish government believed that, for Carter, the issue revolved around 'human rights and relatively little else'.[59] Yet following the incident in Pittsburgh, the INC believed that they had an opportunity to influence the White House, particularly by presenting their organisation as a champion of human rights. Similarly, the Irish government worried that, coming from the South, Carter and his leading advisers were 'notoriously ignorant' about Catholic constituencies in Northeast and Mid-West America. In 1976, the Carter campaign understood that they needed to regain the support of these constituencies. Thus, the Irish government believed that there was 'overkill and oversimplification' of some issues during the presidential campaign, and Northern Ireland was 'a case in point'. The Irish even believed that Carter's advisers saw a 'political advantage' to meeting with the INC. This was due to their 'ignorance of the Irish–American community', which was comprised of people who were either opposed to the violence or disinterested in Northern Ireland. Accordingly, the Carter campaign has been incorrectly 'impressed by the claim that the issue is crucial to securing Irish–American votes'.[60] The INC certainly believed that they had gained assurances from Carter that he would act in accordance with their goals in Northern Ireland. In a *Washington Post* advertisement, the INC wrote directly to the President, calling for him to honour his pledge to pressure British Prime Minister Callaghan to respect human rights and support Irish unification.[61]

Despite making human rights a central focus in their foreign policy, the Carter administration was soon faced with qualifications about that particular agenda. The first challenge was the definition of human rights. It became clear that Carter was interested in individuals' political and civil rights, rather than torture and punishment for political beliefs. This meant that some of the claims of Irish–Americans about Northern Ireland were immediately sidelined. The second challenge was that there were inevitably limitations to what the President could do. For instance, with regard to Northern Ireland, the INC protested about British abuses there, but even though, in 1977, Carter was a signatory to the Economic, Social, and Cultural Rights Covenant and International Covenant of Civil and Political Rights, the US Senate did not ratify even the Civil and Political Rights Covenant until 1992. The third was how to marry together a concern for human rights along with the realities of international politics. For example, whereas the British government, a major ally, became subject to defending a congressional yearly report into human rights in Northern Ireland, the Soviet Union and China did not participate in a similar process with regard to their record on human rights.[62]

The administration certainly kept abreast of developments in the Anglo-Irish process and was interested in continuing efforts to reduce Irish–American support for the IRA. On 10 March, Cyrus Vance, the US Secretary of State (1977–80), met with David Owen, the British Secretary of State for Foreign and Commonwealth Affairs (1977–9).[63] Vance was briefed on a recent consultation between Owen and FitzGerald about the Irish–American dimension to the 'Troubles' and the Anglo-Irish process. Owen remarked that FitzGerald was 'worried about an apparent increase in IRA influence on the new Administration'. Arthur Hartman, the US Assistant Secretary of State for European Affairs (1974–7), simply replied 'that this was not so'. He explained that IRA claims to have contacts in the State Department were 'unfounded', and that representatives, or associates, of the IRA 'had now been banned ever from entering the State Department, by order of the White House'. Nevertheless, Hartman did admit that 'IRA representatives had had discreet contact with a junior White House Staff member'.[64] That this information was shared shows that the Carter administration did not intend to be influenced by the IRA and prioritised Anglo-American relations. Furthermore, the administration ostensibly did not want to risk souring Anglo-American relations by not disclosing a contact that the British may have already known about.

The same day, Prime Minister Callaghan met with members of Congress at a luncheon, in his honour, organised by the chairmen of the Senate Foreign Relations Committee and the House International Relations Committee.[65] On Northern Ireland, Rep. John Bingham (D-NY) enquired about the possibility of a 'negotiated independence', with the European Community serving as guarantors for the right of minorities (an idea initially proposed by Paddy Devlin of the SDLP). Callaghan's reply was the standard British position: 'he would be willing to look at any solution which commanded the support of a majority of both communities in Northern Ireland'. On Devlin's proposal per se, the Prime Minister believed that it 'would not command the support of the Protestants' and, furthermore, he feared that 'independence would cause the present violence to expand into a civil war embracing all Ireland.' Nevertheless, Callaghan was positive about the Anglo-Irish process more generally, saying that the two governments 'now worked more closely than ever . . . on these problems'.[66] This was in keeping with British policy of offering a positive account of Northern Ireland and the Anglo-Irish process.

While Northern Ireland was a topic of conversation between Owen and Vance, and Callaghan and the Congressmen, it was not discussed during the Prime Minister's meeting with the President on 11 March. Instead, the conversation focused on issues such as the SALT talks, the Comprehensive Test Ban, consultation with NATO, nuclear non-proliferation, the Middle East, Concorde, and the Caribbean.[67] Zbigniew Brzezinski, the NSA (1977–81), told Ramsbotham that, in respect of the 'special relationship', the President 'really meant it; he was not just saying it to please'.[68] Thus, now in office, Carter did not act on Northern Ireland despite his campaign statements to Irish–Americans.

Less than a week later, an Irish government delegation visited Washington, DC, and Carter met FitzGerald on 16 March 1977.[69] In contrast to his conversation with Callaghan, the President did discuss Northern Ireland with the Irish Foreign Minister, albeit out of interest rather than as an inquiry as to how to involve his administration in the Anglo-Irish process. The President offered his support for two respective statements in opposition to violence in Northern Ireland, which were being planned for the following day: a joint statement by FitzGerald and Cyrus Vance, and another by the Four Horsemen. Carter enquired about the Anglo-Irish process. Echoing Callaghan's positivity towards the Congressmen, the Irish Foreign Minister explained that 'the Irish Government does not want the British to withdraw from Northern Ireland, nor even to set a date for withdrawal' and that the civil rights situation had improved. He reported that, in recent months, the British government had 'been better . . . about pressing the Protestant majority toward power sharing', while 'the Irish have abandoned "silly" irredentist claims'. FitzGerald 'was hopeful about a new plan for a gradual movement toward real power sharing'.[70] The following day, FitzGerald met with Vance. According to the Irish record, Vance stated that the administration 'would always be happy to do anything they could to help' in ensuring that the 'proper message' on Northern Ireland gets 'across in the United States' and they would continue to tackle IRA fund raising events and gunrunning.[71] The Carter administration's concern was therefore limited to addressing Irish–American support for the IRA, much like its immediate predecessor. On security issues in Northern Ireland, FitzGerald explained that 'there is now close cooperation between the British and Irish Governments', with the RUC 'now quite a good body', which was in 'constant communication' with the Irish police. FitzGerald candidly admitted that 'there are bound to be difficulties at times,' such as occasional border crossings by British troops, as 'their map reading can be faulty at times'. Such problems, however, did not undermine the two governments' 'common determination and . . . common policy'. According to FitzGerald, the British and Irish governments were endeavouring to convince Northern Ireland's politicians 'to join in working together while Northern Ireland still remains under British jurisdiction', as the Irish government did not wish to 'press for any change' in sovereignty against the will of the majority. The Foreign Minister noted that the difficulty was the 'intransigence on the Unionist side by politicians who are not prepared to share power'.[72] Thus, whereas there was cooperation in the Anglo-Irish process, parties in Northern Ireland were not following suit.

The British and the Irish governments agreed that Irish–American activity and any potential intervention by the Carter administration would undermine the Anglo-Irish process by unsettling the parties in Northern Ireland. It was hoped that FitzGerald's visit would help convince the Carter administration that the Anglo-Irish process was progressing and thereby encourage it to hold the line adopted by previous administrations. The subsequent assessment was cautiously optimistic. The British Embassy in Washington, DC, informed the FCO that, according to Donlon (Irish Department of Foreign Affairs, 1971–8), the British and Irish governments were 'by no means out of the wood' with any unwelcome replacement of neutrality by a potential administration-supported fact-finding mission of senior Democratic politicians.[73] Nevertheless, FitzGerald's visit had resulted in a clearer understanding within the administration and Congress of the INC's relationship with the IRA and a renewed conviction by the administration to tackle Irish–American support for the IRA.[74]

In July 1977, Carter met with the new US ambassador to Ireland, William Shannon (1977–81). Brzezinski advised Carter to emphasise the longstanding American policy of 'non-involvement in Northern Ireland' and to reaffirm 'support for a peaceful and just solution involving the two communities which protects human rights'. This security-oriented approach represented continuity with the policy of the NSA's predecessors in the White House, such as Kissinger. Shannon also was to be appraised with a reaffirmation of American efforts 'to combat private, illegal US involvement in the Northern situation'.[75] Yet the British and Irish Embassies were aware that other members of the Carter administration, specifically Vance, were considering the possibility of the President making a statement about Northern Ireland. Following reports of Speaker O'Neill meeting with Vance, the British Embassy concluded that the Horsemen hoped for 'a new initiative by the US, preferably by the administration rather than themselves', which could be 'a statement and possibly some commitment to financial aid'.[76] The FCO informed the British Embassy, 'we are luke-warm about . . . any US government statement', although it 'would certainly be preferable to a fact-finding mission'.[77]

On 26 July 1977, *The Irish Times* reported that O'Neill and Vance had discussed the possibility of an American peace-making initiative in Northern Ireland but concluded that it was best that the US government should avoid direct involvement.[78] Carter was absent from these developments. Beyond the electoral implications in 1976, Carter was disinterested in any involvement in Northern Ireland in preference of pursuing other and broader foreign policy objectives. Nevertheless, it soon became clear that the Horsemen were indeed pressing the administration to make a statement, in addition to their own, calling for an end to the violence and support for violence by Irish–Americans. Thus, the British Embassy advised the FCO that it was 'paramount' to keep the Horsemen 'to the broad line they have now taken'.[79] Although the proposed linkage between American investment and a settlement in Northern Ireland was deemed to be 'a difficult one' for the British government, a carefully worded passage about such a proposal would 'minimise any damage on that score'. The most important issue was to ensure that the Horsemen continued 'disseminating in the Irish–American communities here a better understanding of the true situation and issues in Northern Ireland'. A statement by Carter would achieve this, as the Horsemen could tell their own Irish–American constituents they had successfully lobbied the administration, demonstrating that their approach was the most conducive to a solution in Northern Ireland, and hence underlining their activities as constructive.[80] Peter Jay, the new British ambassador to the US (1977–9), recognised that the discussion of a presidential statement was an example of party politics within the Democratic Party. The Four Horsemen's condemnation of Irish–American support for the IRA in the St Patrick's Day statement that year meant that Carter, in turn, owed them his support for the issue. If the president did not back up the Horsemen, they risked losing the initiative in Irish–American affairs to Mario Biaggi (a public proponent for republicanism and the IRA's paramilitary campaign).[81] They needed political cover from the White House.

The US State Department understood the Horsemen's position. Matthew Nimetz, a counsellor in the US State Department (1977–9), informed the British Embassy that the Horsemen 'probably felt somewhat exposed to criticism from the extremist wing' of Irish–Americans following their St Patrick's Day statement.[82] Carter's support helped them 'to avoid charges of being wholly negative, i.e. condemning fund-raising and violence without proposing anything constructive'.[83] Nimetz did not know 'whether the president was yet personally in the picture' but the 'NSC staff were and he thought it likely that Mr Vance would have mentioned it to him'.[84] For his part, Hume believed that Carter's Protestantism was advantageous, as Ian Paisley would be unable to argue that the President was a supporter of the IRA or biased towards Catholics.[85]

Noting speculation in the British press about a Carter 'initiative' in Northern Ireland, *The Washington Post* was sceptical that any such development would occur, particularly one that went beyond the Horsemen's opposition towards Irish–American support for violence.[86] *The Washington Post* recalled Carter's 'Get England Out of Ireland' button during the presidential election when he was struggling to gain support in American cities, but believed that it was not a signal of potential US foreign policy.[87] Jody Powell, who served as the President's Press Secretary (1977–81), played down reports of Carter's preparedness to offer American economic support as an incentive for peace in Northern Ireland.[88] According to Powell, Carter was not even aware of the discussions between Vance and the Horsemen until 24 August.[89] A potential intervention by the Carter administration was discussed in the British press and, for instance, fiercely condemned in the editorial of *The Sun*.[90] The potential statement from Carter on Northern Ireland was discussed on British television. Appearing on *Face the Nation*, Owen observed that he expected the Carter administration to offer economic support to Northern Ireland but not 'take an active role' in the Anglo-Irish process.[91] This would indeed prove to be the thrust of the announcement.

On 30 August 1977, Carter issued a statement promising American investment if a power-sharing solution could be agreed.[92] He explained that, given the contributions of the British and Irish people, including both Catholics and Protestants, to the US, it was inevitable that Americans 'are deeply concerned about the continuing conflict and violence in Northern Ireland'.[93] Accordingly, the US supported 'a just solution that involves both parts of the community of Northern Ireland', which 'protects human rights and guarantees freedom from discrimination' and is supported by the British and Irish governments. Carter made it clear that his administration had 'no intention of telling the parties how this might be achieved'. However, he stressed that 'the people of Northern Ireland should know that they have our complete support in their quest for a peaceful and just society'. Carter noted that Northern Ireland 'continued to attract investment, despite the violence committed by a small minority', which would 'create jobs' and 'assist in ensuring a healthy economy and combating unemployment'. Consequently, as he explained:

> It is still true that a peaceful settlement would contribute immeasurably to stability in Northern Ireland and so enhance the prospects for increased investment. In the event of such a settlement, the U.S. Government would be prepared to join with others to see how additional job creating investment could be encouraged, to the benefit of all the people of Northern Ireland.

Crucially, Carter's statement also echoed the Four Horsemen's condemnation of Irish–American support for violence in Northern Ireland and the UK generally:

> We hope that all those engaged in violence will renounce this course and commit themselves to peaceful pursuit of legitimate goals . . . . I ask all Americans to refrain from supporting with financial or other aid organizations whose involvement, direct or indirect, in this violence delays the day when the people of Northern Ireland can live and work together in harmony, free from fear.[94]

This was the first time that a US president had stated that there would be American assistance, should there be a resolution to the conflict, albeit along the lines first discussed during the Nixon era (as noted in the previous chapter). By criticising republican supporters of the IRA in the US and promising economic assistance should the conflict be resolved, the precedent was established for subsequent American interventions.[95] The *Irish Independent* praised the statement.[96] So did *The New York Times*, which emphasised Carter's Protestantism as a means to persuade Ulster Protestants to agree a settlement.[97] The *Irish Independent* welcomed Carter's unambiguous and constructive statement that the US desired a solution, which it accepted had to be agreed by the Northern Ireland people, and was willing to offer financial support for it.[98]

The importance that Carter attached to the statement can be disputed. Indeed, it disappeared from the administration's foreign policy; this was perhaps due to the lack of unity amongst Irish–American politicians and lobbyists.[99] Moreover, other events inevitably assumed greater priority: for instance, the negotiations for SALT II, the energy crisis, the Arab–Israeli War and, of course, 1979, which saw the Soviet invasion of Afghanistan and the taking of 444 American hostages following the storming of the American embassy in Tehran, in Iran. Nonetheless, Carter's statement did establish a clear American policy towards Northern Ireland, which would be followed by his successors. Senator Kennedy felt that Vance was due much credit for the statement, while Brzezinski 'was never a part' of the process.[100] He argued that Vance 'understood what we were attempting to do and I think he had a broader view in terms of understanding the dimensions and the implications and the positive aspects that this could provide'. According to Kennedy, Vance 'was empathetic and sympathetic' and he 'was able to use his very considerable skills to try to buck the tradition of the State Department'.[101]

Despite this development, the INC remained frustrated by the Four Horsemen's moderate approach and a lack of intervention by the Carter administration. Its leader, Seán McManus, concluded that a dedicated congressional group was required in order to apply sufficient pressure on the Carter administration to act. It was Rep. Mario Biaggi (D-NY) who decided to take on the mantle. Biaggi organised the Ad Hoc Congressional Committee on Irish Affairs (ACCIA) in September 1977. This was a bipartisan group but the Democratic Party leadership, such as O'Neill, refused to participate, given its connections to groups such as the INC, which was viewed to have connections with NORAID. Nevertheless, the INC and ACCIA continued to ensure that Northern Ireland was on the political agenda. They made 1977 a record year for bills submitted to Congress that related to human rights in Northern Ireland and demanded that Irish republicans receive equal treatment by the State Department with regard to the issuing of visas as those connected with loyalist paramilitary activity.[102] For instance, in October 1977, Nimetz met with Mario Biaggi and other representatives from ACCIA about the refusal of American visas to members of the IRA because of their links to illegal activities.[103] The Irish government did not welcome the activities of Biaggi's committee. Given its ties to the INC and distraction from the Horsemen, Jack Lynch (Taoiseach for the second time, 1977–90) would both publicly criticise and write to Biaggi about this in early 1978.[104]

The possibility of a Northern Ireland settlement was discussed between Vance and Michael O'Kennedy, the Irish Foreign Minister (1977–9), in October 1977. In response to Vance's question about the prospects 'of a long-term solution involving integration between north and south in Ireland', O'Kennedy replied that this 'would have to be by agreement, through negotiation and by consent'.[105] He explained that the Irish government was discussing means to identify potential 'areas of co-operation between the two parts of Ireland'. He suggested that security was an obvious area of such co-operation, coupled with a 'related possibility of creating at some stage All-Ireland Courts' that could act in 'a punitive fashion' but also protect 'young people from an infringement of their rights by institutions of state'.[106] The Irish government's ideas for the Anglo-Irish process were also reported to Carter in a State Department briefing in January 1978. Lynch had offered what the State Department described as 'several controversial remarks on Northern Ireland':[107] he proposed a potential amnesty for members of the IRA should there be a political settlement. Furthermore, in contrast to FitzGerald's remarks to Carter a year earlier, Lynch stated that the British government should declare its intent to withdraw eventually.[108] Carter was aware of developments, but did not advocate intervention beyond his statement in August 1977.

Carter's reluctance to intervene is reflected in his failure to mention Northern Ireland in his remarks at the Hibernian Society dinner in Savannah, Georgia, on 17 March 1978.[109] Instead, the President focused on the need for action on broader priorities, such as energy policy, SALT and nuclear proliferation.[110] Yet Northern Ireland was utilised for political reasons in an attempt to galvanise support for Democratic candidates for federal and state offices, including Carey, at a 'Get Out the Vote Rally' in New York City on 2 November 1978.[111] The President remarked,

> When I have a problem in dealing with international affairs – bringing human rights to Northern Ireland, bringing human rights and peace to the Mideast – I know that I can refer to and depend upon the advice and the counsel and support of your great Democratic Party leadership here.

Appealing directly to voters with familial connections abroad, Carter added: 'It's a very great influence that you enjoy in helping to guide me in making decisions that affect your own ancestors, your own relatives, in troubled areas of the world.'[112]

An ECHR ruling in September 1977 accepted that British soldiers had used illegal, degrading and inhumane interrogation techniques on internees, underlining allegations about human rights abuses. Accordingly, outside of Carter's electioneering, the stalling of the political process in Northern Ireland and human rights abuses dominated Irish–American concerns in 1978. The Four Horsemen's 1978 St Patrick's Day statement again condemned

Irish–Americans who supported violence, but also criticised the British government for the lack of political process. In May 1978, O'Neill voiced his frustration with Callaghan's inactivity, and the following month Kennedy argued that a special prosecutor should be appointed to investigate allegations of abuse by the RUC. Subsequently, an Amnesty International investigation during the summer of 1978 identified seventy-eight cases of abuse of suspects by the RUC while they were at the interrogation centre at Castlereagh. In a visit to London in December 1978, Senator Moynihan informed Roy Mason (Britain's Northern Ireland Secretary) and David Owen (British Foreign Secretary) that the Four Horsemen's attempts to convince Irish–Americans of constitutional nationalism, rather than the republicanism advocated by the likes of Biaggi, were an uphill struggle without a political process. The allegations of RUC abuse prompted the British government to commission an investigation by Harry Bennett (an English Crown Court judge) in March 1979. The Bennett Report quickly confirmed the claims made by Amnesty International: namely, that RUC detectives had physically abused suspects. The Bennett Report recommended the use of physical examinations of suspects and closed-circuit television to monitor RUC interrogations. In turn, Hume encouraged O'Neill to take a delegation to the UK in order to pressurise the Conservative and Labour parties – who, in April 1979, were fighting a general election – into renewing their efforts to restore a political resolution to the 'Troubles'.[113]

## O'Neill's 1979 visit to Europe: a phantom vanguard of a 'peace process'

O'Neill led a bipartisan delegation of US representatives to Great Britain, Belgium, Hungary and Ireland between 11 and 23 April 1979.[114] According to the Speaker's press release, the purpose of the tour was to provide leading figures in Congress with 'the opportunity to gain firsthand knowledge of our defense position in Europe, to explore . . . relations with Eastern Europe, and to assess developments in Ireland'.[115] O'Neill was accompanied by six Democratic and three Republican congressional colleagues.[116] Such expeditions are a typical aspect of congressional service. Before O'Neill's departure, the *Los Angeles Times* mockingly observed that, over the subsequent few days, China would be home to more members of Congress than is sometimes the case in the Senate or House of Representatives.[117]

The Carter administration was convinced that not much could be accomplished by way of progress on Northern Ireland until after the British general election.[118] The consultation between the Horsemen and the administration continued, with the Speaker consulting with the State Department in advance of his European expedition.[119] Despite the general election campaign, the British civil service understood the importance of O'Neill's visit and senior civil servants encouraged Callaghan to meet with him. The FCO explained to Downing Street that O'Neill was 'one of the three or four most influential politicians' in US politics, and 'We look to him for help over a wide variety of issues above all in Northern Ireland.'[120] Callaghan was encouraged to take the line that the government was grateful for O'Neill's 'constructive interest in the problems of Northern Ireland, his condemnation of violence and support for the principle that any solution must be acceptable to all parties'.[121] Moreover, the Prime Minister was advised to add his gratitude for O'Neill's 'efforts to resist the pressure for Congressional Hearings which could only aggravate divisions in Northern Ireland'.[122] Callaghan was to inform O'Neill that, even though 'self-imposed squalor at the Maze prison regrettably continues', the British government would not 'grant political status to those convicted of' what they viewed to be 'criminal acts'.[123]

The Congressional delegation met with Thatcher (leader of the opposition, 1975–9) and Callaghan. According to O'Neill's records, the delegation asked Thatcher about Conservative Party policies towards Northern Ireland.[124] She explained, 'both the Labour and Conservative Parties have adhered to a bipartisan approach to Northern Ireland, and that it was not the subject of public debate in the campaign'. Avoiding any detailed discussion, Thatcher added that her party's manifesto prioritised the 'defeat of terrorism', and a Conservative government 'would move to increase security in Northern Ireland'.[125]

O'Neill, the Congressmen and Kingman Brewster, the US ambassador to Britain (1977–81), then called on Callaghan.[126] In a wide-ranging discussion of issues (East–West relations, trade negotiations, Northern Ireland and energy), one of the Congressmen asked Callaghan about the future of Northern Ireland generally, while O'Neill spoke of his concern about the conditions in the Maze prison. Callaghan admitted that he could not offer a satisfactory response, although his government continued to 'search for a solution to the problems of the province'. With regard to H Block (part of Her Majesty's Prison Maze, in Northern Ireland, where paramilitaries were imprisoned), Callaghan was forthright. He turned the question back on O'Neill, asking what solution he could propose. According to the British record, 'O'Neill acknowledged that he had none' and Callaghan argued that the 'situation of deliberate defilement to which Speaker O'Neill had referred applied only to a part of H block'. In another rebuke, Callaghan noted that 'in the remainder of the block the conditions were in every way superior to . . . most American prisons'. He then explained the British position: they 'would never agree to treat murderers, who had been found guilty by due process of law, as political prisoners'. The Prime Minister even reminded the Congressmen 'that most of the weapons with which their murders had been committed, and money to buy more, came from the United States'. As per his briefings from the FCO, Callaghan emphasised the need for American support in tackling the actions of the IRA and, explicitly, he wanted to remind Irish–Americans of the American contribution to the 'Troubles'.[127] According to the American record, Callaghan advised his guests that there would not be 'any significant policy changes towards the problem of Northern Ireland' and claimed 'that less than 1% of the British electorate have viewed the problem in Northern Ireland as an important national issue'.[128] O'Neill's importance in relation to Irish–Americans was recognised by the British government, but Callaghan had clearly decided to explain the political reality of the situation to the Congressmen.

After these meetings in the UK, the Congressmen met with European leaders before undertaking final stops in Ireland and Northern Ireland. The American record shows that discussions during O'Neill's meeting with Lynch (the Taoiseach) revolved around Northern Ireland.[129] Lynch observed that while the majority of Irish citizens condemned the IRA, continuing violence and tensions meant that 'the British government was limited in its ability or willingness to solve the problem'. The Taoiseach advocated the unification of Ireland, but argued that it was the responsibility of the British government to promote reunification. The Irish government would support this by promoting cross-border economic cooperation. Lynch was 'impressed' by Carter's 1977 statement and was hopeful that the President 'would encourage the next British Government to take positive steps to reach a workable, peaceful solution'. The Taoiseach observed that Irish–American financial aid to the IRA had undermined Irish efforts to solve the problem.[130] The Irish record of this meeting offers a more detailed account.[131] The Speaker explained that Northern Ireland was quickly becoming a key debate in American politics, specifically in foreign policy. He observed that around

> 35% of the Democratic Party were Catholic – and a large number of them Irish. They were saying that if the President could bring about peace between Israel and Egypt, why could he not intervene, on his own doorstep and achieve a similar settlement in Northern Ireland.

The Taoiseach argued that 'British policy now was guaranteeing the continuance of the status quo, with all its uncertainties and instability,' with the British parties believing 'the main issue' to be 'the violence and the killing of soldiers'. O'Neill asked whether Lynch had 'any message' for 'the power of the American Government'. He was offering to use his relationship with the White House. In response, the Taoiseach 'stressed that timing was essential or the whole issue could blow up in our faces'.[132]

Prior to his meeting with the entire congressional delegation, the Taoiseach was briefed that Irish–Americans viewed 'the Northern Ireland problem in very simplistic terms' with 'the British presence in Northern Ireland as the only problem', given their lack of appreciation of 'the strength of unionist sentiment or the explosive nature of inter-community tensions in Northern Ireland'.[133] It is clear that both the Irish and British governments were as exasperated by Irish–American politicians as they were grateful for their support. O'Neill also met with Fitzgerald and Frank Cluskey (Leader of the Labour Party, 1977–81). Fitzgerald noted that O'Neill's 'fact-finding mission' to Northern Ireland would be 'significant', as it would show the rival political groups 'that the outside world was concerned about the problem, and that the interests of Northern Ireland were not perceived in a remote, isolated vacuum'. O'Neill subsequently met with President Patrick Hillery (1976–90) to discuss Irish affairs further.[134]

O'Neill's meetings with various leaders only garnered press attention following his speech at Dublin Castle to mark a dinner in his honour. The Speaker criticised his previous British hosts.[135] O'Neill explained that he was 'deeply concerned by the lack of political progress in Northern Ireland over the last few years' and that 'Britain bears a heavy responsibility for the failures of recent years on the political front'. Appearing to speak on behalf of the US government, O'Neill commented, 'We have been concerned that the problem has been treated as a political football in London or has otherwise been given a low priority.' In order to underline his point, O'Neill added that 'there is no more serious problem on the agenda of British politics than a crisis which has claimed 2,000 lives and caused almost 20,000 serious injuries'. The Speaker then tried to present himself as non-partisan:

> It is not our concern to favour one party or another on the forthcoming elections in Britain but we do insist on an early, realistic and major initiative on the part of the incoming British Government so as to get serious negotiations moving quickly towards a just, realistic and workable solution.[136]

Lynch praised O'Neill and his fellow Horsemen during his speech and noted his appreciation for Carter's statement in 1977.[137] The following day, Thatcher objected to O'Neill's statement.[138] Editorial comment in the British press also showed resentment at O'Neill's remarks; the Massachusetts and the Irish press were inevitably more positive.[139]

O'Neill and a smaller delegation also visited Belfast and held talks with leading Northern Ireland politicians at the residence of the US consul, Charles Stout (1977–80).[140] These 'secret talks' were reported to have been 'unexpected'.[141] O'Neill 'met with

Gerry Fitt, leader of the SDLP; Harry West, official Unionist; Oliver Napier, Alliance Party; and Rev. Ian Paisley, Democratic Unionist Party'.[142] There was press speculation that Carter was planning a Camp David summit to resolve the 'Troubles' and achieve a political resolution, with the 1978 Camp David Accords (that addressed the Egypt–Israel conflict) as a model. The *Irish Independent* reported that O'Neill was acting on Carter's instructions.[143] However, the White House dismissed this notion. *The Sunday Telegraph* reported that O'Neill would deliver a report on his expedition to the President, but any Carter intervention was fantastical.[144] Indeed, O'Neill told *The Boston Globe* that even though he passed on Carter's regards to Lynch, there was no planned summit.[145]

There is no evidence suggesting that O'Neill's 1979 visit to Ireland was the beginning of a Carter administration peace plan. However, O'Neill's influence over the American dimension to the Northern Ireland conflict remained, particularly in his political battle with Biaggi. The State Department's approval for American arms to be sold to the RUC with the issue of a licence on 31 January 1979 was a lightning-rod in the American dimension of the Anglo-Irish process. The RUC were to purchase 3,000 revolvers and 500 automatic rifles from Sturm, Ruger & Co. of Southport, Connecticut. Some Irish–Americans, such as Biaggi, seized this issue and added it to their condemnation of the British government following the publication of the Bennett Report in March 1979, which, as mentioned above, revealed human rights abuses by the RUC.[146]

In June 1979, O'Neill supported the prospect of a ban on American weapon sales to the RUC. The Speaker hoped that the ban would prompt the British government to answer the Northern Ireland question. In August 1979, O'Neill even allowed Biaggi's necessary amendment to be attached to the State Department's Appropriations Bill that passed through Congress, resulting in some friction in the Anglo-American relationship. Carter, prioritising his domestic programme over his relations with the new Thatcher government, did not resist the ban. This action was a message from O'Neill to the new British government: it needed to answer the Northern Ireland question. It was also designed to neutralise Biaggi's argument that, by selling arms to the RUC, the State Department was supporting one side in Northern Ireland but not another.[147] Because of the ban, neither the IRA nor RUC could be supported by anyone in the US. However, any hope that it would lead to a resolution in Northern Ireland was quickly dashed. Furthermore, as discussed below, the RUC would become an issue in Anglo-American relations under Carter and Thatcher, and was a further indication as to how Irish–American politics in the Democratic Party shaped the Carter administration's response to the Northern Ireland conflict. In short, Carter needed O'Neill's co-operation in Congress while O'Neill needed to undercut any grounds for Irish–American support for Biaggi and the INC.

## Northern Ireland and the Carter–Thatcher relationship

Prime Minister Thatcher viewed the 'Troubles' as a domestic issue. Her premiership saw a lower number of deaths related to the 'Troubles' during the 1980s compared to the 1970s. Nevertheless, during the 1980s, 850 people were killed by violence in Northern Ireland. Throughout her time in office, Thatcher was vehemently opposed to terrorism – undoubtedly motivated, in part, by the assassination of Airey Neave (Shadow Secretary of State for Northern Ireland, 1974–9) on the eve of the 1979 general election, for which the Irish National Liberation Army (a paramilitary republican group) claimed responsibility. Thatcher was a unionist, although she was never able to return devolved government to Northern Ireland.[148] The Anglo-Irish process resumed with the 1979–80 Atkins Talks, so named for Thatcher's first Secretary of State for Northern Ireland, Humphrey Atkins (1979–81), which revolved around devolution and power-sharing in Northern Ireland.[149] British sensitivities to the support of some Irish–Americans for the IRA during Thatcher's early premiership were noted by Vance in a briefing for Carter following the assassination of Earl Mountbatten in August 1979.[150]

Carter ensured that the Horsemen remained informed about any conversations that he had with Thatcher about Northern Ireland. Prior to the fifth G7 summit in Tokyo in June 1979, Edward

Kennedy (now viewed by the White House as a likely challenger for the Democratic presidential nomination) wrote to Carter, thanking the President for his willingness to do so and reasserting that his 1977 statement was 'a sound basis for legitimate American involvement in the issue'.[151] Kennedy suggested that 'a constructive next step' would be for the President 'to make a few brief points' to Thatcher: namely, that her government deserved time to develop a Northern Ireland policy and that Atkins was an excellent choice for Northern Ireland Secretary; that Carter's 1977 statement should be re-emphasised; that the Horsemen's opposition to American support for the IRA and support for any settlement to respect the rights of Catholics and Protestants in Northern Ireland were the opposite of a 'vote-catching' strategy; that any British political initiative would be popular in the US; and, if the British government prioritised 'security' and sidelined any political process, Irish–American sentiment would turn strongly against Britain, despite the efforts of the Horsemen.[152]

A few weeks later, Carter replied to Kennedy, 'I discussed Northern Ireland with P.M. Thatcher and will report results of our conversation the next time I see you.'[153] The conversation actually seems to have taken place as a summit telephone conversation, whereby Carter noted that Kennedy and O'Neill requested that he ask her 'briefly about the Northern Ireland question'.[154] He requested 'any analysis that's been done within your own Party or Government that you might send to me that I could read over just to describe both the present situation and any prospects for the future'. Despite his campaign promises and having been briefed about Northern Ireland for two years as president, Carter explained, 'I don't have any background knowledge about it and just hearing directly from you about the present situation and prospects for the future would help to guide me.'[155] It is, of course, possible that Carter's knowledge of Northern Ireland was limited compared to what he knew of issues such as the Soviet Union, China, nuclear weapons (namely, SALT and the neutron bomb), and American economic and energy policies. But, based on Carter's comments to O'Neill below, he clearly did not wish to antagonise Thatcher by appearing to encroach on what she regarded as a domestic issue.

Carter's request was answered. He received four papers about Northern Ireland: the background to the conflict, the Thatcher government's policy, terrorism, and security policy. Thatcher also wrote to Carter, summing up her approach to the conflict.[156] She argued that

> we can best make progress by patient and persistent negotiation with the parties, rather than more precipitate action . . . . There is a wide gap between the outlook and aspirations of the two communities in Northern Ireland, and it will not easily be bridged.

On Lynch's Irish government, Thatcher emphasised that 'they are at one with us that any settlement must have the broad consent of both sides of the community', and reminded Carter that this was 'a principle which you endorsed in your statement of August 1977'. Thatcher clearly wanted to connect her policy to that of the Carter administration. Thus, she offered a discussion about human rights:

> We are as concerned, as I know you are, to safeguard civil liberties to the fullest possible extent: we have a fundamental duty to protect all the law abiding citizens of Northern Ireland from murder and maiming by terrorists, which is the most important human right of all.

Thatcher also reminded Carter of the various American interests in the conflict, noting the concern of O'Neill and his colleagues for human rights, and their appreciated efforts in both reducing Irish–American support for violence and putting 'the record straight' on the 'Irish question' in America.[157] As promised, Carter would pass on Thatcher's comments to O'Neill. He described it as 'a rather basic description, but interesting', which Brzezinski was 'prepared to share . . . with you at your convenience'; in turn, the White House would 'relay back to her your own comments or suggestions'.[158] It is clear that Carter believed his knowledge about Northern Ireland, and that of O'Neill, to rival that of the British Prime Minister.

Despite praising O'Neill and the Horsemen in her letter to Carter, Thatcher was frustrated by American attempts to intervene in the Anglo-Irish process. On 2 August 1979, Atkins met Carey in

London.[159] Carey was thanked for 'his consistent help in condemning terrorism' but his recent *New York Daily News* article, which
accused the British government of 'political neglect of Ulster . . .
had given great offence here because it was not true'. Atkins candidly advised Carey that Irish–American politicians needed to be
careful in their rhetoric as 'political progress could only be achieved
with the support of both communities'. In response, Carey argued
that his 'condemnation of terrorism' was heard in America only
'because he was also known to be working for political progress'.
Thus, the Governor proposed that Atkins should visit New York
to meet Irish–American leaders so that he could explain to them
'what we were trying to do for the political future of Ulster'. Atkins
was polite but cautious, explaining that while he could consider
the offer, 'he would need to consult his colleagues'. A few days
later, Carey telephoned Atkins, suggesting that he would write to
him with more detail in due course. However, four days after his
meeting with Atkins, Carey issued a press statement, claiming that
Atkins (as Britain's Northern Ireland Secretary) and O'Kennedy
(the Irish Foreign Minister) would both visit him in New York in
order 'to continue our work towards peace, security and an end to
violence in Northern Ireland'.[160]

Thatcher was furious. In a meeting with Atkins, the Prime Minister stated, 'there could be no question of talking to Governor
Carey about Northern Ireland'.[161] Thatcher added that, although
Carey was free to visit Britain, he must respect the fact that 'Northern Ireland was part of the United Kingdom', just as she 'would not
think of discussing with President Carter, for example, US policy
towards their black population'. It was simply a breach of proto-
col for the leader of one country to intervene in, and publicly comment on, the domestic affairs of another country. Thatcher argued
that, despite Atkins' subsequent statement to the press that there
would be no such talks, the 'point had not been got across sufficiently.' Atkins' protested that Carey 'was not a complete villain',
given his condemnation of 'the IRA and terrorism, bracketing the
IRA with the PLO and other terrorist groups', yet Thatcher was
clear that the future of Northern Ireland should not be discussed in
the US. Interestingly, Thatcher did not agree with Atkins' assertion
that 'in refusing to continue the supply of weapons to the RUC,

the US was interfering in the internal affairs of another country'. The Prime Minister believed that 'this did not constitute interference, since the right to supply arms or to withhold them was sovereign to any Government'. Indeed – despite Atkins' doubts about the costs and the time it would take – Thatcher argued that Britain 'should make her own weapons and be independent of external sources of supply'.[162] After the meeting, Atkins wrote to Carey about his proposals:

> [I]t would be wrong for a Minister of Her Majesty's Government to take part in a discussion of that nature in the United States or indeed anywhere else outside the United Kingdom . . . . Northern Ireland is a matter for negotiation between Her Majesty's Government, the Parliament at Westminster and the people of the Province.[163]

Thatcher's firm footing and assertiveness on Northern Ireland were in contrast to her inexperience in foreign policy.[164]

The Carter–Thatcher dimension to Northern Ireland revolved around the 'Ulsterisation' of Northern Ireland, particularly the use of the RUC, rather than the British Army, to combat the IRA.[165] She was also frustrated by any unhelpful Irish–American intervention in the situation. Writing in her memoir, Thatcher recalled how the 'emotions and loyalties of millions of decent Irish–Americans are manipulated by Irish Republican extremists', which resulted in 'a continuing flow of funds and arms which helps the IRA', while in 1979 'we were faced with the absurd situation that the purchase of 3,000 revolvers for the RUC was held up by a state department review under pressure from the Irish Republican lobby in Congress'.[166] Between 1977 and 1979 inclusive, the RUC had lost thirty-seven officers to the 'Troubles' but not a single death was attributed to the RUC. Nonetheless, the condemnation of the RUC in the Bennett Report meant that they were subject to criticism by Irish–Americans, including O'Neill and Biaggi. On 31 May 1979, after hearing of a planned second delivery of US arms to the RUC, O'Neill released a statement condemning the sale. The Speaker argued that arms should not be sold by anyone in the US to any group in Northern Ireland and the State Department should ensure that this was the case. Given the RUC's status, demographics and record, O'Neill conjectured that it was not an impartial organisation. On 12 July 1979,

Biaggi opposed the sale in a statement to Congress. He cited human rights violations by the RUC and suggested that, accordingly, the sale was in contravention of Section 502 (B) of the 1961 Foreign Assistance Act.[167] The issue of weapon sales to the RUC was raised not only by Irish–Americans in Congress, but also by Irish–American lobbyists. For instance, in June 1979, Edward M. McCarthy, the President of the Irish Foundation of Arizona, wrote to Carter, claiming that the US government had been selling 'anti-personnel weapons' that would 'increase the number of dead and maimed in Northern Ireland'.[168]

Congressional opposition to the arms sale was an interaction between American and British domestic and foreign policies. Although Thatcher viewed the 'Troubles' as a domestic issue, she was essentially forced to discuss it as a foreign affairs issue with the US because of congressional interest. For Carter, Northern Ireland was a domestic concern because of the politics of dealing with Congress, who framed it as a foreign policy issue on the basis of his broader human rights agenda. Although Carter and Thatcher did not talk about the RUC at length until their meeting in December 1979, it was discussed by the British Embassy and the US State Department during that summer. These talks reveal that the Carter administration was essentially hostage to Democratic Party politics on this matter, particularly on the part of O'Neill and Biaggi's respective Irish–American congressional groups and constituencies. It considered various means to offer political cover to the Thatcher government, in the interests of Anglo-American relations. Given that the Carter administration anticipated that Congress would impose a ban if the issue was taken to a vote in the House of Representatives, and after Vance's consultation with O'Neill, Vance decided to hold back approval of the sales in July 1979 in the hope of avoiding magnifying the issue and further aggravating relations with the British government.[169] The Embassy informed the State Department that the reverse of Vance's objective would be achieved: 'The President's 1977 statement had committed the Administration to impartiality . . . the implication was that the Administration regarded the RUC as partial'.[170] The Carter administration had stumbled into a minefield of domestic politics and international diplomacy.

Nicholas Henderson, the British ambassador to the USA (1979–82), expressed doubts to the FCO about Vance's decision not to battle Congress for the arms sale.[171] Henderson reported that 'Vance's decision was jumping the gun.' He explained to Brzezinski that the problem was not just that America was denying an ally arms 'for the suppression of terrorism', but also that it would encourage 'the terrorists'. Brzezinski argued that supplying the RUC made it more difficult for the administration to conduct its campaign against Irish–American support for the IRA. Henderson rejected the proposition that the two issues could be equated. Looking for a solution, Brzezinski – ostensibly thinking aloud – 'wondered whether the problem could not be resolved if the British government, rather than the RUC, ordered these arms without specifying where they were going to be used'. In response, Henderson enquired whether the US government would be asked about the use of the arms, if the administration would say 'that these arms had been supplied' to the British government and 'their deployment was of no concern to the U.S. Government'. Without wishing this to be a formal proposal, Brzezinski 'said that he would like to give further thought to this'.[172] The NSA was clearly seeking a compromise that would satisfy the administration's foreign policy priorities within the Anglo-American relationship whilst not jeopardising the President's domestic agenda.

In his diary, Henderson was clearly exasperated by the situation.[173] The ambassador wrote that 'discretion is the better part of valour on this subject'. Therefore, the arms should not have been ordered by the RUC but rather by the British government or army. Nevertheless, the overriding aim was now to avoid the IRA claiming 'a famous victory . . . which shows that the USA are on their side'. Thus, Henderson believed that the order should be withdrawn 'in return for a promise that there will be no publicity about it and nothing to suggest that we have been turned down'. Yet the ambassador did not believe that Thatcher 'in her fighting mood is likely to play it that way'.[174] At the end of July, Vance suggested a face-saving measure along the lines of Henderson's withdrawal idea, in order to prevent embarrassing the British government. In an echo of Brzezinski's thinking, Vance's rationale was that the two governments should not worry about any future orders (and the problems they would bring) but should focus on allowing the political situation to thaw. As part of this exercise in damage limitation and prevention of any propaganda victory for the IRA, Vance would avoid discussing the possibility of any future order and maintain that there was no outstanding order.[175] The State Department was set to bow to congressional pressure, although it also sought political cover for the British government.

However, on 3 August, the British government concluded that the Carter administration would not approve the arms sale and the State Department would be undertaking a review of any potential future orders.[176] In turn, on 8 August 1979, the US State Department, under Vance's directions, did begin their review of US policy towards the sale of arms to the RUC (which, tellingly, was never completed).[177] The review was to take into account the Carter administration's commitment to human rights, its policy of supporting 'legally-established governments' in combating and controlling terrorism, and Anglo-American relations more generally. More specifically, it would examine the RUC's role in Northern Ireland and its acceptability to the people there; the role of 'paramilitary/terrorist organisations in Northern Ireland' and their connections with 'international terrorist organizations'; human rights in Northern Ireland, particularly in relation to the Catholic community; the extent of the truth about allegations of RUC human rights abuses and the effectiveness of the British response; the Irish government's attitude towards – and co-operation with – the RUC; whether there were any truth to the claims that paramilitary groups were benefiting from arms meant for the RUC and the British Army; the impact of any suspended arms sales on the ability of the RUC to operate successfully in terms of preventing violence and maintaining order; whether a suspension would change attitudes towards the RUC and 'terrorist organisations' in Northern Ireland; whether a suspension would make a settlement in Northern Ireland more likely; the potential role that a suspension would have in provoking renewed Protestant paramilitary activity; and, more broadly, what the arms sale suspensions would mean for America's reputation as an ally. Vance expected a draft by 22 October 1979.[178]

Vance appeared at a Congressional hearing about the American supply of arms to the RUC at the beginning of September 1979. The Secretary of State was asked about the timetable for the department's review of the RUC and whether he had plans to ask Thatcher about any new political initiative in Northern Ireland.[179] Vance used this as an opportunity to re-emphasise the Carter administration's approach to Northern Ireland: 'It is a position of condemning terrorism and violence . . . which supports the bringing together of the various factions in an attempt to try to move towards a peaceful solution'.[180] On 10 September, Vance informed Carter that Brewster had met with O'Neill to discuss the RUC.[181] While the ambassador 'described the intensity of the feeling in Britain in the wake of the Mountbatten assassination', the Speaker was unmoved with regard to his stance on the RUC. O'Neill argued that the arms sale would problematise his opposition to 'the Irish–American community's desire to support the IRA'. The Speaker was concerned that Biaggi's firebrand republicanism would undermine the Four Horsemen's mission to promote a peaceful resolution to the 'Troubles'. Vance briefed Carter that he had assured O'Neill that further arms sales would not be processed before the policy review had been completed.[182] Later that month, Henderson spoke with George S. Vest (Assistant Secretary for Europe, State Department, 1977–81) about the RUC order.[183] Despite the ambassador's warnings that any delay in or ultimate cancellation of the order would 'provoke a strong political reaction' and be a 'great benefit' for 'the terrorists', Vance believed that arms for the RUC 'would drive the moderates in Congress into the hands of Biaggi and the extremists'. Henderson countered that the US sold arms to other countries, including Israel for use against Lebanon, so the British government was naturally frustrated that they could not use American weapons to combat violence in Northern Ireland. Vest explained that the RUC order remained 'an emotive subject on the Hill' and 'if an order was submitted now the license would be refused'.[184] O'Neill had won the argument. He had utilised his role and influence as Speaker to ensure that any congressional vote on reversing the ban was lost before a motion had even been submitted for consideration by the House of Representatives. Moreover, the State Department would dare not antagonise O'Neill needlessly, particularly should they need his support for approving funding elsewhere.

On 3 October 1979, Carter was informed that the State Department had asked Henderson not to submit the RUC order until the review had been completed.[185] That same day, Vest again spoke with Henderson.[186] He passed on Vance's view 'that it would be best for no new requests for arms for the RUC to be put forward', given that it was a time of 'political liability'. According to Vest, Vance had failed to offer any solution as to how the British could 'find a way round this problem'. For Vest, he hoped that the State Department's policy review would not be rushed. While he was unable to advise Henderson as to how long the suspension of sales would continue, he was certain that it would not end until after the 1980 presidential election. Moreover, O'Neill had informed the State Department that a resumption of sales would ensure that the moderates would be pushed towards Biaggi and the other extremists. Vest was sympathetic towards the British government's frustrations, but, as he explained to Henderson, 'the problem here was that we were dealing with irrational emotions in the Congress which it would be very risky to stir up'. The ambassador's suggestion that he might speak with Harold Brown (US Defence Secretary, 1977–81), as it could be viewed as an issue about arms sales to a NATO ally, was quashed by Vest on the basis that it was 'exclusively a matter for the State Department'. Henderson told Vest that James R. Schlesinger (Energy Secretary, 1977–9) believed that the suspension of sales was 'scandalous' and intended to raise it with Brzezinski. The ambassador again 'floated the possibility that arms needed by the RUC might be ordered by HMG for the armed forces for general purposes without specifying the end use'. Although Vest and Robert Funseth (Director, Office of Northern European Affairs) promised to explore this possibility, 'they were clearly unhappy'. Funseth, obviously sceptical, noted that a specific description of the arms use was required on the application form and that news of the arms sale would inevitably 'create fresh trouble' in Congress.[187] Within a week, Vest informed the British government that he was 'convinced that no solution can be found through changing the form of order'.[188] O'Neill was resolute. At the end of October, Henderson noted in his diary that he had called on the Speaker in advance of Thatcher's forthcoming visit to America. Henderson wanted 'to leave him in no doubt . . . that we were still wanting more revolvers'.[189] Even though the meeting 'started in a very friendly, almost hilarious, fashion' and O'Neill 'exuded Irish charm and flattery', Henderson wrote that when he raised the RUC issue, O'Neill 'stiffened up' and their 'meeting ended on a very different note from that of the start'.[190]

Lynch visited the White House on 8 November 1979, when security issues were central to his discussions with the President.[191] According to the Irish minutes, Carter enquired about the relationship between the RUC and the Irish police force. He clearly wanted to know more about the situation before making a decision on arms sales to the RUC. The Taoiseach explained 'that there was in fact a close co-operation' but 'the British tended greatly to exaggerate the extent to which violence in Northern Ireland originated within the Republic'. He added that, even though the RUC had been working for 'acceptance from the minority in Northern Ireland', there continued to be 'some discriminatory treatment' of Catholics. Indeed, Lynch noted the European Commission and Court of Human Rights identification of suspects in Northern Ireland being subject to 'inhuman and degrading treatment' at the hands of the RUC. The Taoiseach stated that, regardless of these conclusions, nobody from the RUC 'has been brought to justice'. Carter asked if, in the event of British withdrawal, 'was it not better' for the RUC to be a 'well-trained and well-armed police force'? He also enquired about any evidence for recent 'ill-treatment of persons held in custody'. The Taoiseach replied that, even though the most recent cases related to 1978, in political terms they had to allow for any 'residual' feelings.[192] Carter's understanding of the situation impressed the Taoiseach. According to Vance, 'Lynch praised your knowledge and appreciation of the complex Northern Ireland problem' and also observed that Carter's 'policy of impartiality was correct'.[193] Carter certainly had a much better understanding of Northern Ireland than he had previously indicated to Thatcher. Lynch was privately sympathetic to Thatcher's position on the RUC. Before meeting Lynch, the Vice-President, Walter Mondale (1977–81), was advised that Vance had recently raised the issue with the Taoiseach.[194] Mondale was advised not to raise it; should Lynch do so, however, the Vice-President was warned that the Taoiseach 'privately . . . has no problem with such small arms, as the British and the Irish are united in their fight against terrorism' but, publicly, Lynch 'would have to be negative on the subject if he were asked to take a position'. Indeed, the Irish government was concerned that Carter would be pressured by Thatcher to resume the sales when she visited the White House in December 1979.[195] Carter and Lynch both essentially agreed with Thatcher, but they prioritised their own domestic concerns rather than bowing to her priorities.

The British attempted to force the issue, preferably before Thatcher's visit to the US in December 1979. On 20 November 1979, the British Embassy informed Vest that the government would be making a licence application 'in the next week or so'. Vest appreciated the warning about the application and that Thatcher would raise it when she met Carter, although he candidly admitted that the administration still preferred that the sale 'not be pursued at this time'.[196] Yet the situation ostensibly improved for the Thatcher government. Carter minuted, 'I should go ahead and do it' when Vance put a paper to him about the arms sale.[197] A memorandum for Mondale also confirmed that Carter had indicated to Vance that he was willing to authorise the pending weapons sale to the RUC, albeit with a caveat that it would be the last.[198] However, in relaying this news to Henderson, Vest was still cautious, due particularly to O'Neill's attitude. He hoped that the issue would be resolved prior to Thatcher's visit to the US.[199] The Carter administration was clearly determined not to antagonise the British government overly by publicly refusing to allow the arms sale, either completely or indefinitely, so close to Thatcher's visit.

Vest's hope that a solution could be achieved was misplaced. On 11 December, Henderson informed the FCO that Carter would not make a decision until after his meeting with Thatcher.[200] Even then, the ambassador cautioned that the prospects of the arms being authorised were not 'rosy'. The main problem continued to be O'Neill, who, given his opposition to any American support for the IRA, could not credibly continue to oppose the IRA if he allowed American support 'for what he and many Irish/Americans regard, however inadequately, as the other side'. Thus, the Carter administration assured the Speaker that they would not authorise the arms sale to the RUC without his prior approval. According to Henderson, the administration was in a bind, balancing competing domestic and international priorities. The State Department and the White House were privately sympathetic to the British case and wanted to provide the arms 'for the sake of their relationship with the UK'. However, Carter faced domestic 'political realities': a public row with O'Neill could undermine his chances of being nominated by the Democrats for re-election and he needed the Speaker to pass legislation through Congress. Further complicating British hopes was the involvement of Biaggi, who, given his role as a congressional strategist for the President's campaign for renomination, enjoyed 'access to Carter's inner circle'. The situation was even more galling for the British because, as Henderson noted, the Thatcher government was 'giving the USA a lot of help over Iran and they recognise this'. Ultimately, as Henderson advised the FCO, it was Carter's decision. While he was unlikely to be able to offer a 'positive commitment at the moment', changing circumstances – for instance, after his renomination campaign – might allow him to sideline O'Neill. (After all, by mid-1979, the relationship between Carter and O'Neill, which was always mixed, was problematic, driven by Democratic divisions about, for instance, rising oil prices and Carter's proposed budgetary cuts.) Thus, the ambassador advised that Thatcher should aim to convince Carter 'to keep an open mind on the subject and to avoid a negative commitment'.[201]

Thatcher visited America in December 1979 to meet with Carter, leading figures of his administration and members of Congress. Prior to Thatcher's departure for the US, Sir Robert Armstrong (Secretary of the Cabinet, 1979–87) briefed the Prime Minister that one of her objectives was to ensure that the Carter administration was 'in no doubt about the realities of the Northern Ireland situation', and about her government's determination to transfer powers to Stormont while protecting 'citizens of all denominations against terrorism'.[202] Thatcher was also briefed that she was 'to apply pressure on the Americans over arms for the RUC'.[203] Thatcher duly raised these issues with Carter during their plenary meeting.[204] Sympathetically, she expressed her understanding 'of the difficulties the question of the supply of arms from the United States to the RUC raised for the President'. Yet, at the same time, the Prime Minister candidly added that the issue 'also created difficulties for her'. She stressed that the RUC was not sectarian. For instance, the previous Chief Constable (Sir James Flanagan, 1973–6) was a Roman Catholic. Thatcher argued that many other British police forces had similar American arms and, as the RUC already had 3,000 American Rugers, it was 'very strange to deny them the remainder of the order and thereby to deprive a significant number of members of the RUC the right to defend themselves effectively'. Adding flattery to persuasion, she also observed that, having 'handled both the gun which the RUC at present used and that which was on order', she believed that 'the American Ruger was much better'.[205]

Asked by Thatcher whether the difficulty was 'one of principle or one of timing', Carter said that it was the latter. His administration was consulting with Congress but, ultimately, 'the approval of Congress would be necessary if the sale was to take place'. Vance developed this point by citing the rules of the American system of government: in contrast to the Speaker, 'the administration did not have the votes to secure the approval of Congress'. After Thatcher enquired as to the timetable of the process, Carter advised her to speak with O'Neill. While he personally would have approved the sale, he was not willing to be defeated in Congress or risk 'a major altercation'. Moreover, the President believed that 'The political problem of handling the Northern Ireland issue in the United States would be exacerbated if he took on Congress and lost.' He clearly understood the delicate situation that his administration and the Horsemen faced: calls for an end to support for the IRA would be ignored and criticised as hypocrisy if the US armed the RUC. On O'Neill, Carter added that he rarely involved himself in policy debates, but this 'was a personal one for him'.[206]

Given that there was 'nothing the British Government could do that would satisfy the IRA', as the majority of 'Ulster wished to remain part of the United Kingdom', Thatcher presumed that the Speaker's 'attitude was essentially an emotional one'. Distancing himself from the issue, Carter clarified that 'he was persuaded on the merits' of Thatcher's case but she would only be able to advance her position by convincing O'Neill, who 'had in general' supported her government's policy on Northern Ireland. Frustrated, Thatcher argued that the cancellation of the order, or even any delay, 'would be a major propaganda victory for the IRA'. Lord Carrington, the British Foreign Secretary (1979–82), added that it would also prompt a negative reaction in Britain: for instance, through 'a great deal of very adverse comment in Parliament'. In an attempt to change the subject, Carter 'made it clear that he was aware of this' but that Thatcher 'should discuss the matter with Speaker O'Neill'. Carter added that he 'would be interested to learn whether or not Mr. O'Neill showed any flexibility'.[207] Carter was clearly trying to move the conversation onwards and direct Thatcher to the Speaker's office. The President was unmoved by any potential British criticism of his position next to his own political priorities and his relationships with Capitol Hill. The President asked about the forthcoming conference on Northern Ireland (the Atkins Talks). Having chastised her Northern Ireland Secretary previously over American involvement, Thatcher took the opportunity to praise Atkins for his 'considerable diplomatic feat' of securing the involvement of Hume and Paisley. The Prime Minister argued that, whatever the outcome, local government powers should be transferred back to Northern Ireland: 'It was ridiculous to have a Secretary of State and six Junior Ministers working full time on Northern Ireland.' Carrington hoped that, after the conference, there would again be 'some form of representative Government . . . because this was a forum in which moderates could work'. Continuing to move the conversation onwards, Carter asked for an update on the violence, particularly whether it had reduced. Thatcher replied that there had been a 'change of direction rather than a reduction in the level'. She explained that, principally, 'terrorist activity had now moved to the border' and that 'indiscriminate attacks had been abandoned in favour of attacks on the security forces'.[208] It is clear that Carter's interest was limited in this meeting: he had some interest in the Anglo-Irish process and terrorism but sought to distance himself from congressional opposition to weapon sales to the RUC. Indeed, as Henderson noted in his diary, the meeting between Carter and Thatcher 'went well', but the President 'obviously did not wish to speak' about the RUC.[209]

Thatcher also met with members of Congress, including O'Neill.[210] The Speaker, eager to put aside the diplomatic row caused by his remarks at Dublin Castle, noted that Thatcher's calmness on the eve of the UK general election 'was what he liked to see in a leader'. Moreover, in his hopes for a settlement in Northern Ireland, O'Neill, hoping to use his charm to flatter Thatcher, observed, 'If you want anything said, ask a man; if you want anything done, ask a woman.' In response, she expressed her gratitude for O'Neill's 'firm stand on terrorism'. Offering an account of her policy towards Northern Ireland, Thatcher stressed that 'the British Government had enjoyed excellent cooperation' with their Irish counterparts and that the Irish police and RUC 'cooperated well'. She hoped that the forthcoming conference in January 1980 'would lead to the people of Northern Ireland having greater control over their own affairs'. However, Thatcher was adamant about her view of the reality in Northern Ireland: 'Ulster was part of the United Kingdom because that was the way its people wanted it . . . . So long as there was terrorist violence, the Army must stay'.[211]

O'Neill was impressed by Thatcher and continued to support her government's initiative in Northern Ireland. However, his opposition to authorising the arms sale did not waver. If he sanctioned the arms sale, he would have forfeited his claim to impartiality and would have been unable to persuade Irish–Americans not to support NORAID. O'Neill's opposition to Biaggi was concurrent to this: the Speaker convinced Carter that he should not, despite Biaggi's urging, send a message of goodwill to the INC's annual dinner in New York. Likewise, O'Neill's resistance to the sales allowed him to resist pressure for congressional hearings on Northern Ireland on the grounds that Congress had no role in it. Henderson advised the FCO that any further appeals to Carter would be directed to O'Neill, and, therefore, would be in vain. Indeed, Carter would be influenced by such electoral considerations potentially until November 1980.[212]

December 1979 saw Lynch replaced as leader of Fianna Fáil (the Irish conservative party) and as Taoiseach by Charles Haughey (1979–81). Haughey's leadership marked a tougher republican position, with the new Taoiseach insisting that the Thatcher government declare its intention for a British withdrawal from Northern Ireland.[213] Thatcher was clear that this simply would not happen. In her Airey Neave Memorial Lecture on 3 March 1980, she explained, 'No democratic country can voluntarily abandon its responsibilities in a part of its territory against the will of the majority of the population there.'[214] Haughey quickly acquainted himself with Irish–American politicians. The Taoiseach made an abortive attempt to recall Donlon (Irish ambassador to the US, 1978–81) to Ireland (which failed due to the ambassador's excellent relations with both the White House and Irish–Americans in Congress).[215] He also sought to secure American support for his proposals for a federal Ireland, but the White House was inevitably focused on other issues, such as the hostage crisis, while Carter's re-election campaign battled Kennedy for the Democratic nomination. In March 1980, Vance failed to respond to a request made by Brian Lenihan (Irish Foreign Minister, 1979–81) that the Carter administration encourage the Thatcher government to pursue a political initiative to create a political structure – guaranteed by the British and Irish governments – involving both Catholic and Protestant communities.[216]

In another transatlantic expedition, Carrington met O'Neill in the US on 5 May 1980.[217] Despite some discussion about the settlement in Zimbabwe and Afghanistan, the conversation was mostly about Northern Ireland. After the Speaker expressed his preference for devolution in Northern Ireland and the inclusion of the Irish government in any discussion of Northern Ireland's future, arms and the RUC were the dominant topics. When Carrington enquired as to whether O'Neill would be able to help reverse the State Department's ban on the arms sale, the Speaker said that he 'regretted that there was nothing he could do for the present', but the saga 'had been handled very poorly in that it had been a mistake on the part of the British government to say that the arms were for the RUC'. Defending his position, O'Neill explained that a renewal of arms sales to the RUC could lead to 'massive US support for the IRA which would make terrorism worse'. The Speaker candidly admitted that it 'meant nothing to him in votes' and, in fact, any arms order would have brought 'business to a factory in his constituency'. This issue in Anglo-American relations was important in O'Neill's domestic politics. He could not oppose Irish–American funding for the IRA at the same time as permitting the arms sale to the RUC. Moreover, it was a matter of conscience for him. As the record shows, O'Neill explained, 'If he changed his attitude the press of America would handle the issue in such a way as to lead to a flood of money going to the IRA.'[218] Thus, the Speaker prioritised his concern for violence over Anglo-American relations. He was, of course, in a position do this, whereas it was a much more challenging situation for the Carter administration in terms of the development and implementation of US foreign policy.

On 23 May 1980, Edmund Muskie (US Secretary of State, 1980–1) briefed Carter that, while O'Neill's staff believed that the 1980 proposals from Haughey 'for a united, federal Ireland including Northern autonomy' were 'constructive', they did not 'expect the Administration publicly to go beyond our policy of urging a peaceful solution to the parties affected'.[219] This remained the case when Atkins (Britain's Northern Ireland Secretary) entertained Matthew Nimetz, the Undersecretary of State for International Security Affairs (21 February to 5 December 1980) in the House of Commons on 19 June 1980.[220] Nimetz observed that the Carter administration never advocated any 'one particular form of power-sharing' and it 'basically wanted to see a peaceful solution to the problem however that was achieved'. He candidly admitted that the Carter administration still received questions about human rights issues in H Block and about the RUC, but the government's response to the Bennett Report helped the White House respond 'quite easily'. The Undersecretary's frankness extended to the Northern Ireland dimension of Anglo-American relations, manifested by the RUC arms issue: it 'was a small but nevertheless running sore, and it would be in everyone's interests if it could be healed'. In response, Atkins bluntly explained 'that while the embargo ... was not a major issue between the two countries, it certainly caused some to wonder what the US Administration was up to, denying weapons to an ally'. This prompted Nimetz to attribute 'the decision to block the supply of arms to the RUC' as 'a political one', caused by O'Neill's influence, and 'on this issue he and other Irish Americans did not seem receptive to arguments based on logic'.[221]

Unknown to the Carter administration, the RUC had still been able to benefit from a limited supply of Rugers. Prior to Nimetz's arrival, under the heading 'not for disclosure', Atkins was briefed that, despite the ban on the sale of Rugers to the RUC, Viking Arms of Harrogate had still been ordering and receiving their own Rugers totalling 50–70 revolvers every month.[222] This loophole was permitted because the sale was part of Viking Arms' general trade and on their export licence no end-user was specified. In turn, Viking Arms were able to sell the revolvers to the RUC and so they had around 800 additional revolvers a year. Unequivocally, it was argued that, as this number was insufficient and as a matter of principle, the British government 'must continue to press' the Carter administration for the issuing of an export licence.[223] Upon hearing this news, the British Embassy advised that, if this became public knowledge, it would result in a 'souring' of Anglo-American political relations, congressional hearings on Northern Ireland and 'a ready-made propaganda theme' for Biaggi, the INC and NORAID.[224] As the next chapter details, the determination to convince the US government to reinstate the export licence continued into Thatcher's first meeting with President Ronald Reagan (1981–9), even though the Rugers were no longer required. As such, the politics of the export licence surpassed the operational necessity of the revolvers.

## The 1980 presidential election

The Democratic Party platform stated that, consistent with the party's 'traditional concern for peace and human rights', the next Democratic administration would 'play a positive role in seeking peace in Northern Ireland'.[225] While the Democrats condemned 'the violence on all sides', they sought to encourage a long-term settlement 'based upon consent of all parties to the conflict, based on the principle of Irish unity'. They also advocated the creation of political structures that 'should protect human rights', and be agreeable for 'Great Britain and Ireland' and for 'both parts' of Northern Ireland's community.[226]

The involvement of Biaggi in the Carter campaign was a cause of concern for the British government. The British Embassy informed the FCO that, as a result, Biaggi would have 'easy access' to 'the White House inner circle', including Hamilton Jordan, who served both as Carter's Chief-of-Staff (1979–80) and his leading electoral strategist.[227] Thus, Biaggi would be able to influence actors whose 'foreign policy considerations are very much less important than domestic electoral calculations'. It was feared that he would

> build up a nice line of political credit with the President; we can be sure he will try to get Carter to make statements favourable to the Irish National Caucus line on Northern Ireland during the campaign and if Carter is re-elected Biaggi will lose no time in cashing in his political IOUs.[228]

The British Embassy clearly feared that Carter would repeat his controversial statements from Pittsburgh in 1976 and, given Biaggi's influence, such statements could prove to be a hostage to fortune during a second term.

Carter was lobbied by leading Irish–Americans as the general election entered its final stages. As they had met Republican candidate Ronald Reagan's staff, Brzezinski believed that Carter should meet them personally. The proposed meeting would include Pat O'Connor (Co-Chairperson, ethnic-American Committee for Carter–Mondale); McManus; a member of Biaggi's staff; and five other Irish–American leaders.[229] Carter was advised that Irish–Americans wished to support him but sought 'amplification on some of the issues': closer association with the Democratic platform's statement about Northern Ireland; reassurance that the RUC arms embargo would continue; and the President to voice concern about the H Block prison and speak out against British violations of human rights.[230] Although a record of any such meeting is unavailable, Carter issued a statement about Northern Ireland on 27 October 1980.[231] He claimed to have 'formulated this country's first comprehensive policy dealing with the issue'. He reinforced the parameters of his 1977 statement, explaining: 'I condemned the use of violence and stated that a permanent solution will come only from the consent of all the parties . . . with a firm offer for investment and job-creation assistance.'

Carter claimed that, throughout his presidency, he had 'been in close contact' with the British and Irish governments 'to help promote an equitable settlement'. This study suggests that this was an exaggeration on the part of the President, who was motivated by electoral concerns. Carter finished this piece of electioneering by calling for a 'path of reconciliation, cooperation and peace' as the only means that could 'end the human suffering and lead to a better future' in Northern Ireland'.[232] Carter's comments in Pittsburgh in 1976 were ostensibly meant to be 'off the record', while his 1977 statement followed pressure from the Four Horsemen. This election statement in 1980 is indicative of the concern for Northern Ireland amongst key protagonists in the Democratic Party, a need to placate Irish–American politicians, and the campaign team's hope that it would command the support of Irish–American voters. Even though Northern Ireland was not a key foreign policy priority for the President, it was a significant issue within the Democratic Party's political machine, and therefore warranted some attention during the campaign.

## Conclusion

Economic crises at home and seemingly insurmountable challenges abroad battered Carter's White House. In addition, as Hamilton Jordan notes, 'There were two White Houses after November of '79. There was a White House focused almost exclusively on the hostage situation and there was a White House that was working on everything else.'[233] Carter's approach towards Northern Ireland was inevitably symptomatic of the administration's policy-making process. In other words, Carter's policy towards Northern Ireland was shaped by the reality of sharing power with a Democratic Congress, Democratic Party politics and, to a lesser extent, the human rights agenda. The importance of securing a positive working relationship with O'Neill ensured that Carter issued a statement on Northern Ireland in 1977. Democratic Party politics meant that, in the first instance, he commented on Northern Ireland for electoral reasons, and then issued a statement about his administration's policy in 1977 as a means to support the Horsemen's endeavours. As the RUC issue showed, Carter wanted to avoid a further quarrel with Congress. Any challenge to O'Neill would have escalated the Speaker's difficulties with Irish–Americans, such as Biaggi, who opposed the Horsemen's approach to Northern Ireland. Carter was sympathetic to Thatcher's situation, but not sufficiently concerned to jeopardise his domestic agenda by advocating a means to appease Thatcher's demands, such as one final arms sale to the RUC. Furthermore, the continuing role of Biaggi in the Democrats' wider electoral machine in 1980 concerned the British government. The part he played in the congressional gridlock on the RUC issue was indicative of his potential influence on American policy towards Northern Ireland.

Carter did not raise the issue of human rights in Northern Ireland with either Callaghan or Thatcher, preferring to prioritise other issues in Anglo-American relations. Nevertheless, Democratic Party politics meant that he was prepared to disappoint Thatcher over arms sales to the RUC, despite the fact that he sympathised with her position. The President did discuss Northern Ireland with the Irish government. These talks included his asking about a united Ireland, which was typically dismissed by the Irish as, at best, a potential long-term solution rather than an immediate resolution. Carter clearly had not moved on from considering a united Ireland, which was motivated by electoral and political concerns, or, perhaps, even his own interpretation of the Northern Ireland question. Interestingly, he was never so bold to raise the idea of a united Ireland with the British. In short, Carter's concern for Northern Ireland was defined by electoral considerations and the needs of the Democratic Party. Ultimately, Carter failed to secure the White House and party unity. After Reagan's subsequent landslide victory became obvious, O'Neill remarked to Jordan, 'You guys came in like a bunch of pricks . . . . And you're going out the same way'.[234]

## Notes

1. Jimmy Carter, 'Inaugural address', 20 January 1977. Online by Gerhard Peters and John T. Woolley, *The American Presidency Project*, http://www.presidency.ucsb.edu/ws/?pid=6575; Jimmy Carter, 'University of Notre Dame – Address at commencement exercises at

the university', 22 May 1977. Online by Gerhard Peters and John T. Woolley, *The American Presidency Project*, http://www.presidency. ucsb.edu/ws/?pid=7552. Both accessed 15 January 2015.

2. See, for instance, John Dumbrell, *The Carter Presidency* (Manchester: Manchester University Press, 1995); Robert A. Strong, *Working in the World: Jimmy Carter and the Making of American Foreign Policy* (Baton Rouge: Louisiana State University Press, 2000); David F. Schmitz and Vanessa Walker, 'Jimmy Carter and the foreign policy of human rights: The development of a post-Cold War Foreign Policy', *Diplomatic History*, 28:1 (2004), 113–43; Itai Nartzizenfield Sneh, *The Future Almost Arrived: How Jimmy Carter Failed to Change U.S. Foreign Policy* (New York: Peter Lang, 2008); Betty Glad, *An Outsider in the White House: Jimmy Carter, His Advisors, and the Making of American Foreign Policy* (Ithaca, NY: Cornell University Press, 2009); William Michael Schmidli, *The Fate of Freedom Elsewhere: Human Rights and U.S. Cold War Policy toward Argentina* (Ithaca, NY: Cornell University Press, 2013); and Barbara J. Keys, *Reclaiming American Virtue: The Human Rights Revolution of the 1970s* (Cambridge, MA: Harvard University Press, 2014).

3. Dumbrell, *A Special Relationship*, 101–2.

4. Ritchie Ovendale, *Anglo-American Relations in the Twentieth Century* (Basingtoke: Palgrave, 1998), 143.

5. Jimmy Carter, *White House Diary* (New York: Farrar, Straus & Giroux, 2010), entry for 11 November 1977, 133.

6. Hamilton Jordan, *Crisis: The Last Year of the Carter Presidency* (New York: G.P. Putman's Sons, 1982); Cyrus Vance, *Hard Choices: Critical Years in America's Foreign Policy* (New York: Simon & Schuster, 1983); Zbigniew Brzezinski, *Power and Principle: Memoirs of the National Security Adviser 1977–81* (London: Weidenfeld & Nicolson, 1983); Jody Powell, *The Other Side of the Story* (New York: William Morrow & Company, 1984); Stansfield Turner, *Secrecy and Democracy: The CIA in Transition* (Boston: Houghton Mifflin Company, 1985); and Walter F. Mondale, *The Good Fight: A Life in Liberal Politics* (New York: Scribner, 2010). Northern Ireland is also excluded from Jimmy Carter, *Keeping Faith: Memoirs of a President* (London: Collins, 1982).

7. Alex Brummer, 'The greening of the White House', *The Guardian*, Tuesday, 26 November 1985, 21.

8. Richard E. Neustadt, *Presidential Power and the Modern Presidents: The Politics of Leadership from Roosevelt to Reagan* (New York: Free Press, 1990), 29.

9. Despite O'Neill's significance amongst Irish–Americans in Congress, the Speaker surprisingly did not refer to Northern Ireland or anything related to it in his memoir. See Tip O'Neill with William Novak, *Man of the House: The Life and Political Memoirs of Speaker Tip O'Neill* (New York: Random House, 1987).

10. Matthew N. Green, *The Speaker of the House: A Study of Leadership* (London: Yale University Press, 2010), 111.

11. Ibid.

12. Neustadt, *Presidential Power*, 238.

13. Ibid., 239.

14. Ronald M. Peters, Jr, *The American Speakership: The Office in Historical Perspective*, 2nd edn (Baltimore : John Hopkins University Press, 1997), 216.

15. See Peters, *The American Speakership*, 216–32; and Barbara Sinclair, 'Tip O'Neill and contemporary House leadership', in Roger H. Davidson, Susan Webb Hammon and Raymond W. Smock (eds), *Masters of the House: Congressional Leadership Over Two Centuries* (Oxford : Westview Press, 1998), 299–302.

16. Memorandum, written by M. Lillis, Minister's Visit and Problem of contacts between Irish National Caucus and Carter Administration, 6 March 1977, NAI: D/Foreign Affairs: 2007/59/217.

17. Ibid.

18. Letter, Jonathan Davidson, United Kingdom Embassy, Washington (hereafter UKE) to Michael Hodge, Republic of Ireland Department, Foreign and Commonwealth Office (hereafter FCO), 4 May 1976, 'Presidential Election and Northern Ireland', TNA: CJ 4/1835: U.S. Presidential Election and N.I.

19. Ibid.

20. Letter, Jonathan Davidson (UKE, Washington) to Michael Hodge (Republic of Ireland Department, FCO), 16 June 1976, 'Democratic Party Platform and Ireland', TNA: CJ 4/1835.

21. Ibid.

22. Democratic Party Platforms, 'Democratic Party platform of 1976', 12 July 1976. Online by Gerhard Peters and John T. Woolley, *The American Presidency Project*, http://www.presidency.ucsb.edu/ws/?pid=29606, accessed 1 July 2014.

23. Telegram, UK Embassy Washington to FCO, 21 June 1976, 'Democratic Party Platform', TNA: CJ 4/1835.

24. Letter, Jonathan Davidson (UKE Washington) to Michael Hodge (Republic of Ireland Department, FCO), 22 June 1976, 'Democratic Party Platform and Ireland', TNA: CJ 4/1835.

25. Ibid.
26. Miller Center, 'Interview with Edward M. Kennedy (2/27/2006)', University of Virginia, 27 February 2007, http://millercenter.org/oralhistory/interview/edward_m_kennedy_2-27-2006, accessed 2 October 2015.
27. Ibid.
28. Letter, Jonathan Davidson (UKE Washington) to Alan Goulty (Republic of Ireland Department, FCO), 16 September 1976, TNA: CJ 4/1835.
29. Letter, Jimmy Carter to John Michael Keane (National President, Ancient Order of Hibernians in America), 10 August 1976, Jimmy Carter Papers Pre-Presidential, 1976 Presidential Campaign, Ethnic-Urban Affairs – Vickie Mongiardo, Subject File, German–American through Neighbourhoods, 'Irish–American', Box 248, Jimmy Carter Presidential Library (hereafter Carter Library).
30. Ibid.
31. Address by Jimmy Carter, Addressing B'nai B'rith, Washington, 8 September 1976, *Foreign Relations of the United States*, 1977–80, Volume 1, Foundations of Foreign Policy, Document 9, accessed via https://history.state.gov/historicaldocuments/frus1977-80v01/d9, 24 September 2015.
32. Letter, Thomas D. McNabb (President, New York State Board, Ancient Order of Hibernians in America) to Jimmy Carter, 17 September 1976, Jimmy Carter Papers Pre-Presidential, 1976 Presidential Campaign, Ethnic-Urban Affairs – Vickie Mongiardo, Subject File, German–American through Neighbourhoods, 'Irish–American', Box 248, Carter Library.
33. Letter, John J. Finucane (Freedom for All Ireland Committee, Ancient Order of Hibernians in America), to Governor Carter, 7 October 1976, Jimmy Carter Papers Pre-Presidential, 1976 Presidential Campaign, Ethnic-Urban Affairs – Vickie Mongiardo, Subject File, German–American through Neighbourhoods, 'Irish–American', Box 248, Carter Library.
34. Ibid.
35. Ibid.
36. Ibid.
37. The Third Carter–Ford Presidential Debate, 22 October 1976, Debate Transcript, http://www.debates.org/index.php?page=october-22–1976-debate-transcript, accessed 13 June 2014.
38. Thompson, *American Policy*, 71.

39. Letter, Thomas D. Lyons (Consul General, Consulate General of Ireland) to Michael Lillis, Embassy of Ireland, Washington, DC, 27 October 1976, NAI: D/Foreign Affairs, 2007/59/222.
40. Ibid.
41. Memorandum, written by M. Lillis, Minister's Visit and Problem of contacts between Irish National Caucus and Carter Administration, 6 March 1977, NAI: D/Foreign Affairs, 2007/59/217.
42. Ibid.
43. Ibid.
44. Telegram, UKE Washington to FCO, 28 October 1976, 'Carter's Remarks on Ireland', TNA: CJ 4/1835.
45. Ibid.
46. Telegram, UKE Washington to FCO, 29 October 1976, 'Carter's Remarks on Ireland', TNA: CJ 4/1835. (See Express Foreign Desk, 'Carter told: Mind your own business', *Daily Express*, Friday, 29 October 1976, 4. Coverage of the Carter aides denying he had ever worn a badge calling for British withdrawal from Northern Ireland, despite a photograph of the candidate wearing it, was in News, 'So what about that badge, Mr Carter?', *Daily Express*, Saturday, 30 October 1976, 7. Despite the *Express*'s criticism of Carter, it did suggest that Anglo-American relations would thrive under Carter: Peter Bourne, 'Don't worry about Jimmy – he'll be Britain's best friend', *Daily Express*, Thursday, 4 November 1976, 10.)
47. Telegram, UKE Washington to FCO, 29 October 1976, 'Carter's Remarks on Ireland', TNA: CJ 4/1835.
48. Press Release from Mr. John Biggs-Davison, M.P. for Epping Forest and an Official Front Bench Spokesman on Northern Ireland, 28 October 1976, TNA: CJ 4/1835.
49. Ibid.
50. Note of a meeting between the Secretary of State and HM Ambassador, Washington, held at NIO(L) [Northern Ireland Office in London] on Thursday 16 December 1976 at 2.40 pm, TNA: CJ 4/1845, Northern Ireland relations with the United States of America (USA) Foreign and Commonwealth/Policy.
51. Ibid.
52. Note of a meeting between the Secretary of State and Mr John Hume held at Stormont Castle at 5.30 p.m. on the 18th January 1977, TNA: CJ 4/1845.
53. Ibid.
54. DA Hill to Mr Varney, 24 November 1976, TNA: CJ 4/1835.

55. Ibid.
56. EJ Hughes, Atlantic Region, Research Department, 'Governor Carter and Northern Ireland', 3 December 1976, TNA: CJ 4/1835.
57. Ibid.
58. Letter, IM Burns to PLV Mallet, Republic of Ireland Department FCO, 'Carter and Northern Ireland', 13 January 1977, TNA: CJ 4/1835.
59. Memorandum, written by M. Lillis, Minister's Visit and Problem of contacts between Irish National Caucus and Carter Administration, 6 March 1977, NAI: D/Foreign Affairs, 2007/59/217.
60. Ibid.
61. *Washington Post*, 10 March 1977, A4, NAI: D/Foreign Affairs, 2007/59/222, Administration of the USA and the Northern Ireland Situation.
62. Thompson, *American Policy*, 73–4.
63. 'Record of a discussion between the Foreign and Commonwealth Secretary and the United States Secretary of State in the State Department', Friday 10 March, TNA: PREM 16/1486, Prime Minister's visit to United States, March 1977.
64. Ibid.
65. Record of discussion at luncheon in honour of the Prime Minister, given by the Chairmen of the Senate Foreign Relations Committee and the House International Relations Committee, US Capitol, Thursday 10 March 1977, TNA: PREM 16/1486.
66. Ibid.
67. Record of a meeting held at the White House, present: President Carter, Vice-President Mondale, Secretary Vance, Dr Brzezinski, Prime Minister, Foreign and Commonwealth Secretary, Sir John Hunt, Friday 11 March 1977, TNA: PREM 16/1486.
68. Letter, 22 June 1977, John Moreton, British Embassy, Washington, DC, to Sir Michael Palliser GCMH, Permanent Under-Secretary of State, FCO, TNA: PREM 16/1909, USA. Internal Situation; assumption of office by President Carter.
69. Memorandum of Conversation, Participants: President Carter, Garret FitzGerald, Irish Foreign Minister, et al., Wednesday, March 16, 1977, The Oval Office, National Security Affairs – Brzezinski Material, Subject File, Memcons: Brzezinski: 7–8/79 through Memcons: President: 4/77, 'Memcons: President, 3/77', Box 34, Carter Library.
70. Ibid.
71. 'Meeting between the Minister for Foreign Affairs and U.S. Secretary of State Vance at State Department, Washington, 17 March 1977', NAI: D/Foreign Affairs, 2007/111/1997.

72. Ibid.
73. Letter, JK Hickman (British Embassy, Dublin) to PLV Mallet (FCO), 29 March 1977, 'US Interest in Northern Ireland', TNA: CJ 4/1845.
74. Ibid.
75. Memorandum, Zbigniew Brzezinski to The President, Subject: Your meeting with Ambassador William Shannon, July 14, 11:55 a.m, 14 July 1977, Jimmy Carter Presidential Library, RAC Project Number NLC-126-8-19-1-12 (hereafter NLC).
76. Telegram, UKE Washington to FCO, 10 June 1977, TNA: CJ 4/1844, United States of America involvement in Northern Ireland.
77. Telegram, FCO to UKE Washington, US/Northern Ireland, 17 June 1977, TNA: CJ 4/1842, United States attitudes to Northern Ireland situation.
78. News, 'US rule out involvement in the North', *The Irish Times*, Tuesday, 26 July 1977, 5.
79. Telegram, UK Embassy in Washington to FCO, 25 July 1977, U.S. Statement on Northern Ireland, TNA: CJ 4/1844.
80. Ibid.
81. Thompson, *American Policy*, 76.
82. Telegram, UK Embassy Washington to FCO, 21 July 1977, 'US Statement on Northern Ireland', TNA: CJ 4/1844.
83. Ibid.
84. Ibid.
85. Thompson, *American Policy*, 75.
86. Editorial, 'A U.S. "Initiative" in Ulster?', *The Washington Post*, 3 August 1977, A18.
87. Ibid.
88. News, 'Washington weighs "limited" U.S. effort for peace in Ulster', *The New York Times*, 25 August 1977, 45.
89. Ibid.
90. Editorial, '*The Sun* says', 'Memo to President Carter: M.Y.O.B.', *The Sun*, 24 August 1977, TNA: CJ 4/1843, United States involvement in Northern Ireland.
91. Thompson, *American Policy*, 77.
92. Dumbrell, *A Special Relationship*, 247–8.
93. Jimmy Carter, 'Northern Ireland statement on U.S. policy', 30 August 1977. Online by Gerhard Peters and John T. Woolley, *The American Presidency Project*, http://www.presidency.ucsb.edu/ws/?pid=8014, accessed 15 September 2015. (The next series of quotations is from this source.)
94. Ibid.

95. Dixon, *Northern Ireland*, 171.
96. Editorial, *The Irish Independent*, 31 August 1977, TNA: CJ 4/1843.
97. Editorial, 'Fifth Horseman for peace in Ulster', *The New York Times*, 1 September 1977, 20.
98. Editorial, *Irish Independent*, 31 August 1977, TNA: CJ 4/1843.
99. Arthur, *Special Relationships*, 140.
100. Miller Center, 'Interview with Edward M. Kennedy (3/20/2006)', University of Virginia, 20 March 2006, http://millercenter.org/oralhistory/interview/edward_m_kennedy_3-20-2006, accessed 27 October 2015.
101. Ibid.
102. Thompson, *American Policy*, 79–80.
103. Memorandum, Cyrus Vance to The President, 31 October 1977, NLC-128-13-1-20-2.
104. Thompson, *American Policy*, 80–1.
105. Seán Donlon, Minutes of meeting between U.S. Secretary of State and Minister for Foreign Affairs, New York, 1 October 1977, 2 October 1977, NAI: D/Foreign Affairs, 2007/59/222.
106. Ibid.
107. Memorandum, Warren Christopher to The President, 12 January 1978, NLC-128-13-4-5-6.
108. Ibid.
109. Jimmy Carter, 'Savannah, Georgia remarks at the Hibernian Society dinner', 17 March 1978. Online by Gerhard Peters and John T. Woolley, *The American Presidency Project*, http://www.presidency.ucsb.edu/ws/?pid=30520, accessed 24 September 2015.
110. Ibid.
111. Jimmy Carter, 'New York City, New York remarks at a "Get Out the Vote" rally', 2 November 1978. Online by Gerhard Peters and John T. Woolley, *The American Presidency Project*, http://www.presidency.ucsb.edu/ws/?pid=30103, accessed 24 September 2015.
112. Ibid.
113. Wilson, *Irish America*, 151–6.
114. Copy of press release from Speaker's Office enclosed with: letter, JS Wall (Private Secretary, Foreign and Commonwealth Office) to BG Cartledge (10 Downing Street), 11 April 1979, TNA: PREM 16/2291. The PM agreed to see Speaker O'Neill of the American House of Representatives March 1979.
115. Ibid.
116. 'Visit of Speaker O'Neill and Party to London, April 11–14, 1979', in TNA: PREM 16/2291.

117. News report, 'Can't find your elected representative? Try China', *Los Angeles Times*, 13 April 1979, B22.
118. Memorandum, Cyrus Vance to The President, 9 February 1979, 'State Department Evening Reports, 2/79', Box 39, Plains File, Subject File, State Department Evening Reports, 8/78 through State Department Evening Reports, 9/79, Carter Library.
119. Reference Papers, Department of State, April 1979, Box 15, Folder 15/14, Thomas P. O'Neill, Jr. Congressional Papers (CA2009-01), John J. Burns Library, Boston College (hereafter O'Neill Papers).
120. Letter, M Turner (Private Secretary, Foreign and Commonwealth Office) to JDF Holt (Private Secretary, 10 Downing Street), 5 April 1979, in TNA: PREM 16/2291.
121. 'Lines to take, Northern Ireland', author unknown, TNA: PREM 16/2291.
122. Ibid.
123. Ibid.
124. Report on the fact-finding mission to The United Kingdom, Belgium, Hungary and Ireland, April 11–23, 1979, Submitted by Thomas P. O'Neill, Jr. Speaker of the U.S. House of Representatives, Kirk O'Donnell Files, Belgium, Great Britain, Hungary, Ireland Visit, Report, April 1979, Box 15, Folder 15/16, O'Neill Papers. (The recipient of the report is unclear from the documents, but presumably it was for colleagues in the legislative and executive branches.)
125. Ibid.
126. Letter/Minutes, B. G. Cartledge (Private Secretary, 10 Downing Street) to J. S. Wall (Private Secretary, Foreign and Commonwealth Office), Speaker O'Neill's Call on the Prime Minister at 10 Downing Street, 12 April 1979, TNA: PREM 16/2291. (The following notes are from this source.)
127. Ibid.
128. Report on the fact-finding mission to The United Kingdom, Belgium, Hungary and Ireland, April 11–23, 1979, Submitted by Thomas P. O'Neill, Jr. Speaker of the U.S. House of Representatives, Kirk O'Donnell Files, Belgium, Great Britain, Hungary, Ireland Visit, Report, April 1979, Box 15, Folder 15/16, O'Neill Papers.
129. Ibid.
130. Ibid.
131. Memorandum of conversation, 'Visit by Speaker O'Neill', 26 April 1979, NAI: D/Foreign Affairs 2009/93/20.
132. Ibid.

133. Steering Note, 'Visit of U.S. Congressional Delegation April, 1979', NAI: D/Foreign Affairs, 2009/93/20.
134. Report on the fact-finding mission to The United Kingdom, Belgium, Hungary and Ireland, April 11–23, 1979, Submitted by Thomas P. O'Neill, Jr. Speaker of the U.S. House of Representatives, Kirk O'Donnell Files, Belgium, Great Britain, Hungary, Ireland Visit, Report, April 1979, Box 15, Folder 15/16, O'Neill Papers.
135. Speaker Thomas P. O'Neill, Jr., Toast remarks, April 19, 1979, delivered in Dublin, Kirk O'Donnell Files, Ireland – Speakers [sic] 1979 Trip to Ireland, Dublin Castle Speech, April 19th, Box 23, Folder 23/9, O'Neill papers.
136. Ibid.
137. Speech by the Taoiseach, Mr. J. Lynch, T.D. at the dinner for Speaker and Mrs. O'Neill and American Congressmen, Dublin Castle, 19th April, 1979, at 10.00 p.m., Box 23, Folder 23/9, O'Neill Papers.
138. Margaret Thatcher, General Election Press Conference, Friday, 20 April 1979, accessed via *The Margaret Thatcher Foundation* website, http://www.margaretthatcher.org/document/104029, 23 January 2013 (hereafter just URL).
139. See, for instance, Editorial, 'Tip O'Neill and the Irish iceberg', *The Guardian*, 21 April 1979, 8; Daily Express Opinion, 'Go home Mr O'Neill', *Daily Express*, Saturday, 21 April 1979, 8; Editorial, 'Ruffling the lion's mane', *The Boston Globe*, 25 April 1979, 14; and Mary Holland, 'Tip O'Neill was shocked by Callaghan', *Sunday Independent*, 22 April 1979, NAI: D/Foreign Affairs, 2009/93/20.
140. Report on the fact-finding mission to The United Kingdom, Belgium, Hungary and Ireland, April 11–23, 1979, Submitted by Thomas P. O'Neill, Jr. Speaker of the U.S. House of Representatives, Kirk O'Donnell Files, Belgium, Great Britain, Hungary, Ireland Visit, Report, April 1979, Box 15, 15/16, O'Neill Papers.
141. Anne McHardy and Philip Jordan, 'Belfast welcome for Kennedy ally', *The Guardian*, 21 April 1979, 1.
142. Report on the fact-finding mission to The United Kingdom, Belgium, Hungary and Ireland, April 11–23, 1979, Submitted by Thomas P. O'Neill, Jr. Speaker of the U.S. House of Representatives, Kirk O'Donnell Files, Belgium, Great Britain, Hungary, Ireland Visit, Report, April 1979, Box 15, 15/16, O'Neill Papers.
143. James Kelly, 'Carter set for North summit', *Irish Independent*, 21 April 1979, NAI: D/Foreign Affairs, 2009/93/20.
144. Kenneth Clarke, 'O'Neill's trail of rumour', *The Sunday Telegraph*, 22 April 1979, NAI: D/Foreign Affairs, 2009/93/20.

145. Rachelle Patterson, 'O'Neill: Irish trip beneficial', *The Boston Globe*, 22 April 1979, 1.

146. Thompson, *American Policy*, 86–7.

147. Wilson, *Irish America*, 159–60.

148. Richard Vinen, *Thatcher's Britain: The Politics and Social Upheaval of the 1980s* (London: Simon & Schuster, 2009), 214–17.

149. Dixon, *Northern Ireland*, 172.

150. Memorandum For: The President, From: Cyrus Vance, August 28, 1979, NLC-128-14-10-13-9.

151. Letter, Senator Edward Kennedy to President Jimmy Carter, 21 June 1979, White House Central Files: Subject File, Countries, General, CO 73 7/1/79-11/30 through General, CO 73 1/20/77-1/20/81, 'CO 73 Executive 1/1/79-10/31/79', Box CO-33, Carter Library.

152. Ibid.

153. Letter, President Jimmy Carter to Senator Ted Kennedy, 25 July 1979, White House Central Files: Subject File, Countries, General, CO 73 7/1/79-11/30 through General, CO 73 1/20/77-1/20/81, 'CO 73 Executive 1/1/79-10/31/79', Box CO-33, Carter Library.

154. Margaret Thatcher and Jimmy Carter, No. 10 record of phone call, Wednesday, 4 July 1979, accessed via http://www.margaretthatcher.org/document/112212, 25 October 2013.

155. Ibid.

156. Letter, Margaret Thatcher to Jimmy Carter, 'Outline of British policy towards Northern Ireland', Friday, 20 July 1979, accessed via http://www.margaretthatcher.org/document/112217, 25 October 2013.

157. Ibid.

158. Letter, Jimmy Carter to Tip O'Neill, 4 August 1979, Susan Clough File, L [Laney–Lukash] Through Z [Empty], 'O [OAS–O'Neill]', Box 46, Carter Library.

159. Letter, Michael Alison (Northern Ireland Office) to Margaret Thatcher, 'Talks with Governor Carey', 7 August 1979 [Atkins met Carey on 2 August], accessed via http://www.margaretthatcher.org/document/117915, 23 October 2013.

160. Ibid.

161. 'Note for the record, Northern Ireland, Note of a conversation between the Prime Minister and the Secretary of State for Northern Ireland at 10 Downing Street on 23 August 1979 at 12 noon', accessed via http://www.margaretthatcher.org/document/117915, 23 October 2013.

162. Ibid.

163. Letter, Sir Humphrey Atkins to Governor Hugh Carey (D-NY), Thursday, 23 August 1979, accessed via http://www.margaretthatcher.org/document/117915, 25 October 2013.

164. See, for instance, Cooper, 'The foreign politics of opposition', 23–42.

165. Vinen, *Thatcher's Britain*, 215.

166. Margaret Thatcher, *The Downing Street Years* (London: Harper-Collins, 1993), 58.

167. Sanders, 'The role of Northern Ireland in modern Anglo-American relations', 168–9.

168. Letter, Edward M. McCarthy (President, Irish Foundation of Arizona) to President Jimmy Carter, 6 June 1979, White House Central Files: Subject File, Countries, General, CO 71 7/1/79-11/30 through General, CO 73 1/20/77-1/20/81, 'CO73 Executive 1/1/79-10/31/79', Box CO 33, Carter Library.

169. Telegram, 'Arms for RUC', UKE Washington to FCO, Friday, 20 July 1979, accessed via http://www.margaretthatcher.org/document/117869, 25 October 2013.

170. Ibid.

171. Telegram, UKE to FCO, Friday, 20 July 1979, accessed via http://www.margaretthatcher.org/document/117869, 25 October 2013.

172. Ibid.

173. Nicholas Henderson, *Mandarin: The Diaries of Nicholas Henderson* (London: Weidenfeld & Nicolson, 1995), 284.

174. Ibid.

175. Telegram, UKE Washington to FCO, Friday, 27 July 1979, accessed via http://www.margaretthatcher.org/document/117869, 25 October 2013.

176. Telegram, FCO to UKE Washington, 3 August 1979, accessed via http://www.margaretthatcher.org/document/117869, 25 October 2013.

177. Memorandum, Matt Nimetz to Mr. Vest, Mr. Quainton, Mr. Atwood, Ms. Derian, Mr. Bartholomew, Subject: Arms Sales to the Royal Ulster Constabulary (RUC), 8 August 1979, NLC-12-54-10-18–9.

178. Ibid.

179. UKE Washington to FCO, 'Northern Ireland' [Cyrus Vance comments on supply of arms to the RUC], Wednesday, 5 September 1979, accessed via http://www.margaretthatcher.org/document/132493, 6 March 2014.

180. Ibid.

181. Memorandum, Cyrus Vance to The President, 10 September 1979, NLC-128-14-11-6-6.

182. Ibid.

183. UKE Washington to FCO, 'Arms for Northern Ireland', Friday, 28 September 1979, accessed via http://www.margaretthatcher.org/ document/132504, 16 October 2015.

184. Ibid.

185. Memorandum, Warren Christopher to The President, 3 October 1979, NLC-128-14-12-2-9.

186. UKE Washington to FCO, 'Arms for the RUC', Wednesday, 3 October 1979, accessed via http://www.margaretthatcher.org/document/ 117878, 6 March 2014.

187. Ibid.

188. UKE Washington to FCO, 'Arms for the RUC', Tuesday, 9 October 1979, accessed via http://www.margaretthatcher.org/document/ 117883, 6 March 2014.

189. Henderson, *Mandarin*, 309.

190. Ibid., 309–10.

191. Report of meeting between the Taoiseach and accompanying party and the U.S. President at the White House on Thursday, November 8, 1979, NAI: D/Taoiseach, 2009/135/719.

192. Ibid.

193. Memorandum, Cyrus Vance to The President, 8 November 1979, NLC-128-14-13-6-4.

194. Memorandum, Denis Clift to the Vice President, Subject: Dinner with Prime Minister Lynch – Talking Points, 9 November 1979, NLC-133-115-2-11-2.

195. Ibid.

196. UKE Washington to FCO, 'Arms for the RUC', Tuesday, 20 November 1979, accessed via http://www.margaretthatcher.org/document/ 117908, 19 June 2014.

197. UKE Washington to FCO, 'Arms for the RUC', Sunday, 25 November 1979, accessed via http://www.margaretthatcher.org/document/ 117908, 6 March 2014.

198. Memorandum, Denis Clift to the Vice President, Subject: Foreign Policy Breakfast, Friday, November 30, 1979, 7:30 a.m., 29 November 1979, NLC-133-115-2-24-8.

199. UKE Washington to FCO, 'Arms for the RUC', Sunday, 25 November 1979, accessed via http://www.margaretthatcher.org/docu-ment/117908, 6 March 2014.

200. UKE Washington to FCO, 'Margaret Thatcher visit', Thursday, 11 December 1979, accessed via http://www.margaretthatcher.org/document/112132, 6 March 2014.

201. Ibid. For the deteriorating relationship between Carter and O'Neill, see, for instance, John A. Farrell, *Tip O'Neill and the Democratic Century* (Little Brown, and Company: London, 2001), 504–36.

202. Cabinet Office briefing for Margaret Thatcher, Washington Visit, UK Objectives, Wednesday, 28 November 1979, accessed via http://www.margaretthatcher.org/document/112131, 25 October 2013.

203. Ibid.

204. Margaret Thatcher plenary meeting with President Jimmy Carter, Monday, 17 December 1979, accessed via http://www.margaretthatcher.org/document/112136, 25 October 2013.

205. Ibid.

206. Ibid.

207. Ibid.

208. Ibid.

209. Henderson, *Mandarin*, 318.

210. 'Record of a meeting between the Prime Minister and Members of the US Congress at the US Senate, Washington DC on Monday 17 December at 1600 hours', [Prepared by] British Embassy, Washington, 19 December 1979, accessed via http://www.margaretthatcher.org/document/112139, 25 October 2013.

211. Ibid.

212. UKE Washington to FCO, 'Arms for the RUC', Wednesday, 16 January 1980, accessed via http://www.margaretthatcher.org/document/120404, 6 March 2014.

213. Dixon, *Northern Ireland*, 168.

214. Margaret Thatcher, Airey Neave Memorial Lecture, Monday, 3 March 1980, accessed via http://www.margaretthatcher.org/document/104318, 16 January 2015.

215. Thompson, *American Policy*, 91.

216. UKE Washington to FCO, 'Visit of Irish Foreign Minister: 16–18 March: Northern Ireland', Wednesday, 19 March 1980, accessed via http://www.margaretthatcher.org/document/120420, 6 March 2014.

217. Letter, NC Abbott to Buxton (PS/Secretary of State), 12 May 1980, Meeting between Lord Carrington and Speaker O'Neill, Monday 5 May, TNA: CJ 4/3446, Sale of American weapons for use by the Royal Ulster Constabulary (RUC).

218. Ibid.

219. Memorandum, Edmund S. Muskie to The President, 23 May 1980, NLC-128-15-5-12-5.
220. Note of a meeting between the Secretary of State and Mr Matthew Nimetz at the House of Commons on 19 June 1980, TNA: CJ 4/3446.
221. Ibid.
222. Briefing, 'Secretary of State's Meeting with Mr Nimetz – Thursday 19 June 1980', TNA: CJ 4/3446.
223. Ibid.
224. Letter, DC Thomas (British Embassy, Washington DC) to MJ Newington (FCO), 16 June 1980, TNA: CJ 4/3446.
225. Democratic Party Platforms, 'Democratic Party platform of 1980', 11 August 1980. Online by Gerhard Peters and John T. Woolley, *The American Presidency Project*, http://www.presidency.ucsb.edu/ws/?pid=29607, accessed 20 June 2014.
226. Ibid.
227. Letter, UKE Washington to FCO, 13 December 1979, TNA: CJ 4/3242, United States Administrations Attitude to Northern Ireland.
228. Ibid.
229. Memorandum, Vicki Mongiardo to David Aaron, Subject: Meeting with delegation of Irish leaders on Northern Ireland, 21 October 1980, Staff Offices Ethnic Affairs, Aiello, 'Irish: Reference 5/79-12/80', Box 14, Carter Library.
230. Ibid.
231. The White House, Statement, 27 October 1980, Irish Reference 5/79-12/80, Staff Offices Ethnic Affairs, Aiello, Irish: Reference 5/79-12/80 Through Italian: Reference 6/79-12/80, Box 14, Carter Library.
232. Ibid.
233. Miller Center, 'Interview with Hamilton Jordan', University of Virginia, Carter Presidency Project, 6 November 1981, http://millercenter.org/president/carter/oralhistory/hamilton-jordan, accessed 28 January 2015.
234. Farrell, *O'Neill*, 536.

# 3 The Reagan and Bush Administrations, 1981–93

## Introduction

The much-feted partnership between Ronald Reagan and Margaret Thatcher, and that, albeit to a lesser extent, between Thatcher and George H. W. Bush, and then Bush and John Major marked an upturn in Anglo-American relations that, in some ways, had declined since the 1960s and 1970s. The Reagan–Thatcher relationship comprised a personal friendship between the President and the Prime Minister, a commonality in economic philosophies and a broader belief in individual freedom, and a stronger response to the Soviet Union and renewed Cold War tensions.[1] The Bush administration lessened the emphasis on Anglo-American relations with its focus on Germany in the context of the ending of the Cold War, collapse of the Soviet Union and emergence of the new world order.[2] Inevitably, any policy or attitude towards Northern Ireland during the Reagan and Bush administrations must be viewed in these contexts.

In November 1982, the Irish government internally outlined its policy towards the US and Northern Ireland. During the previous ten years, the main components of the policy were: to secure American recognition of and concern about the Northern Ireland conflict as 'a destabilizing factor in Western Europe'; for the US to recognise that it was a political problem and not 'simply a matter of British internal security'; for the US government to agree a solution revolving around consensual 'reunification of North and South'; for the US government to pressure the British government to act along such lines; to secure American cooperation in tackling

Irish–American financial support for dealing with violence; and to achieve American investment in Northern Ireland and the Republic so as 'to create conditions in which violence would cease to flourish as prosperity grows'.[3] By the time of Reagan's presidency, the Irish government could certainly claim to have achieved American co-operation in tackling support for the IRA and the promise of increased investment in Northern Ireland, subject to a political solution being agreed. Whereas Irish–Americans, including some in Congress, satisfied the remainder of the Irish government's list, they had failed to convince successive presidents to intervene to an extent that would have fulfilled the remaining criteria. However, there was a suggestion that some within the Reagan administration favoured a united Ireland, and the President did endorse a political solution in the form of the 1985 Anglo-Irish Agreement (AIA). The AIA prompted American investment in Northern Ireland, and, in turn, this development continued during the Bush administration, along with other contributions to the Anglo-Irish process.

The Reagan epoch also marked the establishment of a congressional group to rival Biaggi's ACCIA. Announced on St Patrick's Day in 1981, the Friends of Ireland (FOI) was a congressional group comprised of familiar protagonists such as Kennedy and O'Neill. Unlike Biaggi's organisation, which relied on grassroots support such as the INC, the FOI enjoyed the support and credibility of congressional leadership. Its mission was to ensure that members of the US Congress, and concerned citizens in the US more generally, were accurately informed of developments in Northern Ireland. The FOI's condemnation of the IRA and related activism meant that their moderation promoted criticism from other Irish–Americans. Politicians such as Speaker Tip O'Neill and Senator Edward Kennedy were therefore not simply electioneering in their concern for Northern Ireland: the positions that they assumed on the issue only infuriated hard-line Irish–Americans.[4]

Edwin Meese (Counsellor to the President, 1981–5, and US Attorney General, 1985–8) later recalled that the President was proud of his Irish ancestry and often quoted Irish jokes. However, he did not remember Reagan ever discussing contemporaneous Irish affairs.[5] Reagan was interested in Northern Ireland, but the extent of his willingness to intervene is clouded by differing views of his administration: namely, William P. Clark, Jr (Deputy Secretary of State, 1981–2; NSA 1982–3; and Secretary of the Interior, 1983–7), Meese and the State Department. During the Bush presidency, the issue became more clear-cut as it reverted to the almost exclusive purview of the State Department.

## Reagan and the Anglo-Irish process

Unlike their Democratic counterparts, the Republican Party made no reference to Northern Ireland in their 1980 platform.[6] After discussions with Senator John Tower (R-TX), the chairman of the platform committee, the Irish Embassy concluded that Tower and the Republicans were 'obsessed' with NATO's weaknesses and the threat posed by the Soviet Union, and prioritised 'uninterrupted good relations with the British government'.[7] During the 1980 presidential election, Reagan's formal stance on Northern Ireland read as follows:

> The divisions in Northern Ireland are deep and of long standing. The wounds can be healed only though the good will of reasonable men and women on both sides. Compromises will be needed and these must be arrived at by those involved. It is not for the United States to interfere in this process or prescribe solutions, but rather to urge the parties to come together to work for a solution and to join in condemnation of terrorism by either side.[8]

This was in accordance with the established position of the US government. Reagan broadened out this position to incorporate his wider anti-terrorism stance:

> Peace cannot come from the barrel of a terrorist's gun. Americans should question closely any appeal for funds from groups involved in the conflict to make sure that contributions do not end up in the hands of gun-runners. Further, as terrorists of either side are apprehended and jailed, extradition procedures should not be relaxed on the grounds these are 'political' prisoners. Terrorism is just that and must not be allowed to be condoned or excused.[9]

On 6 November, President-Elect Reagan was asked at a press conference about Northern Ireland and the possibility of arms sales to the RUC. In reply, Reagan emphasised his Irish heritage and continuity with his predecessors in the White House:

> I cannot answer that specifically. I would say with the name of Reagan the US cannot interfere or intervene but if there is any way we can be helpful we would be more than eager because I think it is a very tragic situation.[10]

The Irish embassy also noted that Irish press coverage focused on Reagan's connections with Thatcher and the possibility of a change in the American government's attitude towards Northern Ireland, particularly with regard to the sales of arms to the RUC.[11]

In February 1981, Thatcher was the first major world leader to visit Reagan. This was a clear signal that the administration expected the British Prime Minister to be a key ally.[12] In anticipation of the meeting, the British government imagined that Reagan would want British support to develop a cohesive foreign and defence policy and share his strong commitment against the USSR.[13] The FCO advised Thatcher 'to give the President and his advisers an account of the realities of the Northern Ireland situation'.[14] The Northern Ireland Office brief suggested that the Reagan administration would 'follow its predecessor in condemning violence unequivocally and taking practical steps to prevent US assistance to IRA terrorists'.[15] Although Thatcher was briefed that the RUC no longer needed Ruger revolvers from the US as an 'operational requirement', politically 'the best position is for the Americans to lift the ban' so that she could 'say that this has happened'. Even so, it was understood that O'Neill would not entertain the prospect and, much like his predecessor, Reagan did not want to oppose the Speaker on that issue.[16] Henderson, following discussions with diplomats in Washington, DC, shortly after Reagan's inauguration, shared this view.[17] This was in contrast to speculation in the *Irish Press* that Thatcher's visit would prompt Reagan to reverse the ban.[18]

According to American documents, Alexander Haig, the US Secretary of State (1981–2), advised Reagan that Thatcher would want to reaffirm the 'special relationship' and that he should '[d]emonstrate publicly and privately that Thatcher is the major Western leader most attuned to your views on East–West and security issues'.[19] However, Haig warned that Thatcher might raise some issues that he 'recommended' the President avoid. Such issues included Northern Ireland. Haig noted, 'Our policy has been to prevent Northern Ireland from disrupting our close cooperation with the UK and Ireland by adopting a policy of strict neutrality.'[20] This represented continuity with the Nixon–Ford approach. A Department of State briefing paper echoed this advice: Reagan should explain (again, only if the issue was raised) that 'US policy has been to prevent the Northern Ireland issue from disrupting our close cooperation with the UK and Ireland on multilateral issues.'[21] The briefing also suggested that the President should maintain continuity with his predecessor's stated policy, which was a 'call for an end to violence, express support for a peaceful solution, and . . . be prepared to join with others to see how job-creating investment there could be encouraged'.[22] But this continuity in policy was not necessarily iron-clad. Reagan admitted to journalists, a month after meeting Thatcher in the White House, that he disagreed with the prohibition of arms sales to the RUC.[23] The President, sympathetic towards Thatcher, was speaking his own mind rather than following the advice of his administration. However, Northern Ireland was not discussed during Thatcher's meetings either with the President or with members of the US Senate.[24]

Reagan's election discouraged many who hoped for American intervention. For instance, P. J. McClean, chairman of the Northern Ireland Civil Rights Association, told *The New York Times* in March 1981 that the Cold Warriors had supplanted Carter's emphasis on human rights, meaning that the US government would not attempt to persuade its British counterparts to act on the issue.[25] Reagan continued to avoid involvement in the Anglo-Irish process. In his first presidential St Patrick's Day statement, he publicly clarified his administration's policy towards Northern Ireland:

> The United States will continue to urge the parties to come together for a just and peaceful solution . . . . We will continue to condemn all acts of terrorism and violence, for these cannot solve Northern

Ireland's problems. I call on all Americans to question closely any appeal for financial or other aid from groups involved in this conflict to ensure that contributions do not end up in the hands of those who perpetuate violence, either directly or indirectly.

I add my personal prayers and the good offices of the United States to those Irish – and indeed to all world citizens – who wish fervently for peace and victory over those who sow fear and terror.[26]

The White House subsequently played down the use of diplomatic language – namely, 'good offices' – that suggested an imminent American intervention, such as a mediatory role between the British and Irish governments. (However, Reagan did gift the Irish Embassy a jar of green jellybeans.)[27] Reagan supported a political solution, but he would not participate in the Anglo-Irish process, and condemned actors such as NORAID. This represented continuity in American policy and the continuity of this neutrality during the 1981 Hunger Strike served only to underline his position. Nevertheless, following a meeting with Reagan on 1 June 1981, Kennedy believed that the President was concerned about Northern Ireland and wanted to act on the issue.[28] Reagan admitted to Kennedy that 'the situation over there really bothers me' and that he would 'give it some serious thought'.[29] Reagan was interested in the situation and sympathetic to the position of Kennedy and like-minded Irish–Americans, but would prove reluctant to intervene.

At this time, the British Embassy advised the FCO about the failings in the Reagan administration's foreign policy team.[30] It judged the team's decision-making to be 'incoherent', as Haig was 'not firmly in the saddle'. In contrast to Casper Weinberger (the Secretary of Defence, 1981–7), the Secretary of State was deemed 'not [to] have the president's trust' and to be 'actively distrusted by Reagan's closest White House advisers, who may well be doing little to counter press criticism of him'. In addition to Haig's failings, the White House played an unclear role in foreign policy: Richard V. Allen's (NSA, 1981–2) 'contribution is uncertain except that he can be relied upon to oppose Haig', and while Meese's 'influence is strong across the whole board of policy', he was 'not a master of the foreign scene'. Reagan was not exempted from criticism: he was judged as ill versed in the nuances of foreign policy, despite his vision of American strength in the relationship with the Soviet Union and being a strong ally to his nation's friends.[31] In such a foreign policy-making milieu, there was scope for the Irish government to secure Reagan's involvement in the Anglo-Irish process while his administration tried to establish and implement its foreign policy.

In a letter handed to Reagan when he visited the Irish Embassy on 14 July, FitzGerald wrote asking for the President's help to prevent the death of hunger striker Kieran Doherty, who had been elected to the Dáil Éireann (the lower house of the Irish parliament) on 11 June 1981. The new Taoiseach essentially pleaded for American intervention in the hunger strike:

> I beg you to use your enormous influence with the British Prime Minister within the next 24 hours to implement immediately an already existing understanding mediated by the Commission of Justice and Peace of the Irish Catholic Hierarchy to avert his death so preventing the very dangerous consequences which would inevitably follow.[32]

By chance, FitzGerald's appeal coincided with the visit of Reagan, his wife and key members of his staff to the Irish Embassy as part of a celebration to mark the conferring of an honorary fellowship on Dr Loyal Davis, Nancy Reagan's stepfather, from the Royal College of Surgeons in Ireland (RCSI). The celebration moved to the White House for drinks for a smaller gathering consisting of members of the RCSI and Irish Ambassador Seán Donlon. According to the Irish record, Donlon, at the first opportunity upon arriving at the White House, emphasised to Michael Deaver (the White House Deputy Chief of Staff, 1981–5) 'the need for an early response' to FitzGerald's message.[33] Deaver confirmed that Reagan had already asked Allen to assess the situation and, given the press interest, the administration would respond 'as soon as possible'. Deaver enquired about 'the precise nature' of the strikers' demands and even asked whether the British government was essentially being asked 'to give in to well calculated blackmail'. Donlon also reported that Allen was not 'very sympathetic to our interests' because Ireland was not a NATO ally and because of his 'somewhat primitive view about how to deal with the IRA'.

In contrast to the sympathy that Reagan revealed to Kennedy, his staff were unenthusiastic for any presidential involvement. Donlon sat with Reagan during dinner and the President candidly admitted that he did not think that 'this is one for me'. After asking Donlon about the situation in Northern Ireland, Reagan offered his own analysis before the ambassador could respond: he 'saw it as a war between two rival religious factions and he wondered why the heads of the churches could not give a more positive lead'. Reagan argued that, even though Paisley was a 'fanatic', the Churches should co-operate without him. After the ambassador informed him 'that the Church leaders had in fact frequently come together to make joint appeals and indeed now met on a regular basis', Reagan 'then asked about external meddling in Northern Ireland', and before Donlon was able to respond, he 'again gave his own reply'. The President claimed that the Communists were 'obviously involved as they had been, for example, on US campuses during the Vietnam era'. Reagan was interested in whether 'the majority in both sections of the Northern Ireland community' would 'rise up' to the terrorists and throw them off 'its back'. Donlon feared that his subsequent account of the history of paramilitary groups in Northern Ireland did not succeed 'in doing much more than confusing the president'. Nonetheless, Donlon recorded that Reagan was, overall, 'well informed and anxious to help in any way he could' regarding the unwelcome American support for violence.[34] This was a surprising conclusion by the Irish ambassador, after his conversation with the President.

Perhaps unsurprisingly, given Donlon's report on the President's visit to the Embassy, Reagan refused to act on FitzGerald's request. In his reply on 23 July, Reagan wrote, 'I appreciate the depth of concern which prompted your letter and want you to know how sorrowfully I, along with millions of other Americans, view this tragic conflict.'[35] He added that, throughout the Hunger Strike 'we have made clear our regret at the deaths', and expressed his 'hope that the hunger strike can be brought to a peaceful conclusion with an end to the violence'. Reagan was clear that American intervention was not a possibility, explaining that 'U.S. policy and my own personal feelings as expressed in my St. Patrick's Day statement are well known to the British Government.'[36] The

White House assured the British Embassy that this letter was 'masterfully non-committal'.[37] This was a diplomatic victory for British policy: Washington was adhering to its traditional neutrality on the issue rather than challenging British policy.

The 1981 Hunger Strike was widely reported in the American media, which served as a further signal to the British government that it could no longer view the 'Troubles' as simply a domestic issue. Even though American coverage supported the British government's stance that republican prisoners should not be awarded political status, the increasing number of deaths matched a mounting level of criticism towards Thatcher. On 6 May 1981, the Four Horsemen released a telegram that they had sent to the Prime Minister, in which they were critical of her 'intransigence'. The President was advised to maintain his non-interventionist stance, despite reports of the letter he received from FitzGerald. Evidently, the President continued to follow Haig's advice, as he only mentioned the Hunger Strike briefly during his meeting with Thatcher in July 1981 at the Ottawa economic summit, and then only to stress that he would not interfere.[38] The issue was not discussed at the lengthy breakfast meeting of leaders, although it was reported that Thatcher briefed Reagan on the Sunday evening before the conference formally began, and that the President and Haig maintained their view that it was an issue for the British government.[39] Furthermore, the Reagan administration reportedly admired Thatcher's response to the Hunger Strike in a speech at Stormont on 28 May 1981. In that speech, the Prime Minister observed that the IRA 'remained inflexible and intransigent', as they 'want their violence justified. It isn't, and it will not be'.[40] She added that peace in Northern Ireland would be achieved only through the 'will, desire and understanding' that 'can only come from the hearts and minds of men and women here in the Province'.[41] The British Embassy informed the FCO that British Information Services (BIS), based in the British Consulate in New York, distributed the speech to newspaper editorials across the US while the British ambassador ensured that copies were sent to Bush, Meese, Haig, Allen, Kennedy, Moynihan and O'Neill, amongst others.[42] Meese told Henderson 'how very much he had admired both the clarity and humanity of the speech' and the Embassy believed that he 'probably . . . showed and commended it to the President'.[43]

The reluctance of the Reagan administration to become involved was reported by the British Embassy to the FCO on 15 July 1981: 'As for the general mood here, there is no sign of weakening in the administration's desire not to intervene, although they are coming under increased pressure to do so.'[44] In addition to 'the enhanced standing of Noraid', the administration was challenged by 'the attitude of Congress'. Irish–Americans were 'not just angry' with the British response to the Hunger Strike, but 'they themselves' were 'under pressure'; for instance, O'Neill's office in Boston was subject to a sit-in while Kennedy was 'also being barracked'.[45] The work of those Irish–American politicians who opposed NORAID and supported the Anglo-Irish process was being undermined, in the view of O'Neill and Kennedy, by Thatcher's policy. This underlines the complexity of the policy-making process towards Northern Ireland. While O'Neill and Kennedy shared the aims of the British government in reducing the influence of NORAID, they also sought action from the White House on the Hunger Strike in order to satisfy the demands of their Irish–American constituents for a settlement and prevent them from turning to groups such as the INC. They wanted the same level of political cover that Carter's 1977 statement afforded them. American policy towards Northern Ireland was therefore determined by competing factors: Irish–American citizens, lobbyists, congressional concerns, the State Department and the White House.

A confusing picture emerges, however, of Reagan's policy towards Northern Ireland. In what was ostensibly intended by Clark to be an 'off-the-record' conversation with Donlon, the Deputy Secretary of State discussed his own Irish heritage and then outlined 'the advice being given to the President' on Northern Ireland.[46] Clark explained to him that the State Department opposed involvement on the basis that it was a British domestic issue and 'astute political advisers', whom Donlon presumed were senior White House aides, briefed Reagan that it was a 'no win situation'. Nonetheless, Clark claimed Reagan 'felt deeply' about the situation. The President was willing to do anything that would be constructive, which would, of course, please Irish–Americans and many members of Congress. Donlon was certain that 'any message delivered by Clark accurately represents the president's position'.[47] It should be noted that Clark was of Irish descent and had an emotional attachment to Ireland. He was a proud Irish–American who visited as often as he could. His interest in Irish affairs ensured that, during his first few months at the State Department, he was the obvious choice when Haig had to deal with Paisley's visa application, which had been greeted by death threats in the US. Clark rejected the visa on the basis that Paisley's safety could not be guaranteed while he was in the country.[48] Also convinced of Reagan's interest was Hume. Citing his conversations with the President, for instance, at a direct meeting at the Speaker's annual St Patrick's Day lunch (a tradition that began in 1983), Hume argued that

> he was very committed to . . . doing anything that he could to support what happened in Ireland . . . he strongly supported anything that Tip O'Neill and Ted Kennedy decided about Ireland because there they were united . . . in their Irish roots.[49]

Based on Clark's conversation with Donlon (and Hume's recollections), Reagan was willing to intervene in Northern Ireland. Nonetheless, the President was cautioned by internal debates in his administration about the issue and wider foreign policy concerns, such as his relationship with Thatcher. Indeed, Kennedy recalled that he had indicated his wish to the White House to discuss Northern Ireland with Reagan at the inaugural Speaker's St Patrick's Day lunch.[50] But the Senator was denied this request:

> I was told very clearly that he did not want to get into any substance whatsoever. He wanted to tell stories and hear stories from the members . . . . He told a couple of stories, Hollywood type stories, gentle stories, kind of amusing.[51]

That Reagan ultimately did not act disappointed Irish–American and Irish government hopes that he could be convinced to petition Thatcher on their behalf.[52] Yet this was unsurprising, given that the Reagan administration prioritised international economic and security interests rather than avoiding a quarrel with Thatcher, the President's friend and closest ally. In November 1981, John Louis, US Ambassador to Britain (1981–3), advised Reagan 'that the best thing we can do on this issue is stick with our present policy as reflected in your St. Patrick's Day statement'.[53] The President followed Louis's advice and supported the next round of discussions between Thatcher and FitzGerald in December 1981. He even endorsed the on-going process in a letter to the Taoiseach.[54]

However, the Reagan administration's neutrality was undermined by a diplomatic error. While visiting Ireland in December 1981, Clark stated that the American people wished to see a united Ireland. Like the President on arms for the RUC, Clark had deviated from the administration's official line. British officials were furious and the State Department quickly clarified that Clark's comment was not indicative of a shift in administration policy.[55] Clark's statement was made in an interview on RTE (Ireland's national public service broadcaster).[56] He also handed a letter to the Taoiseach from the President.[57] After complaints from the British government that Clark did not share this letter's existence with them, the Irish government sent them the full text.[58] The President wrote that Clark would 'want to hear your views on Northern Ireland' as it was 'of tremendous concern to me', albeit adding that he would 'continue to affirm the principles of my St. Patrick's Day statement'.[59] Reagan then used phrasing that was of concern to the British:

> We believe a lasting solution can be found only in a process of reconciliation between the two Irish political traditions and between Britain and Ireland. The United States welcomes the efforts of the Irish and British governments in widening the framework of their cooperation to this end.[60]

Nonetheless, Reagan continued to emphasise American neutrality: 'But as much as our hearts long for a settlement, it is not for the United States to chart the course others must follow. If the solutions are to endure, they must come from the people themselves.'[61] The FCO requested that the British Embassy in Washington subtly raise with the State Department the phrase 'reconciliation between the two Irish political traditions'.[62] The British government believed that the wording 'would cause . . . embarrassment if it were used again', as it 'implies an all-Ireland solution to Northern Ireland's problems' and suggests a 'veiled reference to Irish unity'.[63] Again, Clark was identified as a problematic figure within British correspondence. The British Embassy, confirming that the

State Department will 'try . . . to ensure that the phrase is not used again', observed that 'knowing the attitude of Judge Clark in particular . . . it [is] most unlikely that we will do better than to secure the removal of the word "political".'[64] Embassy staff noted that Clark's remarks about American support for a united Ireland were 'not something which he let slip in the heat of the moment but an idea which he had been determined to get across in public at some point during his visit to Dublin'.[65]

The signals given to the Irish government by the Reagan administration were mixed. Prior to his departure, Clark told Irish Embassy officials 'that there was no change in US policy'.[66] Interestingly, he explained that the President's recent address to the Irish Historical Society had been changed under the influence of Meese. Clark claimed that it originally included a 'helpful' paragraph agreed by Ambassador Donlon and the British about Northern Ireland, but Meese ensured that instead Reagan delivered a humorous and non-controversial address.[67] Meese won the battle amongst Reagan's advisers on this occasion, squashing any hint that the President might intervene. Key members of the administration were attempting to guide the President towards what they viewed to be the most apt policy. As per Meese's wishes, Reagan's comments to the New York audience were light-hearted and autobiographical. His only reference to Northern Ireland was the following passage:

> Today, as has been said here already tonight, there is tragedy again in the Emerald Isle. The Cardinal prayed and His Holiness, the Pope, pleaded for peace when he visited Ireland. I think we all should pray that responsible leaders on both sides and the governments of the United Kingdom and the Republic of Ireland can bring peace to that beautiful Isle once again. And once again, we can join John Locke in saying, 'O Ireland, isn't it grand you look – Like a bride in her rich adornment? And with all the pent-up love in [of] my heart, I bid you top o' the mornin'!'[68]

The State Department's efforts to clarify Clark's remarks in Ireland hardly calmed British concerns. Lord Hurd, former Secretary of State for Northern Ireland (1984–5), recalled that some members of the Reagan administration were instinctively favourable towards

Irish unification.[69] Exasperation with this statement at the time was evident in the House of Commons. Thatcher was asked whether she was willing to 'reassure President Reagan that she will not support the return of Texas to Mexico against the wishes of the majority of the inhabitants of Texas'. She replied, 'I congratulate my hon. Friend on the aptness of that point.'[70]

Clark quickly sought to clarify his position on reunification and apologise for failing to warn the British government about Reagan's reply to FitzGerald's letter. After neglecting to speak with Atkins and James Prior, the Northern Ireland Secretary (1981–4), he telephoned Henderson and distanced himself from the remarks on reunification and blamed the American Embassy for the lack of warning about the President's letter.[71] In his report to the FCO, Henderson noted that the complaint to the US Embassy 'had nettled him' and Clark determinedly, and defensively, explained his remarks line by line.[72] Clark was an on-going concern for the British officials working on Northern Ireland and its relationship with the US. Upon his appointment as NSA, the British Embassy briefed the FCO: 'Clark is one of Reagan's oldest and closest associates . . . and, in his time at the State Department, he has continued to have the ear of the president.'[73] The Embassy warned that there was 'no doubt that Clark will be one of the inner circle at the White House' and 'the one subject which seems to have aroused his personal interest has been Northern Ireland'. There was some optimism that this would change: 'As one NSC staffer put it to us, with luck, Clark will now be too busy to devote much time to that issue.'[74]

Thatcher was certainly unwilling to welcome American intervention in Northern Ireland, even from members of the Reagan administration. Haughey, having recently been elected (and serving briefly) as Taoiseach (March to December 1982), met with the President on St Patrick's Day in 1982. In advance of the meeting, Henderson spoke with Walter John Stoessel, Jr (who succeeded Clark as Deputy Secretary of State, albeit for just eight months in 1982) on 10 March 1982.[75] The ambassador updated him on Prior's talks with the Northern Ireland parties, urging that, given its 'delicate state . . . nothing should be said by the president which could jeopardise our initiative'. The British government was keen

that Reagan would not publicly endorse Haughey's proposed conference for all interested parties in the Northern Ireland issue: 'this
could only have the effect of hardening opinion on both sides'.
Clark was again a point of concern for the British government with
regard to the annual St Patrick's statement, as he was responsible
for Reagan's statement and was likely to be attracted to Haughey's proposal 'and less aware of the damage it could do'. Clark
was even advised by his own staff that the US should not appear
to take sides on Northern Ireland.[76] Also of concern was the proposed presence of Hume at the President's St Patrick's lunch with
Haughey.[77] The NSC informed the British Embassy that it would be
politically embarrassing for the invitation to be withdrawn – it was
just as embarrassing for the British government that it was issued
in the first place. The NSC confirmed with the British Embassy that
Hume was invited, as he was in Washington, DC, at the time to
meet Clark – 'whose idea, of course, it was to invite him'.[78] Clark
was a diplomatic headache for the British government.

Prior to Haughey's meeting with Reagan, the Irish Department of Foreign Affairs reflected on the attitude of the US administration towards Northern Ireland.[79] The Irish government was
pleased that Reagan's interest was 'deeper than might have been
anticipated', although 'it is still by no means certain that we can
hope to retain completely the position established during the
Carter Administration'. With regard to Reagan's 1981 St Patrick's
Day statement, the briefing credited the new President's 'anxiety'
to work with O'Neill as 'the major factor in securing the statement'. However, outside of the realities of American domestic
politics, the President and his administration were 'taking a particularly strong anti-terrorist approach' and, subsequently, Irish
government representatives 'emphasise the terrorist element of
the N.I. problem when talking to senior Reagan officials'. Aside
from Clark serving as an advocate for the Irish position within the
administration, the Irish government's attempts to achieve further
American intervention in Northern Ireland were frustrated by the
State Department's urging of neutrality (which the Irish saw as
de facto 'pro-British') and Allen's anti-Irish sentiments. Moreover,
the key roadblock to American intervention in Northern Ireland
was Meese, who 'believes that it is a no-win situation' and Reagan

'has enough on his plate without taking on one more issue'. The Irish briefing noted that Meese 'is frequently referred to as the real President of the United States'.[80] It is clear that Reagan was interested in the issue; Clark urged him to become involved, while others, in this case Allen and Meese, were opposed to this due to foreign policy and political implications.

During his luncheon toast, Haughey called for Britain to be encouraged to promote 'a change in attitudes and outlooks which would pave the way for unity and so enable her final withdrawal from Ireland to take place with honor and dignity'.[81] Reagan's response was lighter: the President joked that he and Haughey both faced an Irish Speaker in passing legislation.[82] Haughey also visited the White House that day. According to the Irish record, in his meeting with Reagan (who was accompanied by Bush, Haig and Clark), the Taoiseach argued for a 'solution between the two sovereign Governments who had a duty to bring forward new policies and structures to reconcile the communities'.[83] For Haughey, '[t]he ultimate solution to the problem lay in Irish unity and the final withdrawal of the British from Ireland' but in the interim period 'it was his policy to work with them'. Reagan enquired whether 'the people "on the scene in Northern Ireland" want British withdrawal'. Haughey used this as an opportunity to underline his concern about the political process and failings of British policy. Reagan simply responded 'that the majority of the Irish people must yearn for peace but are terrified by the extremists on both sides'. Reagan's interest was clear but non-committal towards any policy of involvement, thus following Meese's guidance. To that end, and perhaps in an attempt to change the topic of conversation, Reagan 'then sought some information on the persons who would be providing entertainment at the lunch'.[84]

Still determined to convince Reagan to intervene in the Anglo-Irish process, the Taoiseach attempted to use the President's Irish heritage to his advantage in a letter following their White House meeting. Haughey wrote to the President, 'to meet on St. Patrick's Day a President of Irish name and descent could not but evoke in me deep feelings of emotion and pride in the achievements of our people in the United States'.[85] He also further flattered Reagan by acknowledging his 'charming wife'.[86] Haughey was determined to secure Reagan's involvement in the Anglo-Irish process, while the British were grateful for him not doing so. On 2 April 1982, Lord Carrington, the Foreign Secretary (1979–82), wrote to Haig:

> We have noted, and warmly appreciate, the helpful attitude of the US administration towards the situation in Northern Ireland. Your firm support during the difficult period of last year's hunger strike, the efforts of your law enforcement agencies to curb the illegal flow of weapons to Northern Ireland and above all the president's wise and constructive statement on St. Patrick's Day, all bear witness to your understanding of the situation.[87]

Carrington shared with Haig the proposals that Prior made for an elected assembly at Stormont, which would consider the devolution of powers to Northern Ireland (hereafter the 'Prior Plan') and noted that Prior would also be sharing the details with Clark.[88] The proposals were not published in a White Paper until 5 April 1982. That relevant members of the British government briefed the two most senior figures in the State Department underlines British acceptance of American interest in the Anglo-Irish process. The fact that Clark was due to receive information from Prior, however, emphasises both his importance to Reagan and his support for American involvement in the Anglo-Irish process. In short, it was better to involve Clark in the process than have him create diplomatic difficulties, as he had done five months earlier. (Prior's Northern Ireland Assembly was dissolved in June 1986 following a series of boycotts and withdrawals on the part of various parties.)

Nonetheless, by June 1982, it seemed that Clark's influence on policy towards Northern Ireland was waning. After discussions with Commander Dennis Blair, a member of the NSC, R. A. Harrington (Northern Ireland Office) informed colleagues that Clark's interest in Northern Ireland 'remained as strong as ever, but he was now too much tied up on other matters as Director of the NSC to involve himself publicly in Irish matters'.[89] Yet despite Clark's interest and 'influence with the President', it was clear that Reagan 'saw the political dangers of involving himself in Irish politics, and would keep right out of it'.[90] Reagan and Thatcher did not discuss the issue during his visit to the UK in June 1982, preferring to focus on the Falklands, the Middle East and the NATO summit that month in Bonn.[91] Nevertheless,

Thatcher was advised on the position to take if Northern Ireland was a topic of conversation. Ostensibly noting potential ethnic influences on US foreign policy, the FCO briefed her that Reagan's Irish heritage had not prevented his condemnation of violence in Northern Ireland and American support for the IRA.[92] Moreover, in his 1982 St Patrick's Day statement, the President 'came down firmly against United States involvement, despite Mr Haughey's attempts to draw the United States in'. The FCO noted that Thatcher could brief Reagan on the aim to devolve some powers 'through the creation of a local Assembly' and to thank the President for his support against NORAID and in 'bringing fugitive terrorists to justice'. Significantly, according to the briefing, any British hopes of reversing the RUC arms sale ban had been abandoned at this stage: 'it would not be appropriate to mention US refusal to license the export of Ruger pistols'.[93] Similarly, prior to Bush's visit to the UK at the end of June 1983, on Northern Ireland, Thatcher was briefed: 'Grateful for US efforts to clamp down on gun-running to Ireland. President Reagan's policies towards Northern Ireland wise and most welcome.'[94] Reagan's neutrality was welcomed in Downing Street.

In October 1982, Gerard Collins, the Irish Foreign Minister (March to December 1982), visited Washington, DC. According to the Irish briefing notes, Collins was to brief congressional allies regarding Northern Ireland and Anglo-Irish relations.[95] After meetings with O'Neill and Kennedy, Collins met Clark. The Irish record reads that there were discussions about the Anglo-Irish process and American interest. The Irish government feared that elections following the Prior Plan would see the IRA fill the void, should moderates not participate. Collins remarked that this government 'hoped our friends would gently nudge the British to deal with this problem, otherwise terrorism might come forward again to the centre of the stage'.[96] In turn, Clark offered administration support to the Irish government, asking if there were 'anything we might do in that relation in a subtle way'. Collins stated that once

> the dust had settled down after the elections . . . we could make contact through the Ambassador in Washington as to how the United States might gently and in a very discreet way nudge the British towards a resumption of a positive process.

Clark remarked that 'he would do nothing before then' and 'would want to consider the situation and discuss it with Secretary of State Shultz'.[97] In light of Shultz's new leadership at the State Department (1982–9), Clark was perhaps reluctant to replicate his diplomatic *faux pas* from the year before. This was also indicative of Shultz's authority. Northern Ireland was not a priority for Shultz: the Anglo-Irish process is not discussed in his memoir.[98]

At the end of 1982, the Irish government again reviewed developments in the Reagan administration's approach to the Anglo-Irish process. After the first two years of the presidency, any fears that interest in Ireland would lessen had been 'debunked' following Reagan's St Patrick's 1981 statement and Clark's visit to Ireland in 1982.[99] The briefing identified the complex nature of American foreign policy with regard to Northern Ireland. The State Department's machinery protected American foreign and security policies 'from the vagaries' of elections and ideological shifts. Subsequently, unless Anglo-American relations deteriorated, 'the preferences in the Department of State will be against doing anything in Ireland which offends its ally, Britain'. However, there was a sense that there were two factors that might challenge America's pro-British and non-interventionist position. The first was Reagan, who emphasised his Irish heritage and viewed Ireland 'with goodwill and affection'. The second was Clark, who considered himself an Irish–American and enjoyed 'a special relationship with the President on foreign policy issues'.[100] Reagan's interest in Northern Ireland was therefore well known to the Irish government. Similarly, the possibility of working with a key aide to the President meant that they might be able to persuade Reagan to intervene.

Reagan did not reference Northern Ireland directly in his congratulatory message to Garret FitzGerald on becoming Taoiseach (1982–7).[101] FitzGerald included it in his response, however, telling Reagan that he valued his 'encouragement of reconciliation and co-operation between Britain and Ireland'.[102] There was a clear determination to convince Reagan to support their nationalist objectives. In November 1982, a telegram from the Irish Embassy in Washington, DC, to Dublin argued that the conclusions to be taken from Reagan's St Patrick's Day statements were:

1. A willingness to assist Britain and Ireland in their efforts against terrorism and to speak out against US support for terrorism.
2. A readiness to speak in encouraging terms of the need for US investment in Ireland (both in the Republic and in Northern Ireland).
3. A willingness to encourage political progress and the process of peaceful reconciliation in Northern Ireland.[103]

The telegram noted that Clark's visit in 1981 saw them come 'very close' to achieving 'a pro-nationalist tilt in American foreign policy on Ireland'. The signals from Clark, combined with State Department policy, led to a conclusion that, despite the White House's willingness 'to view our case sympathetically', there were 'inhibitions on the room for maneuver of those who are well disposed and who would wish to make public concession to our point of view'.[104] The Irish government's agenda was challenged by the inner workings of the Reagan administration. Central to that agenda was the 'national aim of reunification by agreement' in the Anglo-Irish process 'and a call to the U.S. Administration and the American people to support that aim, particularly vis-à-vis the British Government'.[105] The importance of Clark in achieving those aims was noted by the Taoiseach in a subsequent meeting with Peter H. Dailey (the US ambassador to Ireland, 1982–4) in June 1982: Clark's place in the administration 'had not changed policy but had increased the level of interest in Irish affairs tremendously, in recent years'.[106]

The New Ireland Forum (NIF) in 1983–4 was feted by Irish–American leaders and viewed as a means to finding a workable solution to the conflict. In contrast, opinion was divided in Ireland and Northern Ireland about its value, largely due to the exclusion of some interested parties. Constitutional nationalist parties (Fianna Fáil, Fine Gael, SDLP and Labour) were invited to participate, whereas Sinn Féin was excluded due to its connections with IRA activities, and the Unionists were disinterested as they argued that the NIF was a biased process.[107] Reagan's interest in the Anglo-Irish process, but reluctance to be too closely involved, is evident in his telephone conversation with FitzGerald on St Patrick's Day in 1983.[108] The President stated:

> I wanted to take this opportunity to speak to you of my own personal interests in the efforts that you are undertaking to achieve reconciliation between the two Irish communities. You can count on me to do whatever we can to support that effort. Our ambassador, Peter Dailey, keeps me up to date on your thinking, so I hope you will stay in close touch with him.[109]

In turn, FitzGerald explained that, as part of the 'efforts to reconcile the two traditions in Ireland', the NIF had been established. He asked for Reagan's support for it. Cynics would undoubtedly be curious about Reagan's reply: 'Well, we shall retain our good relationship and shall cooperate with you . . . . I think something is happening with our connection. You've begun to fade.'[110] The Taoiseach's connection was fine. Reagan was clearly interested in the progress of the Anglo-Irish process but, following the advice of the majority of his advisers, was manifestly equally keen to avoid commitments to real involvement. Thus, the Reagan administration adhered to a policy of neutrality.

In July 1983, Bush visited Ireland and met FitzGerald and Peter Barry (the Minister for Foreign Affairs, 1982–7). Bush became the highest-ranking official to visit Ireland since Nixon. Although note-takers were not present, the British government learned of the contents of the discussion – albeit at third hand.[111] Half of the meeting was dominated by Northern Ireland. FitzGerald and Barry 'were not seeking any particular action by the Americans, except support against the terrorists and their friends'.[112] Thus, in this meeting, there was no attempt by the Irish government to persuade the Reagan administration to influence the Thatcher government. Following Bush's visit to Dublin, Reagan was invited to visit Ireland. This created some alarm amongst British officials. It was feared that Reagan would be under pressure to refer publicly to the 'Troubles', partly due to the Irish–American lobby, and the Irish government could seek his public support for their policy following the NIF.[113] Thus, the FCO consulted Sir Oliver Wright,

British ambassador to the US (1982–6) about whether the British government should seek to 'discourage' the Reagan administration from accepting the invitation. Wright warned that such a plan was ill advised, as it 'would seem unnecessarily defensive' and have potentially 'serious consequences for Anglo-Irish relations'. Moreover, Wright reassured his colleagues that 'a visit to Ireland by President Reagan might not necessarily be harmful or difficult' to British interests, given that 'the President has so far taken a helpful line on Northern Ireland . . . and that he had refused to become involved in what he regards as a UK internal problem'.[114] Wright's advice was passed on to Thatcher, who agreed with the ambassador's analysis.[115] The British clearly understood the potential influence that an American president could wield in the Anglo-Irish process.

The British were confident of Reagan's stance because Northern Ireland was not raised when Thatcher met Reagan at the White House on 29 September 1983.[116] The President was still reluctant to intervene. Instead, it again fell to members of Congress to discuss it with Thatcher before she visited the White House that day. At a breakfast meeting with members of the Senate Foreign Relations Committee, Senator Paul Tsongas (D-MA) questioned Thatcher about the issue, who noted 'the overwhelming wish of the majority community to remain British', but a republican minority 'chose not to accept the ballot' and instead decided 'to resort [to] terrorism'.[117] Congress had issued a resolution in support of the NIF, and its objective for a united Ireland, on St Patrick's Day in 1983; fifty-three Congressmen and twenty-eight Senators sponsored it. Despite this level of congressional interest and support, the Reagan administration still refused to countenance an intervention in the Anglo-Irish process. Indeed, Reagan rejected Kennedy's appeal to dispatch an American peace envoy in October 1983.[118] This non-interventionist stance continued until after his 1984 visit to Ireland and Britain, and the failure of the NIF.

Before Reagan visited Ireland in June 1984, FitzGerald visited the White House earlier that year on St Patrick's Day.[119] FitzGerald began the meeting by discussing Northern Ireland and the NIF. The Taoiseach 'hoped for a constructive outcome'. Not engaging with the NIF, Reagan instead opened up the conversation more broadly: 'what was happening there was all, ostensibly, happening in the name of God, but it was the same God'. The President pondered whether 'a majority of the people there could get together' or if this was prevented, as 'each side had simply been intimidated by its own radical groups'. This was now a familiar comment from Reagan. FitzGerald engaged with the topic and agreed with the President:

> There had been a massive movement in the early 1970s. Politicians of every persuasion had tried to work together within the constraints of the double majority/minority situation, but there had been great pressures. Paisley had tremendous ability to raise fears and passion.[120]

The Taoiseach also met Bush and stated that 'he would like to describe the work of the Forum'.[121] None the less, the Vice-President turned the conversation to the American supply of arms to the IRA. The Irish record shows that, on this point, the administration was 'extremely anxious to move in any way we wished'. FitzGerald 'thanked the Vice-President for his offer and said it was hard to see anything more the Americans could do'. He then returned to the original topic:

> He said that insofar as the Forum was concerned he would like them to regard what emerged as constructive and, perhaps, say some words encouraging a favourable reaction to it on the part of the British. He was not seeking American intervention which might be counterproductive but American understanding and encouragement of bilateral contacts between the Irish and British Governments.

According to the Irish record, Bush again changed the conversation: he 'then went on to say that we [Ireland] would be assuming the EEC Presidency soon'.[122] The administration did not want to engage with the issue.

In a further meeting, FitzGerald sought to discuss the Forum with Shultz. FitzGerald observed that, whilst the British government shared 'the same objective of peace and stability held by the Irish Government', they wanted 'to avoid taking decisions which they felt might risk making matters worse'.[123] Shultz was sympathetic to the British, commenting that 'this was a good physician's rule – avoid anything which might make the patient worse'.

FitzGerald agreed with this principle, but proposed 'that one had to deal with the malaise as a whole and not just individual symptoms'. Shultz asked about FitzGerald's relationship with Thatcher, who 'indicated that they were a lot better than most people could guess'. On the Falklands War, Anglo-American relations and the personality of the British Prime Minister, Shultz summarised: 'She can get mad at you, even if you're helping.'[124] The pattern of these three meetings is clear: the Reagan administration was not willing to become involved in the Anglo-Irish process. Reagan's obvious interest in the Northern Ireland conflict did not translate into policy, so the administration was following the State Department's traditional stance of neutrality. This lack of engagement with FitzGerald's obvious desire to have a substantive discussion about Northern Ireland is echoed in Reagan's diary: 'He's a fine man. I think we gave him some different insights in Central Am. He's very brave & outspoken about the terrorism in N. Ireland. We held a St. Patrick's Day lunch which was great fun.'[125] *The Washington Post* reported that, according to FitzGerald, his visit, part of an emerging tradition for the Taoiseach to visit the US on St Patrick's Day, highlighted the positive work of the NIF and was not just a reminder of the violence of the 'Troubles'.[126] Reagan publicly praised FitzGerald for his work to reduce Irish–American support for violence. In contrast to the emphasis placed on other topics in his diary, *The Washington Post* reported that in his toast and half-hour meeting with FitzGerald, Reagan encouraged the latest Anglo-Irish discussions on Northern Ireland. Indeed, in his remarks, Reagan welcomed the on-going NIF.[127] This public diplomacy mirrored Nixon's informal private conversations on the topic.

Fortuitously for the Republican Party, Reagan's 1984 visit to Ireland and the UK was an opportunity to create excellent footage for the President's re-election campaign. Reagan would be pictured meeting other world leaders at the London Economic Summit and visiting Normandy's beaches to mark the fortieth anniversary of D-Day.[128] His visit to Ireland followed research done in 1980 by Debrett's of London and Hibernian Research of Dublin, which discovered that Reagan's great-grandfather, Michael O'Regan, had emigrated from County Tipperary to England during the 1845–8 famine. Reagan's political advisers understood the potential electoral advantages of photographs and footage of a trip to his ancestral home in an election year, so the President visited Ballyporeen, County Tipperary, and even claimed to be representing forty million Irish–Americans (or, as one reporter asked, forty million voters).[129] An ambitious Charles Haughey, now the Irish opposition leader, reportedly pressured Reagan to declare while he was in Ireland that Irish unity would become a key plank in American foreign policy after his visit.[130] Reagan faced other potential problems during his visit. As *The Washington Post* reported, on his arrival, hundreds of protestors gathered at Shannon airport, which would be indicative of thousands of other protestors during Reagan's visit demonstrating their disenchantment with American policy in Central America.[131] Moreover, as regards the NIF, the same newspaper observed that it added another dimension to the visit because Reagan was proud of his Irish heritage and was scheduled next to visit Thatcher.[132]

Reagan's speech to a joint session of the Irish parliament discussed American foreign policy, economic prosperity and his approach to the Cold War.[133] The President's 'deepest commitment' was 'to achieve stable peace, not just by being prepared to deter aggression but also by assuring that economic strength helps to lead the way to greater stability through growth and human progress'. On Northern Ireland, he placed his opposition to violence in a wider context: 'I repeat today, there is no place for the crude, cowardly violence of terrorism . . . . All sides should have one goal before them . . . to end the violence, to end it completely, and to end it now'. Reagan was characteristically optimistic about the Anglo-Irish process, citing 'legitimate cause for hope . . . . As you know, active dialog between the governments – here in Dublin, and in London – is continuing'. Likewise, the President praised the 'constructive' NIF: 'The Forum's recent report has been praised. It's also been criticized. But the important thing is that men of peace are being heard and their message of reconciliation discussed.'[134] The NIF had concluded in May 1984, taking the position that a future Irish state should be either a fully reunited state, a federal state of Ireland and Northern Ireland, or Northern Ireland under the joint authority of Britain and the Irish government. This provided further context for Reagan's meetings with the Irish and British governments. However, the Anglo-Irish process did not influence the President's recollection of his speech in his diary, preferring as he did to focus on his policies towards Central America.[135]

Prior to his talks with the Irish and British governments, Reagan was advised about the NIF's potential significance. Robert 'Bud' McFarlane (NSA, 1983–5) briefed him that it called for the British 'to cooperate in facilitating movement toward Irish unity', so he encouraged the President 'to avoid direct involvement, while reaffirming our support for all efforts – by both the Irish and British – to find a peaceful and constitutional solution to the problems of North Ireland'.[136] According to Shultz, Reagan should be prepared for Fitzgerald to ask him to use his 'good offices with Mrs. Thatcher' in support of the NIF proposals. Shultz also advised Reagan to reassert American neutrality and support Anglo-Irish dialogue, but not to comment 'on the merits of the report itself'. Shultz further explained that 'the only workable solution seems to be one which can be supported by both governments and by both communities in the North'.[137] Michael Getler, writing in *The Washington Post*, reported that Irish officials hoped to convince Reagan to accept the proposals.[138] However, based on Reagan's remarks to the Irish Parliament, he prioritised other issues. Indeed, his agenda for the Cold War, and in Latin America, underlined the importance of his relationship with Thatcher.[139] This was clear in Shultz's briefing in advance of Reagan's meeting with her:

> While the issue of Northern Ireland is relatively quiet at the moment, the Prime Minister may have to give it greater attention in the months ahead, in light of the just-issued report of FitzGerald's New Ireland Forum. She may inquire about your impressions after your trip to Ireland. Making clear that the U.S. does not wish to intrude into a problem which should be resolved by Anglo-Irish cooperation, you might ask for her assessment of prospects for progress.[140]

Aides such as Meese were proven to have been correct about the administration's priorities. Moreover, Clark, who was no longer NSA (due to the constant debates and conflict over foreign policy), was now Secretary of the Interior, and therefore foreign affairs was not his immediate concern (although he continued to serve the President in some areas of foreign policy, notably as an emissary).[141]

The Taoiseach clearly sought to convince the President of the merits of the NIF. In his speech at Dublin Castle at the dinner held in Reagan's honour on 3 June, FitzGerald explained that its conclusions were 'courageous, realistic, compassionate'.[142] He endorsed it 'to those who would wish to help us all to make progress, particularly the Government, Congress and the people of the United States of America'. Perhaps deliberately pre-empting Thatcher's position in any talks with Reagan on the topic, FitzGerald argued, 'The Forum goes on to express the belief – the belief, not the demand – of nationalists that unity offers the best solution . . . achieved by agreement and consent'. Concluding his remarks, FitzGerald broadened the issue:

> You will forgive me, Mr. President, for having dwelt for some minutes on a problem that is so close to our hearts . . . . It is, alas, only one of the many problems, and threats of violence, in the world to-day, problems to which you and I will be turning our thoughts together tomorrow morning.[143]

The NIF was the lead topic of conversation during the Taoiseach's meeting with the President the following day.

Once again, FitzGerald marked a break in the previously standard order of conversation, whereby Northern Ireland was raised at the beginning. He observed that, since the publication of the NIF's report, the 'situation was extremely difficult' and so the Irish government 'wished to clear the way by removing obstacles such as that presented by people who said that the only answer is a unitary State now'.[144] The Taoiseach believed that 'Thatcher was genuinely concerned' and the British government was 'considering how they would react to the Forum report'. Acknowledging newspaper reports that Thatcher would discuss the NIF with Reagan, and as predicted by Shultz, FitzGerald 'hoped that the President would have a few words with her of encouragement and support . . . on the Forum report'. In response, Reagan suggested 'that from previous conversations he knew she had one thing in her mind – as in the Falklands. What did the people themselves want?'. He then turned the issue around on the Taoiseach: 'How do you deal with that situation?' FitzGerald reverted to his party's policy: 'to try to help people to change their mind . . . . There could be no new and

Sovereign Ireland without the consent of the people, North and South'. Reagan, again, suggested that he 'had the feeling that the majority want peace' but 'they were afraid to stand up to the terrorist minorities in their own camp'. FitzGerald 'said that there was an element of this' and they then briefly discussed a history of the Provisional IRA.[145]

Recalling the visit in his memoir, Reagan focused exclusively on his visit to his ancestral home of Ballyporeen in Country Tipperary.[146] He made no mention of the 1985 Anglo-Irish Agreement, the Anglo-Irish process, or discussion of them with any Taoiseach that he had met. Reagan's 'Irishness' was ostensibly wrapped up in identity and the 'American dream' success story of Irish immigrants, to which he could relate, given Reagan's paternal great-grandfather's migration from Ireland to the US and his own career in Hollywood and politics. Reagan's visit to London was primarily for the G7 Summit, which was hosted by Thatcher (any record of a discussion between the two of them is unavailable at the time of writing).

A few months later, progress in Northern Ireland was undermined by the IRA's attempt on Thatcher's life. Although the Prime Minister survived the bombing at the Grand Hotel in Brighton in October 1984 during the Conservative Party conference, some of her closest allies and friends were amongst its victims.[147] Reagan could empathise, having himself been victim of an attempted assassination in March 1981 and being a standing target of a Libyan 'hit squad' since December of that same year, as per the orders of Colonel Muammar Gaddafi.[148] In a message to Thatcher, Reagan expressed deep sympathy following 'this barbarous act', and emphasised a shared battle against such violence:

> As we recognised in London during the summit, terrorist violence is becoming increasingly indiscriminate and brutal. Because acts such as the one last night are a growing threat to all democracies, we must work together to thwart this scourge against humanity. In the context of our special relationship, I have directed that my experts be available to work with yours to assist in bringing the perpetrators to justice.[149]

Unsurprisingly, the Brighton bomb stalled the Anglo-Irish process. The bombing, coupled with Thatcher's emphatic rejection of the NIF's conclusions, ensured that the outlook for the Anglo-Irish process was bleak. At a summit with FitzGerald in November 1984, Thatcher made it clear that she did not share the optimism of the Reagan administration about the NIF:

> a unified Ireland was one solution that is out. A second solution was confederation of two states. That is out. A third solution was joint authority. That is out. That is a derogation from sovereignty. We made that quite clear when the Report was published.[150]

Thatcher was clearly frustrated: 'Northern Ireland is part of the United Kingdom. She is part of the United Kingdom because that is the wish of the majority of her citizens. The majority wish to stay part of the United Kingdom.' For the Prime Minister, the key problem with the NIF's proposals was even stressed in its main caveat: 'any change in the status of Northern Ireland could only come about by the consent of the people of Northern Ireland'.[151]

For those who sought a revival of the Anglo-Irish process, it was time to 'play the Reagan card' and exploit the Anglo-American 'special relationship' in order to revise Thatcher's thinking. Yet this was unsurprisingly problematic: Reagan was reluctant to intervene. Lord Powell of Bayswater (who served as Thatcher's Private Secretary, 1983–90) supported such a conclusion. When interviewed for this study, Powell recalled that Northern Ireland was simply not a central issue in Anglo-American relations during the 1980s, at the top level at least. Despite Reagan's solidarity with Thatcher on terrorism, he never pressured her to resolve the Northern Ireland conflict. Reagan respected her view that it was a domestic issue and was therefore not an international concern.[152] Nevertheless, as American archival material shows and as mentioned below, Reagan and Thatcher would briefly discuss Northern Ireland. Reagan received a great deal of credit for the advent of the AIA, and American influence would be a factor during the AIA negotiations and announcement of its implementation. As Kennedy recalled, during Reagan's second term, the administration's approach to Northern Ireland evolved and discussion of the 'Troubles' and Anglo-Irish process were no longer prohibited.[153] Prior to his typical meetings with the President, the White House advised that 'we could talk only about the things we were scheduled to talk about. We were told not to get off on other things. So we didn't have a chance'. However, as his presidency progressed, Reagan's attendance at the St Patrick's lunches and conversations there 'gradually become more substantive'.[154]

## Reagan and the 1985 Anglo-Irish Agreement

Writing in his memoir, FitzGerald recalled that his government 'had been encouraged by the reaction in Britain and abroad' following Thatcher's infamous rejection of the NIF's recommendations for solving the Irish question.[155] Given the pressure on Thatcher, and the context of her relationship with Reagan, FitzGerald resolved to approach him about the issue. Donlon, who had left his post as ambassador to the US but still maintained his American contacts, asked Clark to suggest to Reagan that he 'express his concern about the Anglo-Irish situation'.[156] Indeed, Thatcher's position on the NIF's conclusions prompted outrage amongst leading Irish–Americans. O'Neill wrote to Reagan, expressing his 'deep concern' that Thatcher threatened what was 'the best hope for a peaceful, lawful and constitutional resolution to the tragedy of Northern Ireland'.[157] The Speaker praised the President for 'educating Americans to the real threat posed by Irish terrorists', but he argued that any resolution in Northern Ireland 'must be peaceful and political' and 'must involve the reconciliation of the two identities in Northern Ireland and the active participation of the governments of Ireland and the United Kingdom'. For O'Neill, the NIF represented 'the best efforts of moderate elements ... to fashion a political and constitutional framework for achieving a political solution', but Thatcher had derailed it. The Speaker wanted action from Reagan, requesting that he encourage the Prime Minister to renew the Anglo-Irish dialogue about the NIF's conclusions and that she should recognise its 'significant support in Congress and among Irish–Americans interested in bringing peace to the beautiful land of their forebears'.[158] O'Neill was so determined to see some progress in Northern Ireland that he even wrote to Reagan on a second occasion, albeit as a member of the FOI.[159] The ACCIA also sent a letter to Reagan, urging him to discuss Northern Ireland with Thatcher during her forthcoming visit to America. In the letter, Biaggi explained, 'We are cognizant of the need for the United States not to be in the position of advocating or imposing a particular solution', but hoped that Reagan would practise 'some quiet diplomacy . . . in the just pursuit of peace and justice in Northern Ireland'.[160]

Irish–American lobbying provided an opportunity for some political quid pro quo. Considering these appeals, the Reagan administration saw a political advantage to responding favourably to O'Neill's request: it hoped that by directly raising Northern Ireland with Thatcher, the President might gain the Speaker's support for the funding of Contra rebels in Nicaragua. Indeed, an NSC memo noted, 'we hoped to use this as a lever against Tip to get Contra aid moving'.[161] O'Neill frustrated Reagan in this case: the subsequent Iran–Contra affair, in which the Reagan administration illegally financed the Contras, was such a serious scandal that it threatened Reagan's presidency.[162] The Nicaraguan Contras obsessed the President. He even declared them to be 'the moral equal of our Founding Fathers'.[163] Not everyone shared Reagan's sentiments, including O'Neill and the majority in Congress, which resulted in a ban on any US government financial support for the Contras in their struggle against the Marxist Sandinista regime in 1984.

The Reagan administration revised its settled position of non-intervention in Northern Ireland and the President was briefed to discuss the Northern Ireland conflict with Thatcher during their Camp David meeting in December 1984. Shultz suggested that the President should urge the Prime Minister to achieve some progress at the next Anglo-Irish summit, in order to prevent 'a radicalization of Irish–American opinion which would endanger our current bipartisan policy toward Northern Ireland'.[164] Just in case Thatcher raised the failure of a New York court to extradite Joseph Doherty (a 'convicted murderer and IRA gunman'), Shultz's brief said that the US government was 'sympathetic to British concerns' and continued to explore 'possible avenues to prevent future denials on these grounds'. On terrorism, Shultz briefed Reagan that, although the 'IRA continues as the primary British concern', the

British government was 'now also focusing on the threat to NATO, and the threat from terrorism of Middle Eastern origin'. Indeed, given that 'Irish terrorism' was 'now recognized as one facet of a wider international problem', cooperation between Britain and the US was 'excellent' in combating such activities.[165] Despite Shultz's briefing, and the appeals from O'Neill and members of Congress, Reagan failed to raise the subject. It was Thatcher who brought up the issue, perhaps as an act of political pre-emption. As the American record reads, 'Mrs Thatcher said she wished to address the situation in Northern Ireland. Despite reports to the contrary, she and Garret FitzGerald were on good terms and we are work-ing toward making progress on this difficult question.'[166] Only then did Reagan express congressional concerns: 'The President said making progress is important, and observed that there is great Congressional interest in this matter. Indeed, Tip O'Neill has sent him a personal letter, asking him to appeal to Mrs. Thatcher to be reasonable and forthcoming.'[167] Reagan subsequently wrote to O'Neill, overstating the extent of his comments to Thatcher:

> During my meeting with Mrs. Thatcher at Camp David on Decem-ber 22, I made a special effort to bring your letter to her personal attention and to convey your message of concern. I also personally emphasized the need for progress in resolving the complex situation in Northern Ireland, and the desirability for flexibility in the part of all the involved parties.[168]

Reagan's neutrality was clear: nothing specific was mentioned in his meeting with the Thatcher, who conceded nothing. He passed on Thatcher's report:

> While emphasizing the complexity of the situation, Mrs. Thatcher made a point of stressing to me that press reports of her alleged differences with Prime Minister FitzGerald were exaggerated. She also noted that she would be continuing her discussions with Prime Minister FitzGer-ald early in the new year.[169]

Reagan's message to O'Neill was clear: the Anglo-Irish process was progressing and, accordingly, any American intervention was unnecessary, although he had discussed the issue as requested. In contrast to this documentary record, FitzGerald wrote in his memoir that Reagan expressed his concern to Thatcher about the Anglo-Irish process and it was also 'somewhat to the surprise' of the State Department and his advisers. FitzGerald argued that Reagan's 'expression of concern must have been a factor contributing to the more positive approach the British adopted'.[170] However, it was Shultz – along with O'Neill and Biaggi – who had encouraged Reagan to raise the issue. Balancing the competing priorities of his relationship with Thatcher alongside his interest in Northern Ireland and the demands of members of Congress, Reagan displayed political astuteness. He waited for Thatcher to raise the issue in the first instance, and subsequently voiced the concerns of O'Neill and his colleagues. Thus, it was not Reagan criticising Thatcher – he was simply passing on the message from the Speaker that she be 'reasonable and forthcoming'. Reagan brought up the subject without criticising Thatcher himself. He balanced domestic politics and foreign affairs: he had satisfied O'Neill without condemning Thatcher and passed on Thatcher's stance that the Anglo-Irish process was progressing and would not require American intervention. Thus, the President had cooperated with the Speaker, satisfying his demand for action and, similarly, that of other Irish–American Congressmen, while not forcing a quarrel that would have problematised his meeting with the British Prime Minister, soured Anglo-American relations, and taken time away from his foreign policy priorities.

Thatcher again visited Reagan in the US in February 1985, when she also addressed a joint session of Congress. The opportunity to do this was in the gift of the Speaker. Ambassador Wright was informed that O'Neill expected Thatcher to include Northern Ireland in her speech.[171] Thatcher did just that, although she actually used her remarks to criticise NORAID and explain that she and FitzGerald were working together and the Anglo-Irish process was progressing.[172] O'Neill discussed Northern Ireland with Thatcher on the day of her address. It was reported that he sought a resolution but was cautious of telling another government what course to follow.[173] After Thatcher's speech, Reagan once again discussed the issue of Northern Ireland in their White House meeting. Shultz briefed him that the Irish press reported Reagan's correspondence with the Speaker about his previous meeting with Thatcher, which 'sparked interest' in the British government, and that O'Neill and other congressional members of the 'Friends of Ireland' would spend St Patrick's Day in Ireland with leading political figures.[174] Reagan was advised to emphasise to Thatcher that 'Our policy on Northern Ireland has not changed. Despite urgings by some US politicians that we get directly involved, we have no intention of injecting ourselves into this complex and emotional issue.' The message was clear: despite press discussion of the Reagan–O'Neill correspondence, the administration remained detached from the issue and they did not wish to interfere. Nevertheless, the President was advised to explain that he was 'concerned that unless there is the appearance of progress at the next Anglo-Irish Summit, a radicalization could occur in Irish–American opinion which would endanger the current bipartisan support that our Northern Ireland policy enjoys'.[175] Such 'radicalization' of opinion amongst congressional Irish–Americans could, for instance, threaten Anglo-American co-operation with regard to extradition and the tackling of American financing of violence in Northern Ireland. Although the record of this meeting is unavailable, in his memoir, FitzGerald claims that Reagan told the Irish ambassador that he had raised the Irish question with Thatcher and 'the discussion had led him to believe that the Prime Minister really wanted to do something about the problem'.[176] The threat of the consequences of radicalised opinion in Congress had a precedent: Thatcher would not want a repeat of the type of circumstances that banned arms sales to the RUC. As such, Reagan could present his concerns to Thatcher, as an example of the American domestic political debate about matters abroad – in this case, Northern Ireland – influencing US foreign policy – or practical relations with an ally.

Such radicalised opinion, urged on by the INC, threatened the UK–US Supplementary Extradition Treaty in October 1985. In advance of Thatcher's meeting with Reagan at the UN in New York on 23 October 1985, Wright advised that she should convince the administration to work towards the treaty's passage.[177] The Prime Minister should briefly 'describe progress on the Anglo-Irish dialogue' and then 'point to the importance for the fight against terrorism, of the supplementary treaty's going through on the Hill'. She would then be able to 'link the two issues by enquiring about the desirability of a drive to get the treaty successfully through the committee before the recess, so maintaining momentum for the renewed battle, on the senate floor next year'.[178] Thus, Thatcher would be able to offer a positive update on the Anglo-Irish process, which could provide political cover for the administration and sympathetic members of Congress to support the treaty. Sir Geoffrey Howe (UK Foreign Secretary, 1983–9) concurred with this advice, suggesting that, if time allowed, it would be opportune for Thatcher to brief Reagan on the Anglo-Irish discussions and 'it would be worth putting down a marker with the president about the importance to us of the UK/US supplementary extradition treaty'.[179] However, as for securing Reagan's direct involvement, Howe was much more strategic. He stressed 'the need to keep some ammunition in reserve for later, if it becomes clear that there is a real risk of the Treaty being blocked or unacceptably amended, for example when it reaches the floor of the senate'.[180] Evidence that this was discussed is not available. However, that it was deemed worthy of inclusion in Thatcher's meeting with Reagan is indicative of the importance attached to the President and to briefing him on the Anglo-Irish process and his influence in Congress to secure passage of a favourable extradition treaty.

Clark Judge, a former speech-writer for the President, observed that Reagan's intervention was low-key in the Anglo-Irish process, which was in keeping with his approach to friends and allies. Judge speculated that Reagan would have viewed the British position as increasingly untenable, and so he offered some advice in order to be helpful to a political leader with whom he was allied. This advice was meant on the friendliest of terms and it was not a case of political pressure or the official position of the US government.[181] The caveat of Reagan's briefing before his 1985 meeting with Thatcher, and the emphasis that his administration's position was unchanged, are certainly in accordance with Judge's observation. William Clark explained Reagan's intervention on the basis of the domestic political impact of approximately 40 million Irish–Americans and Congress: 'President Reagan had to remind Mrs. Thatcher a time or two to treat her counterpart in Dublin with more dignity, because each time that she did not we'd hear about it from congressional members. She responded.'[182] There would be significant progress in the Anglo-Irish process when the AIA was signed on 15 November 1985.

The AIA meant that the Irish government would be consulted over the affairs of Northern Ireland.[183] FitzGerald credited this development to American pressure on the Thatcher government.[184] Indeed, the British and Irish governments privately acknowledged the importance of Irish–Americans at this stage in the Anglo-Irish process, particularly Reagan and O'Neill. McFarlane briefed Reagan that 'emissaries who came on a private mission' on behalf of Thatcher and FitzGerald requested 'that the president and speaker would endorse the AIA and reiterate their condemnation for violence and terrorism in a joined public appearance'.[185] It was suggested that a joint statement from 'America's two most prominent Irishmen' would 'send a signal of hope and moderation to the people of troubled Ireland'. McFarlane also told Reagan that the British and Irish governments had expressed their hope for American 'tangible, financial support to assist with the economic and social development of those areas that have suffered from the instability'. Thus, the President's statement would 'lay the groundwork for possible future U.S. funding', even though the British government had requested 'some distance between the agreement and a formal request for funding'. A political dimension shaped Reagan's intervention. Likewise, Reagan was balancing domestic and foreign affairs: he wanted to satisfy both Thatcher and O'Neill. McFarlane explained, 'The Speaker is impressed that you are willing, on the eve of your trip to Geneva, to address the Irish question personally in public.' (Reagan was due to meet Mikhail Gorbachev.) Nonetheless, the Reagan administration was serious about the American response to the AIA. Prior to their statements, Reagan met with O'Neill to discuss 'bipartisan, public support' for the AIA and 'to lay the groundwork for possible future U.S. funding in support of the rebuilding of Northern Ireland'. The attendance of other dignitaries underlined the administration's efforts to convince O'Neill of its commitment: Vice-President George Bush, Shultz, Donald T. Regan (White House Chief of Staff, 1985–7), McFarlane, M. B. Oglesby, Jr (Head of Legislative Affairs), Ros Ridgway (Assistant Secretary of State), Ronald K. Sable (NSC), Peter R. Sommer

(NSC), Kirk O'Donnell (O'Neill's senior aide), Wright and the Irish Ambassador, Pádraig MacKernan (1985–91).[186]

In his statement, the President praised the AIA:

> Given the complex situation in Northern Ireland, all may not applaud this agreement . . . the United States strongly supports this initiative, which pledges to both communities in Northern Ireland respect for their rights and traditions within a society free from violence and intimidation.[187]

In his diary, Reagan simply wrote, 'At 9 A.M. Wash. Time P.M.s Thatcher & FitzGerald (Ireland) signed an agreement on bringing peace to Northern Ireland. Tip O'Neill came down & we were photographed together endorsing their action & making statements of support.'[188] In claiming that the AIA would 'bring peace', Reagan either failed to understand the extent of the challenges in Northern Ireland or, perhaps characteristically, viewed the AIA through the prism of his own optimism.

The Reagan administration initially sought to connect the aid programme to their broader policy objectives. Kennedy recalled that the President offered $50 million over five years, although, reflecting the Reaganite agenda, 'most of it was all incentive for the private sector to come in'.[189] When Kennedy and O'Neill approached Donald T. Regan about direct aid, Regan

> indicated he was prepared to get us the money if we were prepared to call off the dogs on the [Edward Patrick] Boland Amendment, which was to end the war with the Contras, in Nicaragua. It was sort of a quid pro quo, and we weren't going to have that.[190]

The political wrangling for aid even saw disagreement between O'Neill and FitzGerald. Frustrated at the lack of activity in the White House on the issue, the Speaker was candid towards the Taoiseach about his conversations with the President: 'Cut the bullshit . . . . Is President Reagan going to go for the larger money or isn't he?' Much to O'Neill's irritation, FitzGerald accurately replied, 'This is a matter that's going to have to be solved here in this country.'[191] Ultimately, American aid to Northern Ireland proved to be a final flourish prior to O'Neill's retirement in 1987, with the House of Representatives unanimously voting in March 1986 for a $250 million aid package (over five years) to Northern Ireland.[192]

Reagan's presidency coincided with two other key developments in Irish–American contributions to the Anglo-Irish process: the extradition of Joseph Doherty and the MacBride Principles. Both cases also came to the attention of the Bush administration. As discussed above, Doherty was the subject of discussion between the Reagan administration and the Thatcher government. Having entered the US illegally using a bogus passport, Doherty was initially subject to deportation by the US Immigration and Naturalization Service in 1982. After some years in custody, Meese (as the US Attorney General) earmarked Doherty for extradition, as he had managed to escape prison following his conviction for murdering a British officer while a member of the IRA. In response, the INC was outraged and 132 members of Congress signed a resolution demanding that Doherty be granted bail and an asylum hearing. In February 1992, the US Supreme Court sided with the Bush administration on the matter.[193]

The objectives of the MacBride Principles can be traced back to the campaign of ACIF during the late 1960s, which wished to highlight discrimination against Catholics on the part of American companies in Northern Ireland. During Reagan's first term, American business activities made the US the largest foreign investor in Northern Ireland's economy. For instance, eleven per cent of Northern Ireland's manufacturing jobs were dependent upon American investment. Allegations of anti-Catholic discrimination in these companies prompted concern from the INC. Collaboration between the INC and Harrison Goldin, the New York City Comptroller (1974–89), resulted in the MacBride Principles: nine fair-employment guidelines for US companies to adhere to in Northern Ireland. They were so named after Seán MacBride, a colleague of McManus, who had served as Ireland's Minister for External Relations (1948–51) and helped establish Amnesty International, despite his past connections with the IRA. Initially, the MacBride Principles were criticised by the British and Irish governments and some leading protagonists, including Hume and Kennedy. For instance, Hume argued that they would deter American investment, just when it should be encouraged. The British government, similarly, suggested that employers could not guarantee security, as many of the principles designed to increase Catholic employment were potentially illegal under the 1976 Fair Employment (Northern Ireland) Act. In this period, MacBride activists failed to see federal legislation passed in the US Congress but, during the 1988 presidential election campaign, Michael Dukakis (D-MA) highlighted his signing of the principles into law while governor of Massachusetts and promised to do so again as president. There was a wider impact. After 1985, the Fair Employment Agency confirmed the MacBride campaign's claim about anti-Catholic discrimination in Northern Ireland. Furthermore, the 1989 Fair Employment (Northern Ireland) Act ensured that all private and public sector employees should be monitored for discrimination; thus, a Fair Employment Commission and a Fair Employment Tribunal were created.[194] Just as Dukakis promoted his support for the MacBride Principles, they would be an important factor in Irish–American politics during the Clinton administration.

## The Bush administration

As Vice-President, George H. W. Bush indicated some interest in Northern Ireland and the Anglo-Irish process, albeit nothing out of the ordinary. For instance, Atkins wrote a letter to him on 3 July 1981, which was dispatched via the diplomatic pouch, about British policy in Northern Ireland.[195] In Bush's role as President of the Senate, he was also briefed on the status of O'Neill's funding bill after the Anglo-Irish Agreement.[196] Following the involvement of the Reagan administration with the Anglo-Irish process, at the 1988 Republican National Convention, the following on Northern Ireland was adopted by the party platform:

> We share a deep concern for peace and justice in Northern Ireland and condemn all violence and terrorism in that strife-torn land. We support the process of peace and reconciliation established by the Anglo-Irish Agreement, and we encourage new investment and economic reconstruction in Northern Ireland on the basis of strict equality of opportunity and non-discrimination in employment.[197]

Bush was elected President of the US in November 1988. As he had been Reagan's Vice-President, Bush's victory was, in many respects, an electoral mandate for continuing with the Reagan epoch.[198]

Although the ending of the Cold War and the collapse of the Soviet Union changed Bush's plans for continuity in Europe and the Middle East, his administration's policy towards Northern Ireland was broadly consistent with the preceding eight years. Nevertheless, developments in Northern Ireland ensured that the foundations of the 'peace process' were secured before Bush handed over the White House to President Bill Clinton (1993–2001) on 20 January 1993. For instance, the American consul-general in Belfast improved its contacts across Northern Ireland, ensuring that the US government enjoyed greater accuracy in reports from there. Thus, the State Department was not surprised by secret talks between Gerry Adams (President of Sinn Féin, 1983 to present) and John Hume in 1988 to establish common ground for nationalists and republicans, or between the British government and the IRA in 1991. Another key development was talks arranged by Peter Brooke, the British Northern Ireland Secretary (1989–92), who was able to bring together all interested parties in Northern Ireland. Brooke's success in holding 'talks about talks' led to the declaration of a temporary ceasefire in 1991. The talks and ceasefire established a model and foundation for similar initiatives during the Clinton era. [199]

Given broader international concerns, continuity of Reagan's policy on Northern Ireland was clear within a few months of Bush's presidency. On St Patrick's Day in March 1989, in the presence of Haughey, Bush explained,

> The U.S. supports the efforts of the Irish and British Governments to use the Anglo-Irish accord and the International Fund for Ireland to address the problems which have too long plagued Northern Ireland. We will continue to support efforts to promote fair employment and investment.[200]

The International Fund for Ireland (IFI), however, proved to be a controversial issue. The fund was designed to support economic and social investment in areas of Northern Ireland that had been subject to the worst of the 'Troubles'. A seven-member board that was appointed by the British and Irish governments would distribute the money. In the period 1986–9, the fund supported 1,299 projects, which, in turn, created more than 8,000 jobs. Many of these projects revolved around recreation and tourism, which resulted in the INC and the ACCIA challenging the distribution of money. In January 1989, Tom King (the British Secretary of State for Northern Ireland, 1985–9) was asked by the FOI to respond to Irish–American accusations that the fund was giving money to those who were not victims of the 'Troubles'. Consequently, the fund supported large awards to two West Belfast-based projects, which stated they would offer jobs to 500 nationalists. These controversies prompted the State Department to reduce American contributions to the fund to $10 million. This was reversed by the efforts of Speaker Thomas Foley (D-WA). He secured American contributions of $20 million for the 1992 and 1993 fiscal years and the appointment of Eugene McCaffrey as America's observer of the fund on 21 March 1990. By the end of Bush's presidency, 70 per cent of the fund's money supported community-regeneration projects in the most disadvantaged parts of Northern Ireland.[201]

Shortly after Bush's inauguration, he received a letter from John J. Finucane, on behalf of the Council of Presidents of Major Irish–American Organizations.[202] In addition to offering his congratulations to the new President, Finucane's motivation for writing was 'a meeting with the appropriate officials . . . to discuss U.S. policy with regard to Irish reunification, the Northern Ireland situation'. His organisation was 'disappointed that our views were dismissed without a hearing by the previous Administration'.[203] The response came, not from the White House, but rather from the Office of Northern European Affairs at the State Department.[204] Eileen Heaphy stressed that American policy was to advocate 'peaceful solutions to the political, economic and social issues of Northern Ireland' and the policy was to support the AIA, while extraditing 'those convicted of serious offenses', such as Doherty, and continuing to 'oppose admitting to the U.S. those who support terrorism, as in the case of Gerry Adams'.[205] Given that his priorities focused on the Soviet Union and the Middle East, Bush was content for the State Department to direct policy for Northern Ireland's affairs.

Irish–American lobbying of the President continued in 1990. Elizabeth Lee (Director, Women's Issues, American Protestants for Truth about Ireland) wrote to Bush, asking him 'to exert all the pressure possible on Great Britain to withdraw from Ireland both politically and militarily'.[206] Lee pointed to wider international politics: 'Ireland has as much right to be re-united as Germany or any other country.'[207] Again, it was Heaphy who replied on behalf of the administration.[208] After reminding Lee of American support for the AIA and the International Fund for America, she stressed that members of the administration 'have found it desirable to raise human rights issues with British officials on several occasions' and that it 'is our understanding that the majority of the people of Northern Ireland still oppose political unification of the Island'.[209]

Northern Ireland was not discussed when the President met with Gerard Collins, the Irish Foreign Minister (1989–92), in January 1990.[210] After seeing Haughey again on 27 February 1990, Bush afforded Northern Ireland a relatively fleeting reference: 'we . . . appreciate Ireland's efforts to promote economic development, security, reconciliation, and peace in Northern Ireland'.[211] In what was presumably an act of electioneering, the Bush administration proclaimed March 1990 to be 'Irish American Heritage Month'. The positive response from Irish–Americans meant that the White House saw the value of another such event, or even a conference about Northern Ireland, which could attract the support of Irish–Americans at the ballot box.[212] During this second year of the Bush administration, Ralph R. Johnson (Deputy, and later Principal Deputy, Assistant Secretary of State, 1989–93) outlined administration policy towards Northern Ireland at a conference on the conflict at the Woodrow Wilson Center in Washington, DC, on 14 May 1990.[213] Again, it was the State Department taking the lead on this issue. According to Johnson, the Bush administration supported the AIA as a means 'to address the social, economic, political and security problems of Northern Ireland'. Furthermore, the administration would promote dialogue, reconciliation, economic development, human rights and opposition to terrorism. However, again it was stressed (by a State Department official) that

> We recognize that while the U.S. can play a positive supporting role, it is up to the Government and people of the United Kingdom, in cooperation with the Government and people of Ireland, to solve the problems of Northern Ireland.[214]

Policy towards Northern Ireland was outlined in support for Brooke's talks and because Irish–American leaders wanted a clear explanation of American policy. The five plans for US policy were dialogue and reconciliation, support for economic development, support for human rights, opposition to terrorism, and support for the IFI.[215] The following day, the 'Council of Presidents' of leading Irish–American organisations was denied entry into the White House for their meeting with an NSC representative because a number of them supported violence in Northern Ireland.[216] The White House was clearly avoiding any involvement.

Despite the President's attempts to avoid involvement in Northern Ireland, the Bush administration was dragged into some controversy due to comments made by Paisley in April 1992. *The Irish News (Belfast)* reported that, following a meeting with Raymond Seitz, the US ambassador to the UK (1991–4), Paisley claimed that Seitz was willing to meet them regularly and he would pass on what was discussed that day to Bush.[217] McManus wrote to Bush asking that he 'immediately deny this claim if it is not true'.[218] Brent Scowcroft, again serving as NSA (1989–93), replied that 'no offer or promise was made to the Reverend Ian Paisley about a "direct line" to the President'.[219] McManus's fury at Paisley's remarks underlines the significance of any involvement by the US President in Northern Ireland.

## Conclusion

Reagan was undoubtedly interested in the Northern Ireland conflict and considered the role the US could play in ending the 'Troubles'. His understanding of the issue lacked nuance and the US government was divided over it (namely, congressional Irish–Americans and Clark, compared to the stance taken by the State Department and Meese), so Reagan ostensibly followed his instinct to remain neutral. During his first term, Reagan discussed it collegiately with Thatcher and her Irish counterparts. Thus, he was a cautious conduit for various interested protagonists and parties who were concerned by, and lobbied about, the 'Troubles'. This interest in, and discussions about, Northern Ireland echoed Nixon's approach. Members of the Reagan administration were aware of the nuanced aspects of the situation, and therefore attempted to guide and control administration policy accordingly. The advice and appeals of other protagonists betrayed the evolving influences on American foreign policy: members of Congress, lobbyists, Clark, the State Department and Meese. The British and Irish governments also sought to influence Reagan.

Reagan, a proud 'Irishman', is relatively ignored in the history of the Anglo-Irish process. This arguably mirrors the Thatcher government's hopes that they would be able to avoid an obvious connection between the AIA and American financial aid to Northern Ireland in 1986. The Anglo-American relationship, particularly its security aspects, was prioritised ahead of intervention in the Anglo-Irish process. Nevertheless, domestic concerns triumphed when Reagan exaggerated to O'Neill that he raised the issue with Thatcher in 1984. Having won re-election, and therefore entering into his final years in office with the prospect of patronage slipping away, Reagan was willing to discuss the issue with Thatcher as a means to gain favour with O'Neill. As such, Reagan's stance towards the Northern Ireland conflict was similar to that of his predecessor. Carter also spoke about Northern Ireland as a means to a political end with his Democratic supporters and allies. Regardless of Reagan's motivations (be they O'Neill, opposition to terrorism generally, or friendly advice for Thatcher), he did intervene more directly than any of his predecessors. This established a trend of increasing US involvement in Northern Ireland. Just discussing the issue with Thatcher meant that Reagan could claim to have encouraged her to act positively, thus satisfying demands from Congress. This credibility was enhanced when the British and Irish governments sought his public support for the AIA.

The British hoped for American neutrality on the Anglo-Irish process, coupled with support for extradition cases and reduction of support for NORAID. Successive Irish governments endeavoured to 'play the Reagan card' in order to influence the Anglo-Irish process to further their objectives. Essentially, both governments failed: Reagan was ultimately prepared to urge Thatcher to act positively in the Anglo-Irish process, but he refused to become consistently and publicly involved, and to the extent that the Irish pressure had hoped to achieve. In addition, advisers to the President were influential in his administration's approach. After Clark's diplomatic errors in 1981, the administration avoided the issue until domestic political pressure and approval from Shultz prompted it to be discussed with Thatcher at Camp David in December 1984. Reagan was able to navigate a middle ground between the competing opinions around him and the evolving situation in Northern Ireland. The Bush administration, concentrating on the end of the Cold War, returned any Northern Ireland policy to the State Department. Yet, as the Paisley–McManus dispute highlights, a curious paradox emerges: even a president that ostensibly is disinterested in a subject could, simply by having their name and office invoked, have a fundamental impact on the Anglo-Irish process. Those interested in Northern Ireland attached great significance to what Reagan and Bush thought about the topic, even if the presidents themselves tried, to varying degrees, not to become involved at all.

This study of the Reagan–Bush administrations and Northern Ireland is revealing. It has demonstrated the importance of the White House, in terms of president and advisers, in the ranking of foreign policy priorities. Moreover, the differing emphases attached to domestic politics that influence foreign policy are clear. Likewise, how foreign policy and domestic politics relate to electioneering is underlined. Reagan courted the Irish–American electorate. In contrast, Bush failed to earn its support, and vacated that political territory in favour of his Democratic opponent in 1992. Indeed, Reagan and Bush's contribution to international affairs more generally also enabled President Bill Clinton to focus on Northern Ireland in a way that his predecessors, even if so inclined, could not. The ending of the Cold War meant that the

Clinton administration could downgrade Anglo-American relations in favour of an intervention in Northern Ireland, despite its status as a major domestic issue for the British government. This marked the beginning of a deeper involvement on the part of the American government during the 1990s. As that decade unfolded, the US overcame any intransigence in British policy and was able to help move the peace process towards a positive conclusion. Reagan's involvement in Northern Ireland represents an embryonic, no matter how symbolic, internationalisation of the Northern Ireland conflict.

## Notes

1. Dobson, *Anglo-American Relations*, 148–50. Alternatively, for recent works that problematise the Reagan–Thatcher relationship, see Richard Aldous, *Reagan and Thatcher: The Difficult Relationship* (London: Hutchinson, 2012); and James Cooper, *Margaret Thatcher and Ronald Reagan: A Very Political Special Relationship* (Basingstoke: Palgrave, 2012).
2. Dumbrell, *A Special Relationship*, 123.
3. 'The Northern Ireland Problem in the USA', NAI: D/Foreign Affairs, 2012/59/1603.
4. Thompson, *American Policy*, 106–7.
5. Interview with Mr Edwin Meese, 19 November 2012. (Meese served as Reagan's Chief-of-Staff when the latter was Governor of California, and later became Special Counsellor to the President and the US Attorney General.) For a discussion about the use of oral history when interviewing protagonists in the political process, see Cooper, *Thatcher and Reagan*, 25–7. For oral history and the use of 'memory' generally, see, for instance, Paul Thompson, *The Voice of the Past: Oral History* (Oxford: Oxford University Press, 2000); and Geoffrey Cubitt, *History and Memory* (Manchester: Manchester University Press, 2007).
6. Republican Party platforms, 'Republican Party platform of 1980', 15 July 1980. Online by Gerhard Peters and John T. Woolley, *The American Presidency Project*, http://www.presidency.ucsb.edu/ws/?pid=25844, accessed 5 December 2014.
7. Report on Republican Convention, 21 July 1980, 'Ireland', NAI: D/Foreign Affairs, 2012/59/1603.

8. Brief, provenance unknown, 'President Reagan and Northern Ireland', NAI: D/Foreign Affairs, 2012/59/1603.

9. Ibid.

10. Ibid.

11. Telegram, R Murphy to Sharkey (Washington), 6 November 1980, 'Gov Reagan and N Ireland', NAI: D/Foreign Affairs, 2012/59/1603.

12. See James Cooper, '"I must brief you on the mistakes": When Ronald Reagan met Margaret Thatcher, 25–28 February, 1981', *Journal of Policy History*, 26:2 (2014), 274–97.

13. Steering Brief, Brief by Foreign and Commonwealth Office, 19 February 1981, Prime Minister's Visit to the United States, 25–28 February, TNA: FCO 82/1110, Visit by Margaret Thatcher, Prime Minister of the UK, to the USA, February 1981: briefs.

14. Ibid.

15. Northern Ireland (If Raised), Brief by the Northern Ireland Office, 19 February 1981, TNA: FCO 82/1110.

16. Ibid.

17. Telegram, From British Embassy (Washington, D.C.) to FCO, 21 February 1981, TNA: CJ 4/3446, Sale of United States weapons for use by the Royal Ulster Constabulary (RUC): consultation between officials and advice to the Secretary of State.

18. Peter Fearon, 'Carter's ban on RUC arms sale may be lifted by Reagan', *Irish Press*, 6 February 1981, TNA: CJ 4/3446.

19. Memorandum, Alexander Haig to Ronald Reagan, 'Visit of Prime Minister Thatcher', Briefing Book re: visit of British Prime Minister Thatcher, February 25–28, 1981 (Binder 1/2), Box 91434 (RAC 1), Executive Secretariat, NSC: VIP Visits, Ronald Reagan Library (hereafter Ronald Reagan Library).

20. Ibid.

21. Department of State Briefing Paper, Northern Ireland, Briefing Book re: Visit of British Prime Minister Thatcher, 02/25/1981-02/28/1981 (2 of 2), Box 91434 (RAC Box 1), Reagan Library.

22. Ibid.

23. Reuters, 'Deny aid to guerrillas in Ireland, Reagan asks', *The Globe and Mail*, Wednesday, 18 March 1981, accessed via LexisNexis, 3 June 2013 (a Canadian newspaper; page number unknown).

24. See 'No.10 record of conversation (MT-US Senate Members) *[Reagan Administration, defence, nuclear weapons, Soviet Union, Poland, economy, socialism, NATO]*', Thursday, 26 February 1981, accessed via http://www.margaretthatcher.org/document/127292, 11 August

2014; 'No.10 note of conversation (Reagan–Thatcher meeting) *[plenary session]*', Thursday, 26 February 1981, accessed via http://www.margaretthatcher.org/document/113943, 11 August 2014.

25. Francis X. Clines, 'About Washington: A nonlyrical view of the Irish Troubles', *The New York Times*, Monday, 16 March 1981, A10.
26. Ronald Reagan, 'Statement on St. Patrick's Day', 17 March 1981. Online by Gerhard Peters and John T. Woolley, *The American Presidency Project*, http://www.presidency.ucsb.edu/ws/?pid=43547, accessed 31 July 2013.
27. Lee Lescaze, 'Reagan offers "good offices" in Ulster strife', *The Washington Post*, Wednesday, 18 March 1981, A5.
28. Telegram, Ambassador (Wash DC) to Asst Sec Neligan (HQ), 2 June 1981, 'President Reagan and Senator Kennedy', NAI: D/Foreign Affairs, 2012/59/1603.
29. Ibid.
30. Telegram, From Washington to FCO, 13 July 1981, 'US Foreign Policy', TNA: PREM 19/1152, USA. United States foreign policy; nuclear non-proliferation; part 1.
31. Ibid.
32. Telegram, M Burke (HQ) to Ambassador London, 15 July 1981, 'Following for your information is the text of a letter handed over to President Reagan on 14 July, 1981', NAI: D/Foreign Affairs, 2012/59/1603.
33. Telegram, Ambassador (Washington DC) to Asst Sec Neligan (HQ), 'Representations to President', 15 July 1981, NAI: D/Foreign Affairs, 2012/59/1603.
34. Ibid.
35. Letter, Ronald Reagan to Garret FitzGerald, 23 July 1981, NAI: D/Foreign Affairs, 2012/59/1603.
36. Ibid.
37. UKE Washington to FCO, 'Irish Prime Minister's Letter to President Reagan', Thursday, 30 July 1981, accessed via http://www.margaretthatcher.org/document/125275, 11 August 2014.
38. Wilson, *Irish America*, 194.
39. News, 'Reagan still steers clear of jail fast', *Belfast News Letter*, 21 July 1981, TNA: CJ 4/3914, Security issues in Northern Ireland. For the breakfast meeting, see Memorandum of conversation, 20 July 1981, 'Bilateral meeting with President Reagan', TNA: FCO 82/1093, Bilateral talks between Ronald Reagan, US President, and Margaret Thatcher, UK Prime Minister, Chateau Montebello, Ottawa, 20 July 1981.

40. Margaret Thatcher, Speech at Stormont Castle lunch, Thursday, 28 May 1981, accessed via http://www.margaretthatcher.org/document/ 104657, 11 August 2014.

41. Ibid.

42. Letter, UKE Washington to FCO, 'Prime Minister's Stormont Speech, 28 May', Friday, 5 June 1981, accessed via http://www. margaretthatcher.org/document/126188, 1 August 2014.

43. Ibid.

44. Telegram, From Washington to FCO, 'Northern Ireland Hunger Strikes', 15 July 1981, TNA: CJ 4/3914.

45. Ibid.

46. Telegram, Ambassador (Washington) to HQ, 13 August 1981, 'Conversation with Deputy Secretary of State William Patrick Clark', NAI: D/Foreign Affairs, 2012/59/1603.

47. Ibid.

48. Paul Kengor and Patricia Clark Doerner, *The Judge: William P. Clark, Ronald Reagan's Top Hand* (San Francisco: Ignatius Press, 2007), 232.

49. Miller Center, 'Interview with John Hume', University of Virginia, 29 September 2005, http://millercenter.org/oralhistory/interview/ john_hume, accessed 2 October 2015.

50. Miller Center, 'Interview with Edward M. Kennedy (3/20/2006)', University of Virginia, 20 March 2006, http://millercenter.org/ oralhistory/interview/edward_m_kennedy_3-20-2006, accessed 2 October 2015.

51. Ibid.

52. Wilson, *Irish America*, 195.

53. Memorandum, Richard V. Allen to Ronald Reagan, 'Your Meeting with John Louis: A Few Key Points for the Record', Monday, November 9, 1981, United Kingdom 9/1/81–3/31/82 [4 of 4], Box 20, Executive Secretariat, NSC: Records, Country File, Reagan Library.

54. Reuters, 'Reagan backs Ulster's efforts', *The New York Times*, Saturday, 5 December 1981, 3.

55. William Borders, 'Haig aide's remark on Irish unification stirs furor in Britain', *The New York Times*, Wednesday, 9 December 1981, A1.

56. 'U.S. Administration attitudes to Northern Ireland', Brief for Minister, Anglo-Irish Affairs, December 1982, NAI: D/Foreign Affairs, 2012/59/1559.

57. Ibid.

58. Letter, PKC Thomas (Republic of Ireland Department, FCO) to JS Wall (British Embassy, Washington D.C.), 'President Reagan's letter to Dr FitzGerald', 1 February 1982, TNA: CJ 4/3914.
59. Telegram, From Dublin to FCO, 7 December 1981, TNA: CJ 4/3914.
60. Ibid.
61. Ibid.
62. Letter, PKC Thomas (Republic of Ireland Department, FCO) to JS Wall (British Embassy, Washington D.C.), 'President Reagan's letter to Dr FitzGerald', 1 February 1982, TNA: CJ 4/3914.
63. Ibid.
64. Letter, JS Wall (British Embassy, Washington D.C.) to PKC Thomas (Republic of Ireland Department, FCO), 'President Reagan's letter to Dr FitzGerald', 22 February 1982, TNA: CJ 4/3914.
65. Ibid.
66. Telegram, Ambassador (Washington) to Secretary HQ, 25 November 1981, NAI: D/Foreign Affairs, 2012/59/1603.
67. Ibid.
68. Ronald Reagan, 'Remarks in New York, New York, at the 84th annual dinner of the Irish American Historical Society', 6 November 1981. Online by Gerhard Peters and John T. Woolley, *The American Presidency Project*, http://www.presidency.ucsb.edu/ws/?pid=43221, accessed 5 December 2014.
69. Interview with Lord (Douglas) Hurd, 20 June 2012.
70. Margaret Thatcher, House of Commons P[M]Qs, Tuesday, 8 December 1981, accessed via http://www.margaretthatcher.org/document/104757, 5 September 2013.
71. Letter, AKC Wood (APS/Lord Privy Seal) to AJ Coles (10 Downing Street), 'Northern Ireland: Mr Clark's remarks', 10 December 1981, TNA: CJ 4/3845, United States Involvement in Northern Ireland and visits to the USA by Northern Ireland politicians.
72. Telegram, From Washington to FCO, 9 December 1981, 'Clark visit to London', TNA: PREM 19/1152.
73. Telegram, From Washington to FCO, 'President Reagan's National Security Adviser', 7 January 1982, TNA: CJ 4/3914.
74. Ibid.
75. Telegram, Washington to FCO, 'Northern Ireland: St Patrick's Day Statement', 10 March 1982, TNA: CJ 4/3846, United States Investments in Northern Ireland.
76. Ibid.
77. Telegram, Washington to FCO, 'Northern Ireland: St. Patrick's Day', 10 March 1982, TNA: CJ 4/3846.

78. Ibid.
79. 'Attitudes of current U.S. Administration on Northern Ireland', March 1982, NAI: D/Foreign Affairs, 2012/59/1604.
80. Ibid.
81. AP, 'Irish leader celebrates the day with Reagan', *The New York Times*, Thursday, 18 March 1982, B8.
82. Ibid.
83. 'Meeting between the Taoiseach President Reagan, White House, March, 17th 1982', NAI: D/Foreign Affairs, 2012/59/1603.
84. Ibid.
85. Letter, Charles Haughey to Ronald Reagan, 17 April 1982, NAI: D/Foreign Affairs, 2012/59/1603.
86. Ibid.
87. Telegram, FCO to British Embassy in Washington, 1 April 1982, 'Northern Ireland Constitutional Proposals: Message from Lord Carrington to Mr Haig', TNA: CJ 4/3914.
88. Ibid.
89. Letter, RA Harrington (Northern Ireland Office) to Patrick Eyers (Republic of Ireland Department), Foreign and Commonwealth Office, 'Commander Dennis Blair, National Security Council', 7 June 1982, TNA: CJ 4/3914.
90. Ibid.
91. 'Record of a meeting between the Prime Minister and the President of the United States of America on Wednesday 9 June 1982 at 10 Downing Street at 0945', TNA: PREM 19/943, USA. Visit to UK by President Reagan, June 1982: meetings with Prime Minister; part 2.
92. 'President Reagan's visit to London, 7–9 June 1982, Talks with the Prime Minister, 9 am Wednesday, 9 June, Steering brief, Brief by the Foreign and Commonwealth Office, 4 June 1982', TNA: PREM 19/943.
93. Ibid.
94. Visit of American Vice President, 23–25 June 1983, 'Northern Ireland Anglo/Irish Relations, Points to Make', TNA: FCO 82/1373, Visit by George H W Bush, Vice President of the USA, to the UK, June 1983.
95. Visit of Minister for Foreign Affairs to Washington DC, 29 September 1982, NAI: D/Foreign Affairs, 2012/59/1581.
96. 'Meeting with Judge William P Clark, National Security Adviser, at the White House, 4 October, 1982', NAI: D/Foreign Affairs, 2012/59/1581.
97. Ibid.

98. George P. Shultz, *Turmoil and Triumph: Diplomacy, Power, and the Victory of the American Ideal* (New York: Charles Scribner's Sons, 1993).

99. 'U.S. Administration attitudes to Northern Ireland', Brief for Minister, Anglo-Irish Affairs, December 1982, NAI: D/Foreign Affairs, 2012/59/1559.

100. Ibid.

101. Letter, Ronald Reagan to Garret M. FitzGerald, 20 December 1982, NAI: D/Foreign Affairs, 2012/59/1603.

102. Letter, Garret FitzGerald to Ronald Reagan, 21 December 1982, NAI: D/Foreign Affairs, 2012/59/1603.

103. Telegram, J Sharkey (Washington) To M. Hennessy (HQ), 4 November 1982, NAI: D/Foreign Affairs, 2012/59/1603.

104. Ibid.

105. D. M. Neiligan, Call by American Ambassador, 13 May 1982, NAI: D/Foreign Affairs, 2012/59/1603.

106. Roinn an Taoisigh, 9 June 1982, 'The Taoiseach today, in the absence of the Minister for Foreign Affairs, met Ambassador Dailey, at the Ambassador's request', NAI: D/Foreign Affairs, 2012/59/1603.

107. Wilson, *Irish America*, 240–2.

108. Ronald Reagan Presidential Library, Head of State Files, Memorandum of Telephone Call between Reagan and FitzGerald, 17 March 1983, accessed via *The Reagan Files*, http://www.thereaganfiles.com/19830517-hos.pdf, 9 August 2015.

109. Ibid.

110. Ibid.

111. Letter, AC Goodison (British Embassy, Dublin) to PHC Eyers (Republic of Ireland Department, FCO), 'Visit of Vice President Bush to Dublin: 4–7 July', 15 July 1983, TNA: FCO 82/1379, Relations between the USA and Northern Ireland.

112. Ibid.

113. Letter, RB Bone (Private Secretary, Foreign and Commonwealth Office) to AJ Coles (10 Downing Street), 'Possible visit to the Irish Republic by President Reagan', 22 December 1983, TNA: PREM 19/1292, Possible visit to Republic of Ireland by President Reagan.

114. Ibid.

115. Letter, From the Private Secretary (10 Downing Street) to Roger Bone (Foreign and Commonwealth Office), 'Possible Visit to the Irish Republic by President Reagan', 28 December 1983, TNA: PREM 19/1292.

116. Thatcher and Reagan held two meetings: a tête-à-tête with just note-takers and a working lunch, which was attended by Howe, Shultz,

Clark, Regan, Louis and other aides from each country. See 'Record of a conversation between the prime minister and the president of the United States at the White House at 1137 hours on Thursday, 29 September 1983' and 'Record of a conversation at a working lunch given by the president of the United States for the prime minister at the White House at 1240 on Thursday, 29 September 1983', TNA: PREM 19/1153, Prime Minister's visit to Washington, September 1983; part 3.

117. Prime Minister's Visit to Washington: Summary record of breakfast with Senate Foreign Relations Committee on 29 September 1983, TNA: PREM 19/1153.

118. Wilson, *Irish America*, 240–1.

119. 'Taoiseach's Meeting with President Reagan, White House, 16th March, 1984', NAI: D/Taoiseach, 2014/105/824.

120. Ibid.

121. Taoiseach's Visit to America, 'Meeting with Vice-President Bush, 14 March, 1984', NAI: D/Taoiseach, 2014/105/824.

122. Ibid.

123. Cable, Washington to HQ, 'Meeting between Taoiseach, Dr Garret FitzGerald and U.S. Secretary of State George Shultz: 16th March 1984, Washington DC', NAI: D/Taoiseach, 2014/105/824.

124. Ibid.

125. Douglas Brinkley (ed.), Ronald Reagan, *The Reagan Diaries* (New York: HarperCollins, 2007), Friday, 16 March to Sunday, 18 March 1984, 226.

126. Michael Getler, 'Reagan praises Irish leader's peace tries', *The Washington Post*, Saturday, 17 March 1984, A18.

127. Ibid.

128. See, for instance, Cannon, *President Reagan*, 424–87.

129. Ibid., 406.

130. Alfred McCreary, 'Americans don't know Ireland', *Christian Science Monitor*, Monday, 16 April 1984, 18.

131. Lou Cannon and Michael Getler, 'Reagan pledges U.S. will meet threats to peace; his arrival in Ireland greeted by protestors', *The Washington Post*, 2 June 1984, A16.

132. Ibid.

133. 'Address Before a Joint Session of the Irish National Parliament June 4, 1984', *The Public Papers of Ronald W. Reagan*, Ronald Reagan Presidential Library, accessed via http://www.reagan.utexas.edu/archives/speeches/1984/60484a.htm, 3 September 2013 (hereafter just URL).

134. Ibid.

135. Reagan, *The Reagan Diaries*, Monday, 4 June 1984, 243.
136. Memorandum for the President, From: Robert C. McFarlane, Subject: Your European Trip: Bilateral Aspects, 18 May 1984, The President's Trip to Europe: Ireland, UK and Normandy (1 of 6) RAC Box 20, 06/01/1984–06/10/1984 (Binder), Office of Coordination, NSC: Records, Box 10, Reagan Library.
137. Memorandum, George P. Shultz to The President, Subject: Your Trip to Ireland: Setting and Issues, The President's Trip to Europe: Ireland, UK and Normandy (1 of 6) RAC Box 20, 06/01/1984–06/10/1984 (Binder), Office of Coordination, NSC: Records, Box 10, Reagan Library.
138. Michael Getler, 'Reagan told of growing violence; President tells Irish U.S. "will not interfere"', *The Washington Post*, Tuesday, 5 June 1985, A10.
139. See, for instance, Sally-Ann Treharne, *Reagan and Thatcher's Special Relationship: Latin America and Anglo-American Relations* (Edinburgh: Edinburgh University Press, 2015).
140. Memorandum for: The President, From: George P. Shultz, Subject: Your Trip to the United Kingdom: Setting and Issues, 14 May 1984, The President's Trip to Europe: Ireland, UK and Normandy (1 of 6) RAC Box 20, 06/01/1984–06/10/1984 (Binder), Office of Coordination, NSC: Records, Box 10, Reagan Library.
141. See Kengor and Doerner, *The Judge*, 230–326.
142. 'Address of An Taoiseach, Dr. Garret FitzGerald T.D. at Dinner in Honour of President Ronald Reagan, Dublin Castle, 3 June, 1984', NAI: D/Taoiseach, 2014/105/487.
143. Ibid.
144. 'Taoiseach's Meeting with President Reagan, 4th June, 1984', NAI: D/Taoiseach, 2014/105/824.
145. Ibid.
146. Ronald Reagan, *An American* Life (London: Simon & Schuster, 1990), 373.
147. Vinen, *Thatcher's Britain*, 216.
148. Our own Correspondent, 'Gadafy denies ordering Reagan's assassination', *The Guardian*, Monday, 7 December 1981, 6.
149. Cable, Ronald Reagan to Margaret Thatcher, 12 October 1984, United Kingdom: Prime Minister Thatcher, (8407695 – 8409063), Executive Secretariat, National Security Council: Head of State File: Records, Box 36, Reagan Library.
150. Margaret Thatcher, Press Conference following Anglo-Irish Summit, Monday, 19 November 1984, http://www.margaretthatcher.org/document/105790, accessed 31 July 2013.

151. Ibid.

152. Interview with Lord (Charles) Powell of Bayswater, 20 June 2012.

153. Miller Center, 'Interview with Edward M. Kennedy (3/20/2006)'.

154. Ibid.

155. Garret FitzGerald, *All in a Life: An Autobiography* (London: Macmillan, 1991), 527.

156. Ibid.

157. Letter, Thomas P. O'Neill to Ronald Reagan, 13 December 1984, 8434471, Congressional Correspondence by member (L-Z), Box 90520, Chris Lehman, Files (4/18) [0], Reagan Library.

158. Ibid.

159. Letter, Thomas P. O'Neill, Jr. et al. to Ronald Reagan, 20 December 1984, Thatcher Visit – Dec 84 [3], Box 90902, European and Soviet Affairs Directorate, NSC: Records, Reagan Library.

160. Letter, Mario Biaggi et al. to Ronald Reagan, 17 December 1984, 834470, Congressional Correspondence by member (L-Z), Box 90520, Chris Lehman, Files (4/18) [0], Reagan Library.

161. Farrell, *Tip O'Neill*, 624.

162. See, for instance, Michael Schaller, *Ronald Reagan* (Oxford: Oxford University Press, 2011), 73–80.

163. Ronald Reagan, 'Remarks at the Annual Dinner of the Conservative Political Action Conference, Friday 1 March, 1985', accessed via: http://www.reagan.utexas.edu/search/speeches/speech_srch.html, 13 November 2013.

164. Memorandum, George P. Shultz to Ronald Reagan, 20 December 1984, 'Your meeting with Margaret Thatcher, Prime Minister of the United Kingdom, December 22, 1984', United Kingdom: Prime Minister Official Visit, 22 December 1984 (2/3), Box 91440 (RAC 6), Executive Secretariat, NSC: VIP Visits, Reagan Library.

165. Ibid. (Interview with Sir Bernard Ingham, 28 May 2012: Ingham (Margaret Thatcher's Chief Press Secretary, 1979–90) recalled that, whereas the subject of Northern Ireland was always on the margins of discussions between Reagan and Thatcher, the two governments shared their vehement opposition to terrorism generally. For Ingham, Reagan's contribution to the Anglo-Irish process was his opposition to violence.)

166. Memorandum of Conversation, Meeting with British Prime Minister Margaret Thatcher, Participants: The President, The Vice President, Secretary Shultz, Robert C. McFarlane, Ambassador Price, Assistant Secretary Burt, Peter R. Sommer, NSC, Mrs. Thatcher, Ambassador Wright, Robin Butler, Principal Private Secretary to

Mrs. Thatcher, Charles Powell, Private Secretary to Mrs. Thatcher, Date, Time and Place: December 22, 1984, Camp David, 10: 40 a.m.–11: 10 a.m., Private Meeting, Aspen Lodge, 11:30 a.m.–1:25 p.m., Expanded Meeting and Lunch, Laurel Lodge, 22 December 1984, Thatcher Visit, Dec 84 [1], Box 90902, European and Soviet Affairs Directorate, NSC: Records, Reagan Library.

167. Ibid.
168. Letter, Ronald Reagan to Thomas P. O'Neill, 9 January 1985, Congressional Correspondence by member (L-Z), Box 90520, Chris Lehman Files (4/18) [0], Box 3, Reagan Library.
169. Ibid.
170. FitzGerald, *All in a Life*, 527.
171. Brummer, 'The greening of the White House', 21.
172. Margaret Thatcher, Speech to Joint Houses of Congress, Wednesday, 20 February 1985, accessed via http://www.margaretthatcher. org/document/105968, 1 August 2013.
173. Brummer, 'The greening of the White House', 21.
174. Memorandum, George P. Shultz to Ronald Reagan, 15 February 1985, 'Your meeting with Margaret Thatcher, Prime Minister of the United Kingdom, February 20, 1985', United Kingdom: Prime Minister Thatcher Official Visit, 02/20/1985 (1 of 2), Box 91440 (RAC Box 6), Executive Secretariat, NSC: V.I.P. Visits, Reagan Library.
175. Ibid.
176. FitzGerald, *All in a Life*, 535.
177. Telegram, From Washington to FCO and UKDEL NASSAU, 'UK–US Supplementary Extradition Treaty', 17 October 1985, TNA: PREM 19/1660, Prime Minister's visit to New York and the United Nations, October 1985; part 5.
178. Ibid.
179. Telegram, From FCO to UKDEL NASSAU and Washington, 21 October 1985, 'Following for prime minister's and secretary of state's parties', TNA: PREM 19/1660.
180. Ibid.
181. Interview with Clark S. Judge, 19 November 2012.
182. Miller Center, 'Interview with William P. Clark', University of Virginia, 17 August 2003, http://millercenter.org/oralhistory/interview/william-clark, accessed 2 October 2015.
183. Vinen, *Thatcher's Britain*, 217. For the Anglo-Irish Agreement, see, for instance, Thomas Hennessey, *The Northern Ireland Peace Process: Ending the Troubles?* (Dublin: Gill & Macmillan, 2000), 19–66; and Feargal Cochrane, *Unionist Politics and the Politics of*

*Unionism since the Anglo-Irish Agreement* (Cork: Cork University Press, 1997).

184. Wilson, *Irish America*, 245.
185. 'Meeting with House Speaker Tip O'Neill, Date: November 15, 1985, Location: Oval Office and Press Room, Time: 10:00–10:15 a.m., From: Robert C. McFarlane/M.B. Oglesby, Jr.', Meeting with Tip O'Neill & Irish & UK Ambassadors 11/15/85, Box 10, Coordination Office, National Security Council: Records, Reagan Library. (According to FitzGerald, the emissaries were Donlon for the Irish and Robert Armstrong, Secretary of the Cabinet, for the UK: FitzGerald, *All in Life*, 542.)
186. Ibid.
187. Ronald Reagan, 'Statement on the United Kingdom–Ireland Agreement Concerning Northern Ireland, November 15, 1985', accessed via http://www.reagan.utexas.edu/archives/speeches/1985/111585a.htm, 1 August 2013.
188. Brinkley, Reagan, *The Reagan Diaries*, Friday, 15 November 1985, 368.
189. Miller Center, 'Interview with Edward M. Kennedy (2/27/2006)', University of Virginia, 27 February 2006, http://millercenter.org/oralhistory/interview/edward_m_kennedy_2-27-2006, accessed 2 October 2015.
190. Ibid.
191. Ibid.
192. The package was delayed due to debates about a new extradition treaty between the UK and US. Ultimately, the American contribution to the International Fund for Ireland was passed at $120 million – over three years – in July 1986. See Wilson, *Irish America*, 254–6.
193. Thompson, *American Policy*, 157.
194. Wilson, *Irish America*, 269–75.
195. Letter, Nicholas Henderson to The Honorable George Bush, 8 July 1981, Ireland – 1981 [19767-017], Donald P. Gregg Files – Country Files, Office of National Security Affairs, Restrictions: Ireland 1981 through Brazil 1982, Office of Vice President George Bush, George Bush Library (hereafter Bush Library).
196. Memorandum, Don Gregg and Samuel Watson to the Vice President, 'Northern Ireland: Will Tip O'Neill's $50 Million Help?', 27 March 1986, Ireland – 1986 [OA/ID 19814-202], Donald P. Gregg Files – Country Files, Office of National Security Affairs, Restrictions: Bahrain 1986 through Italy 1986, Office of Vice President George Bush, Bush Library.

197. Republican Party platforms, 'Republican Party platform of 1988', 16 August 1988. Online by Gerhard Peters and John T. Woolley, *The American Presidency Project*, http://www.presidency.ucsb.edu/ws/?pid=25846, accessed 5 December 2014.

198. For George H. W. Bush's presidency, see, for instance, Meeneskshi Bose, Meena Bose and Rosanna Perotti (eds), *From Cold War to New World Order: The Foreign Policy of George H.W. Bush* (London: Praeger, 2000); and John Robert Green, *The Presidency of George H.W. Bush* (Lawrence: University Press of Kansas, 2015).

199. Thompson, *American Policy*, 145–7.

200. George Bush, Statement on Meeting with Prime Minister Charles Haughey of Ireland, 17 March 1989, *The Public Papers of George H. W. Bush*, George Bush Presidential Library, accessed via http://bush41library.tamu.edu/archives/public-papers/203, 5 December 2014 (hereafter only URL).

201. Thompson, *American Policy*, 147.

202. Letter, John J. Finucane (Council of Presidents of Major Irish American Organizations) to Honorable George Bush, 25 January 1989, 009746, CO073, WHORM: Subject File, Bush Presidential Records, Bush Presidential Library (hereafter Bush Library).

203. Ibid.

204. Letter, Eileen M. Heaphy (Acting Director, Office of Northern European Affairs, United States Department of State) to John J. Finucane (National President, American Irish PEC [Political Education Committee]), 22 March 1989, no document ID, CO073, WHORM: Subject File, Bush Presidential Records, Bush Library.

205. Ibid.

206. Letter, Elizabeth B. Lee, Ph.D. to President Bush, 29 March 1990, 129952, CO167, WHORM: Subject File, Bush Presidential Records, Box 1, Bush Library.

207. Ibid.

208. Letter, 27 April 1990, Eileen M. Heaphy (Director, Office of Northern European Affairs) to Elizabeth B. Lee, Ph.D (Director, Women's Issues), no ID, CO167, WHORM: Subject File, Box 1, Bush Presidential Records, Bush Library.

209. Ibid.

210. Memorandum of Conservation, Meeting with Gerard Collins of Ireland, 12 January 1990, Oval Office, accessed via George Bush Library, http://bush41library.tamu.edu/files/memcons-telcons/1990-01-12-Collins.pdf, 5 December 2014.

211. George Bush, Remarks Following Discussions with Charles Haughey, Prime Minister of Ireland and President of the European Council, 27 February 1990, accessed via http://bush41library.tamu.edu/archives/public-papers/1592, 5 December 2014.
212. Thompson, *American Policy*, 150.
213. Statement by Ralph R. Johnson, Deputy Assistant Secretary of State for European and Canadian Affairs, before the Woodrow Wilson Center, Washington, D.C., 14 May 1990, 'U.S. Policy Towards Northern Ireland', National Security Council, Adrian Basora Files, Country File, Ireland, [CFO1429-011], Country Files, OA/ID CF01429-012 to CF01429-014, Bush Presidential Records, Bush Library.
214. Ibid.
215. Thompson, *American Policy*, 151.
216. Letter, 15 May 1990, Kathy Jeavons (Assistant Director for Public Liaison) to Mr. Michael Cummings, White House Office of Public Liaison, Kathy Jeavons Files, Irish American Briefing [07227-031], Kathy Jeavons Files, OA/ID 07227 through OA/ID 07228, Bush Presidential Records, Bush Library.
217. Stephen O'Reilly, 'Paisley claims "direct line" to Bush', *The Irish News* (Belfast), 15 April 1992, 9203352 [OA/ID CF00996], National Security Council, NSC: Confidential Files, 9203281 through 9203483, Bush Presidential Records, Bush Library.
218. Letter, Father Seán McManus (President, Irish National Caucus, Inc.) to The Honorable George H.W. Bush, 23 April 1992, 9203352 [OA/ID CF00996], National Security Council, NSC: Confidential Files, 9203281 through 9203483, Bush Presidential Records, Bush Library.
219. Letter, Brent Scowcroft to Father Sean McManus, 12 May 1992, 9203352, [CF00996], National Security Council, NSC Confidential Files, 9203281 through 9203483, Bush Presidential Records, Bush Library. (N.B. Seán is spelt as Sean in American documents unless otherwise stated.)

For further discussion about Reagan and Northern Ireland, please see: James Cooper, '"The situation over there really bothers me": Ronald Reagan and the Northern Ireland conflict', *Irish Historical Studies*, May 2017, 41:159.

# 4   The Clinton Administration, 1993–2001

## Introduction

The Good Friday Agreement (GFA) is viewed as a successful example of Bill Clinton's foreign policy.[1] Clinton's rhetoric about Northern Ireland established both his opposition to violence and his view that it was comparable with other situations, such as those in Bosnia, the Middle East and Haiti.[2] His engagement with the 'Troubles' thus represented a new and broader mission for US foreign policy, which recognised that it had to reflect a new era of globalisation and interdependence.[3] However, credit for the peace process should not be afforded only to the President's activities. The Clinton administration coincided with a willingness by unionists and nationalists to secure a sustainable peace, an acknowledgement by the republican movement that the war between the IRA and the British government had resulted in a stalemate, and that the 'armed struggle' had negative electoral consequences for Sinn Féin.[4]

Clinton's approach to Northern Ireland is also revealing because of the impact that it had on his administration and, more broadly, America's anti-terrorism policies before 11 September 2001, particularly the internal power struggle between the NSC and the State Department.[5] The focus of the academic literature on the Clinton administration and the 'peace process' is the internationalisation of the Northern Ireland question and the 'Troubles', meaning the involvement of other countries, particularly the US, in chairing and facilitating discussions about the development and implementation of governmental institutions and agreements, including, for instance, the decommissioning of arms and how the peace process began and unfolded.[6] The peace process has also been contextualised by scholarship that argues that the 'Troubles' were indirectly sustained by the Cold War. The ending of the Cold War ultimately ended the environment for revolutionary republicanism to thrive and turned the West's attention to national and ethnic conflicts such as that in Northern Ireland. Subsequently, the importance of the Anglo-American 'special relationship' was essentially downgraded after the Cold War. Furthermore, Anglo-Irish relations benefited from improving trust within the process of European integration.[7] Therefore, this chapter contends that, while Clinton was a significant factor in the GFA, his importance stems from an ability to take advantage of the opportunity for an agreement in Northern Ireland that was the result of a combination of various historical processes.

## The 1992 presidential election

As a candidate for president of the US, Clinton sought to secure the support of Irish–Americans, in a similarly explicit fashion to the Carter campaign sixteen years earlier. Governor Clinton spoke at an Irish–American political meeting in New York in April 1992. He promised that, as president, he would dispatch a special envoy to Northern Ireland and Gerry Adams would be granted a visa to enter the US. Clinton's opponents claimed that he was attempting to secure Irish–American votes for the primary campaign and, ultimately, the general election. In response, Clinton was adamant that his interest in Northern Ireland was a result of his Rhodes scholarship at Oxford University during the late 1960s.[8] Nonetheless, his renewed interest in Northern Ireland and the concerns of Irish–Americans were undoubtedly inspired by the realities of primary politics: in New York, Clinton faced a strong alternative in Jerry Brown, who served as governor of California (in 1975–83 and, again, since 2011).[9] In his memoir, Clinton recalled of his 1992 campaign: 'The most important and enduring encounter I had with an ethnic group was with the Irish.'[10] Even though it risked angering the British, he was 'convinced that the United States, with its huge Irish diaspora . . . might be able to facilitate a breakthrough'.[11]

Anthony Lake, who served as Clinton's foreign policy adviser during the presidential election campaign and as NSA (1993–7), was critical of this electioneering strategy, describing it as 'inflammatory and . . . ill advised'.[12] He added that Clinton was not the first candidate to follow this course.[13] Clinton's campaign echoed the efforts of Carter sixteen years earlier and, similarly, divided opinion. Writing in *The Irish Times*, Conor O'Clery noted that Clinton's criticism of British policy and his vow to appoint a special envoy were welcomed by Irish–American groups but dismayed British diplomats.[14] In her senior thesis at Stanford, Chelsea Clinton would note that her father's involvement in Northern Ireland was a consequence of New York politics.[15]

Clinton believed that Irish–Americans could be relied upon to vote 'as an ethnic bloc' and he was able to convince his audience to set aside their cynicism towards another politician's promises. Clinton's audience believed he understood and empathised with their view on Northern Ireland. An embryonic 'Irish–Americans for Clinton/Gore Association' quickly evolved into the 'Americans for a New Ireland Agenda'. This group sought to convince the new Clinton administration to engage in Northern Ireland in a similar fashion to how, for instance, Seán Donlon and John Hume secured congressional interest during the Carter and Reagan epochs. This new effort was led by Bruce Morrison, a former member of the US House of Representatives (1983–91, D-CT) and peer of Clinton at Yale, and Niall O'Dowd, who founded *The Irish Voice* newspaper in 1987.[16]

The Democratic Party again included Northern Ireland in its 1992 platform. It pledged 'a more active United States role in promoting peace and political dialogue to bring an end to the violence and achieve a negotiated solution' in the context of America's longstanding connections to the British and Irish people and the 'country's commitment to peace, democracy and human rights'.[17] Reflecting Reagan's involvement in the Anglo-Irish process, this pledge was matched by the Republican Party in its own platform: 'We urge peace and justice for Northern Ireland. We welcome the newly begun process of constitutional dialogue that holds so much promise. We encourage investment and reconstruction to create opportunity for all.'[18] However, neither Clinton nor Bush referred to the 'Troubles' at their respective national conventions.[19] Neither was it raised in the presidential debates.[20] Likewise, Clinton did not mention Northern Ireland in his inaugural address as president.[21] Regardless, Northern Ireland was positioned as a factor in American politics. Although the majority of Americans who could claim Irish descent were Protestant in the 1990s, Irish–Americans were typically assumed by political strategists to be a significant component of the Roman Catholic electorate. Catholics were key 'swing voters' and supported the winners of the general elections in the seven presidential contests between 1972 and 1996 inclusive. Therefore, if candidates addressed Catholic concerns, including, presumably, Northern Ireland, that would translate into winning votes.[22]

Clinton won the presidency, albeit with the support of 43 per cent of the popular vote and benefiting from Ross Perot's independent candidacy. Before Christmas 1992, Prime Minister John Major (1990–7), who had succeeded Margaret Thatcher in Downing Street, met with President-Elect Clinton in Washington, DC.[23] According to the *Daily Mail*, Major intended to raise Northern Ireland with Clinton and explain the British position.[24]

## 1993–7

Clinton's involvement in Northern Ireland stemmed from a combination of factors: campaign promises based on longstanding personal interest; lobbying by Irish–Americans, including prominent Democrats; peace-making objectives in foreign policy; and the need for political success. Clinton's interest in the issue was summarised by Senator Kennedy: 'I think he wasn't having a lot of successes in a lot of different places, and this was a process that was going through and that looked like it had some real prospect of making it.'[25] Nevertheless, the President's involvement was significant. For example, Donlon observed that it was impossible to exaggerate Clinton's importance to the development of the peace process.[26] Recalling his time as a special adviser to John Bruton (Taoiseach, 1994–7), Donlon explained that Clinton appeared more informed than even the Taoiseach.[27] Such commitment to the issue arose largely from Clinton's personal connection with key American protagonists. In the summer of 1993, Clinton appointed Jim Lyons as US Observer to the IFI at the US Department of State (1993–7). Lyons was close to the Clintons. He had been Attorney General in Arkansas during Clinton's governorship. Lyons's appointment, and NSC support, prompted the State Department to include $20 million in its 1994 Budget for the IFI.[28]

Irish–Americans expected Clinton to deliver on his campaign promises in his talks with Major. Despite a positive working relationship with Major, Anglo-American relations were initially problematised by Clinton's election success. This came about firstly because Conservative Central Office in London was clearly supporting Bush's re-election campaign, and secondly, related to the first issue, because of a Home Office search of British passport files to see if Clinton had applied for British citizenship while at Oxford in order to avoid the Vietnam draft.[29] Initial relations between Clinton and Major were going to be somewhat awkward.

Major visited the White House in February 1993. Prior to his arrival, members of Congress lobbied Clinton, emboldened by the President's campaign statements. Sixteen members of the US House of Representatives, including Hamilton Fish (R-NY) and Thomas J. Manton (D-NY), asked the President to 'make the issue . . . a top priority in our relations with the United Kingdom'.[30] The members of Congress were 'heartened' by Clinton's public support for the MacBride Principles and supported his 'pledge to appoint a Special Envoy . . . to facilitate the peace process'.[31] Members of the Senate, including Kennedy (D-MA), Christopher J. Dodd (D-CT) and John F. Kerry (D-MA), wrote to Clinton along similar lines.[32] Irish–Americans in Congress were determined to see action from the President. Lake recalls an incident in which a letter about Northern Ireland was sent to Clinton from a member of Congress, who in turn received a presidential response, which 'was absolutely the British, traditional State Department formulation on this issue'.[33] Lake explained that, after Clinton signed it, 'all hell broke loose' on Capitol Hill because the White House was seen to be 'taking the British side', after indications during the presidential campaign that Clinton was more sympathetic to the nationalist position. Now, the administration was 'suddenly coming under pressure politically to do more'. Remembering his meeting with the Irish lobby, which included 'moderates' such as Kennedy, and 'hard-edged folks' like Richard Neal (D-MA), Peter King (R-NY) and Joseph P. Kennedy, Jr (D-MA), Lake commented, 'I was feeling ill. I didn't know much about any of this stuff and they're all over me, "Live up to Clinton's pledges, we need to do the envoy," et cetera.'[34]

The White House's initial failure to grasp the complexities of Northern Ireland was underlined by Clinton's first meetings with the British and Irish prime ministers. Clinton and Major did discuss the possibility of a special envoy to Northern Ireland from the US but Major opposed the plan. Clinton's failure to deliver on his promise of a special envoy prompted the INC to claim that the British government overly influenced the administration on the issue. However, it was the Irish government that was primarily responsible for stalling the envoy proposal. In March 1993, a month after his meeting with Major, Clinton met Albert Reynolds, the Taoiseach (1992–4). Reynolds convinced Clinton to postpone the envoy, as he did not believe it would succeed. He wanted to develop a peace process and accepted that the voices of paramilitaries on both sides of the 'Troubles' would need to be included in the political talks. Reynolds did not wish to frighten either side and thought that an American envoy would be viewed as pronationalist and cause difficulties for Major. Reynolds was public with both of these views and his political efforts culminated in the 1993 Downing Street Declaration (see below).[35] O'Dowd was unsurprised by Clinton's immediate failure to deliver on his campaign promises, although he does recall it within the context of the President's ultimate engagement: 'What's promised and what's delivered are two different things. There were some early setbacks with President Clinton, which really had to do with the time not being right.'[36]

In June 1993, Clinton appointed Jean Kennedy Smith as US ambassador to Ireland (1993–8). The appointment of a Kennedy to such a sensitive post was illustrative of Clinton's savviness both in Democratic politics and in his assurances to Irish–Americans of his sincerity in seeking a solution to the 'Troubles'. However, Smith's appointment was of grave concern to US Ambassador Raymond

Seitz in London. He was concerned by Smith's outlook on Northern Ireland, recalling that 'she wanted to promote the reunification
of both parts of Ireland', and even described her as 'an ardent
IRA apologist'.[37] The longstanding internal debate about Northern Ireland between Irish–Americans, republican lobbyists and the
State Department had been exported back to the British Isles.

In a statement on the peace process in Northern Ireland on
30 October 1993, the President condemned an IRA bombing in
Belfast a week earlier and praised the 'common resolve' of Reynolds and Major in their endeavour 'to work for peace, justice, and
reconciliation in Northern Ireland'.[38] Clinton stressed that America
was 'ready to support this process in any appropriate way'.[39]
Regardless of his interest in the issue, events either side of the Irish
Sea were arguably more influential. On 2 November 1993, the
Irish government leaked a plan for Northern Ireland to the *Irish
Press* that had been written by officials at the Department of Foreign Affairs. The plan essentially was for the British government
to advocate Irish unity. A few weeks later, on 28 November, *The
Observer* reported that the British government – in contrast to
its official position –had engaged for three years in secret communications with the IRA and Sinn Féin. The British government
argued that the consent principle – nothing could be done without
the majority approval of the people of Northern Ireland – had
been maintained during these discussions. On 2 December, Sinn
Féin published *Setting the Record Straight: A Record of Communications between Sinn Féin and the British Government October
1990 – November 1993*. These documents contradicted the British
government's claim that the IRA had informed them that they recognised an end to the conflict and accepted the principle of consent. It would become clear that intermediaries had been the cause
of this confusion. The resulting public mood demanded a policy,
which would clarify the situation and outline the future of the
Anglo-Irish process.[40]

The public was granted its wish. The Downing Street Declaration (DSD, or the 'Joint Declaration') of 15 December 1993
established (in accordance with the Hume–Adams agreement)
that the British government conceded the self-determination of
the Irish people, coupled with a similar concession from the Irish

government that respected the application of self-determination to Northern Ireland, which would become part of a united Ireland if so wished by the majority in the North. Thus, the British government agreed to act as a facilitator for an agreed Ireland, not a united Ireland (until there was majority consent in Northern Ireland for that). The Irish government demanded that, as an act of good faith, the IRA decommission its arms. Moreover, the Irish government's negotiations with Britain – which, for republicans, resulted in a limited achievement with the DSD – were contextualised by economic realities. Ireland simply could not afford the economic cost of Irish unity: Northern Ireland was subsidised to the tune of £5 billion by the British government, which would be unsustainable under rule from Dublin.[41] Also significant was the Taoiseach's relationships with Clinton and Major and, crucially, Clinton's telephone conversation with Major, in which he urged him to 'go the extra mile for peace'.[42] The IRA ultimately declared a ceasefire on 31 August 1994, which enabled Adams and Sinn Féin to participate in subsequent talks. There was much cautious optimism in the American press coverage.[43]

As the British and Irish governments were in agreement, the US administration would not have to worry about appearing to side with one ally over another, and could therefore play a supporting role in any peace process. Responding to the declaration, Clinton described the DSD as 'an historic opportunity to end the tragic cycle of bloodshed'.[44] Again, the President noted his determination to contribute to the peace process: 'I reaffirm the readiness of the United States to contribute in any appropriate way to the new opportunities which lie ahead in Northern Ireland.'[45] Within weeks of the DSD, Clinton told *The Irish Times* that despite the 'special' Anglo-American relationship, the US had an equitable approach to the British and Irish government with regard to Northern Ireland.[46] *The Irish Times* viewed this to be a reversal of successive administrations' traditional policy of adhering to State Department priorities in the Cold War, in which the US sided with British interests, including over Northern Ireland.[47] In his memoir, Clinton wrote that that the DSD 'was a wonderful Christmas present'.[48]

The year 1994 saw the Clinton administration become increasingly involved in Northern Ireland. In January, the President controversially granted Adams a visa to enter the US. Clinton's decision to intervene in the Anglo-Irish process to this extent was problematic. There was much debate about the visa.[49] In his memoir, Clinton acknowledged the division amongst Irish–Americans on Northern Ireland: while some Irish–Americans supported the IRA, Sinn Féin enjoyed the backing of others who opposed violence, and another constituency in America aligned itself with the British and Irish Protestant view that the US 'had no business meddling in the affairs of the United Kingdom, our strongest ally'. He noted that, while a largely non-interventionist stance 'had carried the day with all my predecessors, including those sympathetic to the legitimate grievances of Northern Ireland's Catholics', the DSD meant that he felt obliged to review this longstanding policy, given that 'the British and Irish governments clearly had created pressure on all the parties to work with them for peace'. Since the DSD, Adams' supporters in the US had advocated the granting of a visa to the Sinn Féin president, as it would enable him to convince the IRA to renounce violence and include his party in the peace talks. Clinton noted that Hume had revised his position on Adams' visa: he now believed that 'it would advance the peace process'. Kennedy, Dodd, Moynihan, Kerry, King and Manton supported Hume's view. Speaker Tom Foley (D-WA, 1989–95) continued to oppose the visa. Reynolds favoured a visa for Adams while the British government was fervently opposed to it.[50]

Clinton concluded that he would address the question if Adams were invited to an event in the US. Adams – along with other leaders in Northern Ireland – was subsequently invited to a peace conference in New York City. In turn, this issue became a major foreign policy debate within the Clinton administration. Opposing the visa were Warren Christopher and the State Department, Seitz, the Justice Department, the Central Intelligence Agency (CIA) and the FBI. Three members of the NSC proposed an alternative view: Lake, Nancy Soderberg and Jane Holl. They argued that Adams wanted to end the IRA's violent activities, lead Sinn Féin into the peace process and for Northern Ireland to enjoy a democratic future. Indeed, Ireland was prospering as a member of the European Union, tolerance towards the violence was collapsing in Ireland, and the principle of consent combined with the demographics in Northern Ireland meant that it would remain in the UK 'for some time to come'.[51] The NSC argued that Clinton 'should grant the visa, because it would boost Adams' leverage within Sinn Féin and the IRA, while increasing American influence with him'.[52] Seitz was extremely critical of this advice to the President. He suggested that Soderberg's 'influence flowed from her previous ten years on Senator Kennedy's staff, and she became the in-house coach for the Irish lobby'.[53] Seitz was equally critical of Lake, claiming that he represented the Wilson–Roosevelt wing of the Democratic Party and, as such, opposed any remnants of colonialism: 'for him, no country was more imperial than Britain and no place more colonized than Ireland'.[54] Donlon recalled how Hume, his close ally, influenced the President, who told Clinton that the visa was the 'best chance' to secure a ceasefire, as Adams could persuade Irish–American supporters of the IRA that the talks needed to be supported and it would help enable Sinn Féin to become part of the talks with the unionists. He also observed that the visa was a unique occasion when Northern Ireland caused a 'rupture' in Anglo-American relations, and proved to be the State Department's 'last stand' on their long-held position on the Anglo-Irish process.[55] Seitz, despite noting that Hume was 'a man of considerable courage and faith', claimed that the SDLP was clearly 'ready to put hope ahead of experience' as he essentially 'legitimized Gerry Adams' in the US.[56]

In contrast to Hume's optimism, Seitz attempted to persuade the President not to issue the visa. In his memoir, Seitz summarised the cable that he dispatched from London to Washington, DC: 'Adams was involved with the IRA right up to his elbows . . . . A visa would confer respectability on him and condone the violence he advocated.'[57] The ambassador warned that unless Adams renounced violence before receiving his visa, Clinton 'should make no mistake about the severity of the British reaction in the Parliament, the press and the public'.[58] The Embassy was simply told to invite Adams to the consulate-general in Belfast, where he could be asked to renounce violence and commit Sinn Féin to the Joint Declaration.[59] In his memoir, Major's scepticism and fury are wrapped in diplomacy. He noted that Adams failed to renounce violence yet, 'to my astonishment and annoyance, the White House gave him his visa'.[60] Soderberg's account of the British reaction – and that of the US State Department – was much more colourful:

> When the President ultimately decided to go with the recommendation to give the visa, the entire State Department just had a fit as did the entire British Empire and they were so angry about it they just really weren't capable of coordinating anything anymore.[61]

The White House simply believed that the proximity of British diplomats to the issue meant that they failed to understand that the US could offer constructive assistance.[62]

Clinton candidly admitted in his memoir, 'For days Major refused to take my phone calls.'[63] However, he was satisfied that the decision was the right one: 'Seven months later the IRA declared a cease-fire' and the visa marked 'the beginning of my deep engagement in the long, emotional, complicated search for peace in Northern Ireland'.[64] In terms of the positive result that Clinton pointed towards, Major claimed that the ceasefire was not announced as quickly as the Clinton administration hoped: 'American hopes that the visit would lead to an early ceasefire were unfulfilled . . . . When Adams applied for a further US visa in July, the White House turned him down – evidently without damaging the chances of a ceasefire.'[65] Nevertheless, Adams' visa was indicative that an Anglo-Irish process exclusively between the British and Irish governments could not end the Northern Ireland conflict. Instead, the future of Northern Ireland was in the hands of its nationalist and unionist parties and any peace process revolved around talks between them.[66] Soderberg has offered a similar explanation: 'I asked Gerry Adams once whether, if Clinton had been President in the early and mid-'80s, he could have made a difference. He said, "No, we weren't ready." I think that's probably right.'[67] Indeed, Adams recalled that the visa coincided with other timely developments, such as the growth of Sinn Féin and his discussions with Hume.[68] On the visa, Adams succinctly described its importance, in his view, in the context of American foreign policy: 'Really, in the scheme of things, it arguably wasn't huge, but it was symbolically very big, because U.S. foreign policy, up until that point under previous Presidents, had been broadly speaking in support of the British position.'[69]

This break with traditional American policy towards Northern Ireland angered the British government. On the receiving end of the British government's fury over Adams' visa was, inevitably, Seitz. In his memoir, Seitz recalled visiting 10 Downing Street after the news broke that Clinton had issued the visa against the wishes of the British government. As Major was occupied in the House of Commons, it fell to Sir Roderic Lyne, the Prime Minister's Private Secretary (1993–6), to express the government's view to the American ambassador. Seitz recalled, 'I did not recollect ever having been spoken to by a British colleague in such a prepared and formal manner.'[70] The British government's view was that Adams had failed to meet the conditions as laid down by the US: namely, the renouncement of violence and commitment to the principles of the DSD. They believed that the visa undermined the purpose of the DSD: that is, its desire to isolate Sinn Féin and apply pressure on them to participate in the talks.[71] For Seitz, the visa issue implied that the Clinton White House was not overly concerned with British interests.[72] Moreover, just as the White House was clearly willing to downgrade the 'special relationship' on this issue, in the domestic sphere the visa served as a boon to Senator Kennedy, who was fighting for re-election and 'was an anxious man in the market for favour'.[73] Clinton's decision to issue the visa was, in turn, supported by Kennedy's 'powerful congressional machine'.[74]

The Clinton administration was willing to discomfit the British government, as taking a risk for peace in Northern Ireland was not a political gamble for the President – in contrast to the British and Irish governments. Despite the diplomatic fallout between London and Washington, DC, Adams' visa was simply an embarrassing incident and certainly not comparable to the 1956 Suez Crisis in Anglo-American relations. The visa showed that Clinton could utilise Northern Ireland to his political advantage at home and cultivate a legacy abroad: Clinton, the peacemaker.[75] Nonetheless, the domestic politics surrounding the visa cannot be marginalised. Steven Greenhouse, writing in *The New York Times*, explained that Moynihan and Kennedy, whom Clinton needed to support his healthcare plan, supported the visa.[76] R. W. Apple, Jr, also writing for *The New York Times*, noted Moynihan and Kennedy's key chairmanships of Senate committees, which would influence the fate of Clinton's healthcare and welfare proposals.[77] According to Apple, a White House staffer remarked that, in addition to the gains in domestic politics, the visa would potentially be a boon to the peace process, meaning that it was acceptable to disgruntle their British counterparts.[78]

The IRA announced a ceasefire on 31 August 1994. However, it was contingent on the Clinton administration issuing another controversial visa. The IRA informed Reynolds via an intermediary, Father Alex Reid (who resided in Belfast's Clonard Monastery), that they wished to dispatch an emissary to the US in order to reassure their American republican supporters. The chosen emissary was Joe Cahill. Although Cahill was a seventy-four-year-old man in 1994, he had been involved in leadership positions in the IRA since the 1930s – he had been reprieved of a sentence to hang for the murder of a Catholic policeman in Northern Ireland in 1942 – and was a key figure in establishing the Provisional IRA after 1969. Cahill was even one of the founders and initial promoters of NORAID in 1970 and had been arrested off the Waterford coast for gunrunning in March 1973 (with five tins of explosives and weapons courtesy of Gaddafi). He was released early from a three-year prison sentence due to ill health and was banned from entering the US (although he had successfully entered and left illegally in 1981, campaigning for financial support for the IRA and all the while escaping the attempts of the FBI to bring him to justice). Reynolds was able to convince the Clinton administration that a visa for an IRA hardliner such as Cahill was the final step towards the ceasefire. On 30 August 1994, Cahill arrived in New York City and the following day the ceasefire was declared. Having had his visa extended from five days to fifteen, Cahill toured major cities and spoke to supporters of Sinn Féin and the IRA. Journalists were barred from the meetings.[79] However, Conor O'Clery notes that, amongst Cahill's reasons for the ceasefire, he explained that 'Clinton had changed Irish republican thinking. For the first time an American President was not automatically linked up with the British. They wanted to take advantage of that.'[80]

The Clinton administration also sought to reassure the unionists, who feared that they were seeking to impose a republican-led solution. At Reynolds' urging, Vice-President Al Gore (1993–2001) met with James Molyneaux, the leader of the Ulster Unionist Party (1979–95), a few days after the ceasefire. The Taoiseach advised that, as the unionists viewed Clinton to be a nationalist sympathiser, the Vice-President would have to balance out that perception. Lake and Admiral William J. Crowe, the US ambassador to the UK (1994–7), encouraged Molyneaux (or representatives of the Ulster Unionist Party) to visit the White House as his political opponents had done. Thus, on 21 September, Gore welcomed an Ulster Unionist Party (UUP) delegation of David Trimble (party leader, 1995–2005), Ken Maginnis, William Ross and Jeffrey Donaldson to the White House for talks.[81] Lake recalls that, having achieved success with Adams' visa and the ceasefire, it was clear that the Clinton administration were firmly involved as honest brokers:

> As it happens, we turned out to be right on this issue. Progress was made. So we'd gotten drawn into it. I talked to most of the leaders in the Northern Ireland parties once every week or two . . . . And the British and the Irish.[82]

The White House worked to dispel any notion that it was conspiring against the unionists. For instance, on 1 November 1995, Trimble was reported to have had a thirty-minute meeting with Gore, with Clinton joining their discussion of the peace process for ten minutes.[83] In the mean time, the British and Irish governments sought to agree a common vision for Northern Ireland.

On 22 February 1995, the British and Irish governments agreed and announced the Joint Framework Document (JFD), which described the two governments' view of the political future of Northern Ireland. The main difficulty was that the JFD outlined cross-border arrangements; unionist would have to be reassured of Northern Ireland's position in the UK while nationalists sought an indication that Irish unity was the ultimate outcome of the Anglo-Irish process. The JFD did not accomplish this feat. After extensive negotiation up to the eleventh hour, it was published on 22 February; it failed to address Ireland's constitutional claim to Northern Ireland, with ambiguous language in regard to the territorial issue underlining this point. Republicans were frustrated by the lack of progress while other parties waited for republican disarmament. Talks reached an impasse. The situation was complicated further by the arms conditions of the DSD: Sinn Féin's participation in the talks was contingent on decommissioning.[84] The only way that Sinn Féin would be permitted to participate in the talks was on terms that satisfied all parties. These developments coincided with the appointment of George Mitchell (D-ME) as the US Special Envoy to Northern Ireland (1995–2001) in January 1995, following the end of his fifteen-year career in the US Senate.[85] Mitchell's initial appointment was as the president's Special Adviser for Economic Affairs in Northern Ireland – a role that he anticipated would revolve around a trade conference and essentially total a few days of his time. But events would demand more than that.[86]

Clinton's third St Patrick's Day as president marked his first meeting with Adams. The President had come to view the celebrations as 'an annual opportunity for the United States to advance the peace process in Northern Ireland'.[87] Having issued Adams with a second visa, based on his promise to engage with the British government on the issue of IRA decommissioning, Clinton invited him, Hume and other Northern Ireland leaders to a reception at the White House. The President even reversed the ban on Sinn Féin's fundraising in the US. Before the White House event, Clinton shook hands with Adams at Newt Gingrich's St Patrick's Day Speaker's luncheon, albeit after encouragement by Hume. In his memoir, Clinton remarked that, at the White House celebration, Adams and Hume would sing a duet. These developments in American policy were quite stunning. The British government continued to view Adams as a terrorist; thus, they and members of the US State Department opposed the President's stance. Clinton, however, was working with Adams and Hume – and eventually Trimble would also participate in the annual St Patrick's Day celebrations at the White House.[88]

In November 1995, within the context of the ceasefire, Clinton became the first American president to visit Northern Ireland. Thousands lined the streets of Belfast and Derry to welcome him, eager to hear an American president make unprecedented comments on the Northern Ireland situation in Northern Ireland. Clinton was able to speak to all concerned parties: he urged unionists and the British government to maintain dialogue, while calling on republicans to maintain the ceasefire.[89] In his speech in Derry on 30 November, Clinton recalled that, during his three years in the White House, he had met with both nationalists and unionists, and listened 'to their sides of the story'.[90] Having done so, the President believed that 'The deep divisions, the most important ones, are those between the peacemakers and the enemies of peace.' Clinton explained that it was now time 'for the peacemakers to triumph in Northern Ireland, and the United States will support them as they do'. He concluded, 'I ask you to build on the opportunity you have before you . . . . Have the patience to work for a just and lasting peace. Reach for it. The United States will reach with you'.[91] In his memoir, Major praised Clinton's contribution during his visit to the UK and Ireland, noting that the President 'did not put a foot wrong'.[92] Clinton recalled that this visit constituted 'two of the best days of my presidency', his mission being to convince Protestants in Northern Ireland that 'I was working for a peace that was fair to them, too', as all that 'most of the Protestants knew about me was the Adams visa.'[93] Clinton's visit was an occasion for all the party leaders to be together at the same event, although Paisley refused to shake hands with Catholic leaders. Clinton remarked,

> Though he wouldn't shake hands with the Catholic leaders, he was only too happy to lecture me on the error of my ways. After a few minutes of his hectoring, I decided the Catholic leaders had gotten the better end of the deal.[94]

*The Irish Times* noted the electioneering implications for Clinton. Conor O'Clery observed that Clinton's re-election campaign would benefit from the footage showing cheering crowds and that he could point to such a success in foreign policy.[95] An anonymous member of the Clinton administration remarked that Clinton's visit to Belfast was the second day of the re-election campaign.[96] Mandy Grunwald, the media director for Clinton's 1992 election campaign, hoped that some of the people of Belfast had relatives who could vote in America in 1996.[97] Three weeks after Clinton's visit to Northern Ireland, R. W. Apple, writing in *The New York Times*, argued that in 1996 the President would be able to win Irish–American votes but also to show that he was leading a broader international peace movement.[98] Regardless of the electioneering implications, Clinton's importance to the Irish government in their hopes to resolve the 'Troubles' was obvious. One Irish diplomat praised Clinton as the first president to possess a policy on the issue, whereas his predecessors just smiled and ducked it.[99]

The issue of decommissioning proved to be a roadblock to talks. Major refused to begin talks that included Sinn Féin until the IRA agreed to decommission its arms. However, the British government did agree to an independent group – the International Body on Arms Decommissioning – reviewing the process; it was led by Mitchell, General John de Chastelain (a leading Canadian military advisor) and Harri Holkeri (Finland's former Conservative Prime Minister).[100] On 22 January 1996, Mitchell published his *Report on the International Body on Arms Decommissioning*.[101] In short, he advised that decommissioning should not have to take place before Sinn Féin was admitted to the talks, but rather that decommissioning of all paramilitary groups would take place during the talks. This advice was accepted, although the British government, seeking to maintain the involvement of the unionists, focused on his advice for an electoral process in Northern Ireland as a means to build confidence in the talks.[102]

The process stalled on 9 February 1996 when the IRA's ceasefire came to a murderous end with a bomb in Canary Wharf in London.[103] The White House was stunned: only five days beforehand, Adams had assured Clinton that the ceasefire would continue and the administration had publicly supported the Mitchell Report. Although nationalists and republicans criticised Major's slow movement on the talks following the report, it was Adams who now saw his credibility doubted in Northern Ireland and the US. Nevertheless, Sinn Féin still secured 16 per cent of the vote in the 30 May elections for a non-executive forum that would provide negotiators for the forthcoming talks; Adams' party were clearly still vital protagonists in the peace process. Yet when talks commenced on 10 June, chaired by Mitchell, Sinn Féin representatives were absent due to the ending of the ceasefire.[104] Clinton recalled that he 'decided to maintain contact with Adams, waiting for the moment when the march toward peace could resume'.[105] Regardless, Sinn Féin opted to disengage until after the 1997 UK general election. They (correctly) anticipated that it would lead to a Labour government. Moreover, Sinn Féin correctly believed that Tony Blair's government (1997–2007) would not necessarily be sympathetic towards Ulster Unionism.[106]

It was in this context that Clinton first met Tony Blair on 12 April 1996, when the latter was serving as Leader of the Opposition (1994–7). Northern Ireland was a priority in this meeting. Clinton was keen to emphasise that he believed the Labour leader's 'non-partisan approach to Northern Ireland' was 'courageous and helpful to peace process'.[107] The topic was the first issue discussed when Blair met with Clinton in the Oval Office. An increase in the time allotted for the meeting (from twenty minutes to thirty minutes), as well as the list of those attending, underlines the fact that Clinton saw the meeting as significant. A long list of senior people took part: Warren Christopher, the US Secretary of State (1993–7); Lake; Robert Rubin (Secretary of the Treasury, 1995–9); Leon Panetta (Chief of Staff, 1994–7); Soderberg; Rudolf Perina (Deputy Assistant Secretary of State for European and Canadian Affairs, 1996–7); and Mary Ann Peters (Director for European Affairs, NSC Staff, 1995–7).[108] Clinton enquired as to the latest news on Northern Ireland, to which Blair responded that the 'key question is whether the IRA will call the cease-fire'. As a signal to his approach towards negotiations in government and acceptance of American involvement, Blair explained:

> We have a clear path with the Mitchell Principles. The only condition is the cease-fire; the talks would have to focus on decommissioning but that is not an absolute precondition. It is all there if they get the cease-fire back; if not, we will have to carry on with the process. It will be difficult and it is important to reinforce the message with Sinn Fein [sic]. If the Irish nationalists and SDLP are both saying they should get into talks, it does not make sense for them to do otherwise.[109]

Blair stressed that his party would maintain its 'bipartisan approach' so that they 'will have credibility when we are in government'.[110] The contrast between the seriousness attached to this meeting and the controversial reception of one of Blair's predecessors as Labour leader, Neil Kinnock (1983–92), at the Reagan White House was staggering.[111]

Northern Ireland would emerge as a factor in another policy area for Clinton. On 12 April 1996, the President vetoed H.R. 1561, the Foreign Relations Authorization Act, Fiscal Years 1996 and 1997. In his message to the House of Representatives, Clinton explained that he had vetoed the legislation because it included 'unacceptable provisions that would undercut U.S. leadership abroad and damage our ability to assure the future security and prosperity of the American people'.[112] Clinton was unwilling to approve any legislation that restricted 'the President's ability to address the complex international challenges and opportunities of the post-Cold War era' and even 'restrict Presidential authority needed to conduct foreign affairs and to control state secrets, thereby raising serious constitutional concerns'.[113] Section 1615 of the Act related to the IFI, urging 'the use of U.S. contributions to increase employment opportunities in communities with high unemployment in Northern Ireland'.[114] That the Clinton administration had been slow to act on the MacBride Principles ensured that this veto antagonised McManus (the INC President).[115] The furore that McManus created following Clinton's decision to veto H.R. 1561 prompted the President to neutralise the issue prior to the Democratic National Convention. The President wrote to Lyons about this veto.[116] He emphasised that the IFI was a 'significant force in promoting investment and jobs in Northern Ireland and adjacent areas of the Republic of Ireland', which had also 'actively promoted reconciliation and . . . established an excellent record on equal opportunity and fair employment issues'. He reassured Lyons that his veto was 'entirely unrelated to the language in section 1615' and therefore asked that, when administering America's contribution to the IFI, he should 'ensure that the intent of Section 1615 of HR 1561 is carried out to the greatest extent possible'.[117]

The domestic implications of Clinton's peace-making were becoming increasingly clear. Equal to the positive image that he was able to project to the world following his visit to Northern Ireland, which in turn was utilised by his aides and allies at home to strengthen his domestic position, policies towards Northern Ireland offered political threats. In addition to frustrating Irish–Americans on the MacBride Principles, the Anglo-American aspects of Clinton's policies were challenged by his political opponents. At the 1996 Republican National Convention, James Baker (US Secretary of State, 1989–93) told the GOP (Grand Old Party, or Republican Party):

> We have seen a representative of the IRA hosted in the White House just prior to its resumption of terrorist bombings in London. The result has been the worst relationship with our closest ally, Britain, since the Boston Tea Party in 1773.[118]

Nonetheless, both the Republicans and Democrats identified the political value of including Northern Ireland in their platforms. The Republican platform stated,

> We support efforts to establish peace with justice in Northern Ireland through a peace process inclusive of all parties who reject violence . . . we encourage private U. S. investment in the North, fully consistent with the MacBride principles for fair employment . . . . We call on all parties to renounce terrorism.[119]

Despite the platform representing the concerns of Irish–American Republicans and an attempt to garner Irish–American votes for the GOP, their presidential nominee, Senator Robert J. 'Bob' Dole (R-KS), did not include a reference to Northern Ireland in his speech.[120] The reference in the platform was probably indicative of the concern of those Republican members of Congress who had taken an interest in the 'Troubles' since the 1980s. The Democratic Party's platform in 1996 contextualised Northern Ireland within similar foreign policy successes for the Clinton administration. It proclaimed:

> Four years ago, the Middle East process had not moved beyond a set of principles, and there were no signs of peace in Northern Ireland. Today, in the Middle East we have seen real agreements toward peace, and handshakes of history, and the people of Northern Ireland have seen a 17 month cease-fire and historic negotiations among the parties . . . .[121]

This was emphasised further:

> We are committed to promoting democracy in regions and countries important to America's security, and to standing with all those willing

**214**

to take risks for peace, from the Middle East to Northern Ireland, where President Clinton was the first U.S. president to engage directly in the search for peace, including making an historic visit to Northern Ireland.[122]

A final flourish earmarked specifics (again with similar objectives for other minorities and challenged regions), ostensibly in order to satisfy Irish–American Democrats: 'The Democratic Party supports the aspirations of all those who seek to strengthen civil society and accountable governance. To this end, we support the MacBride Principles of equal access to regional employment in Northern Ireland.'[123] In his convention speech, Clinton recalled his impression that a 'deep desire for peace that Hillary and I felt when we walked the streets of Belfast and Derry must become real for all the people of Northern Ireland'.[124] He also contextualised his endeavours in Northern Ireland:

> I have spent so much of your time that you gave me these last 4 years to be your President worrying about the problems of Bosnia, the Middle East, Northern Ireland, Rwanda, Burundi. What do these places have in common? People are killing each other and butchering children because they are different from one another. They share the same piece of land, but they are different from one another. They hate their race, their tribe, their ethnic group, their religion.

For the benefit of the electorate, the President ultimately connected his interventions abroad with the success of America at home:

> In our own country, we have seen America pay a terrible price for any form of discrimination. And we have seen us grow stronger as we have steadily let more and more of our hatreds and our fears go, as we have given more and more of our people the chance to live their dreams.
>
> That is why the flame of our Statue of Liberty, like the Olympic flame carried all across America by thousands of citizen heroes, will always, always burn brighter than the fires that burn our churches, our synagogues, our mosques – always.[125]

This use of Clinton's Northern Ireland policy within a broader narrative of his administration's accomplishments is symptomatic of a more nuanced approach by Democrats to Irish–American voters in 1996. Dodd, who served as Chairman of the Democratic

National Committee (1995–7), did not believe that Clinton's engagement with Northern Ireland alone would be sufficient to convince Irish–Americans to support his re-election. Nevertheless, he accepted that Northern Ireland could become a key deciding issue for Irish–Americans who were otherwise undecided. Thus, the Democratic Ethnic Coordinating Committee produced advertisements, such as one that included Irish–Americans advocating the President's re-election because of his 'commitment to peace in Ireland' and support for more police, Medicare and tackling illegal drugs.[126] Clinton's efforts did not entirely convince the Irish–American community, however. Although some Irish–American groups lauded the President, others condemned his veto of the 1995 Partial-Birth Abortion Ban Act. Ultimately, Clinton secured the support of 53 per cent of Catholic voters.[127] The country as a whole was more convincing in its decision: Clinton secured 49 per cent of the popular vote, compared to Dole's 41 per cent, and the electoral college vote was 379 to 159, respectively. The President was re-elected in 1996 for similar reasons to his victory in 1992: the economy was central to the campaign, not foreign policy.[128]

## 1997–2001

There was much admiration within the Clinton administration for Major's approach to the Anglo-Irish process. For instance, Lake explained,

> Major was on a razor thin majority, in the end of one vote, and if the Unionists walked, his government fell . . . . Despite that, Major . . . always took it as far as he could within the realm of political possibility. I really admire him greatly.[129]

Yet Major's negotiations reached an impasse, mainly due to the loss of his Conservative parliamentary majority and the opposition from some within his party to his efforts to achieve a settlement. However, it was because of Major's work in Northern Ireland that Tony Blair, the Opposition and Labour Party leader (1994–7), upon his landslide victory on 1 May 1997, believed that he had a unique opportunity to resolve the Northern Ireland conflict.

By the time that Blair became British prime minister, the 'Troubles' had caused the death of over 3,000 people in thirty-five years.[130] He informed Clinton that Northern Ireland would be a leading priority during his time at 10 Downing Street.[131] Fifteen days into his premiership, on 16 May 1997, Blair visited Northern Ireland. In his address to the Royal Agricultural Society, Blair directly addressed Sinn Féin and gave his view of the peace process:

> The settlement train is leaving. I want you on that train. But it is leaving anyway, and I will not allow it to wait for you. You cannot hold the process to ransom any longer. So end the violence. Now.[132]

In addition to this rebuke to republicans, Blair also made explicit his expectations of loyalists:

> Loyalist terrorism is equally contemptible, equally unacceptable, just as futile and counter-productive. The Loyalist paramilitaries have so far maintained their cease-fire in formal terms. I welcome that signal of restraint, as far as it goes, and urge them and those with influence on them to hold fast to it.[133]

Clinton was surprised that Blair had turned his attention towards Northern Ireland as soon as he had done.[134] The advent of the Blair government raised the hopes and expectations of Irish–Americans that a resolution to the conflict could be achieved. On behalf of the ACCIA, Rep. Benjamin A. Gilman (R-NY), King, Manton and Neal wrote to Clinton on 19 May 1997. They observed that the British election result was 'a genuine opportunity to revive the Irish peace process'.[135] The Congressmen asked that Clinton prioritise the issue during his forthcoming meeting with Blair: 'You can play a key role in ensuring that the opportunity now before us is not missed. We are ready to work with you to do whatever it takes.'[136] The Congressmen would not be disappointed. James Steinberg (Deputy NSA, 1996–2001) has succinctly explained the relationship between Blair and Clinton, particularly with regard to Northern Ireland:

> It was a little bit of the big-man, smaller-man thing. Clinton tried to use his magnetism more, whereas Blair tried to use his ideas, his mind, and his arguments more. Clinton thought he could do it with force of

personality. This is one case where I think he was able to use his force of personality as a big mover.[137]

Northern Ireland was unsurprisingly a topic of conversation when Clinton visited Blair in London, shortly after the latter's general election victory in May 1997. Although it was not discussed when Clinton met with the Cabinet, it was the first issue raised in the restricted session between the President and the Prime Minister.[138] The American record of the closed discussion underlines the level of Clinton's engagement towards Northern Ireland.[139] The President explained to Blair that 'when it comes time that you think it would be helpful for us to say something about a cease-fire or decommissioning, let me know . . . . I have some pull and can call in chits'. In Clinton's view, the political leadership in Northern Ireland was moving too slowly for its constituents: 'One problem is that the people are farther along than the leaders. For people like Sinn Fein [sic] and Ian Paisley, the conflict is their whole life.' Indeed, Clinton believed that 'if there were no political leaders, we could get the people to agree'. The President praised Mo Mowlam, the UK Secretary of State for Northern Ireland (1997–9): 'She is good, great on TV. Her happy face inspires confidence. She seems solid and not full of herself; you don't need another person over there posturing like a peacock.' (Unfortunately, any comments made by British protagonists in the meeting, including Blair, are redacted.)[140] Lake echoed this praise. He described Mowlam as 'great' and symptomatic of the Labour government's greater receptivity to American involvement in Northern Ireland.[141]

On 2 July 1997, Clinton briefed the ACCIA on his prior discussions with Blair in London in May and (at the G8 Summit) in Denver in June 1997. The President wrote,

> I share your conviction that there is now a historic opportunity for peace in Northern Ireland. Tony Blair and I discussed this subject at length during my recent visit to London and in Denver, and I believe he wants to get a meaningful negotiating process underway as soon as possible.[142]

Clinton observed that the 'IRA's murder of the two policemen in Lurgan June 16 can be understood not only as a brutal crime, but also as a deliberate provocation aimed at the peace process,' which, coupled with the Marching Season (discussed below), meant that 'both nationalists and unionists must show a spirit of compromise and political courage.' He concluded,

> Please rest assured that my Administration will spare no effort in our attempts to help move the peace process forward. I look forward to working with you and with other members of the Ad Hoc Committee for Irish Affairs on this important issue.[143]

American pressure continued to be directed at the IRA for another ceasefire. In the meantime, on 3 June 1997, Mitchell resumed his negotiations and Clinton argued in favour of Sinn Féin's readmission, should the IRA deliver a ceasefire. Blair also sought to convince the IRA to renounce violence by criminalising two unionist paramilitary groups and abandoning Major's stance that the IRA must announce a timetable for decommissioning in order for Sinn Féin to participate in the talks. Blair and Clinton's strategy proved successful: the IRA ceasefire recommenced on 19 July 1997. Adams and Sinn Féin agreed to adopt the Mitchell Principles. Blair had agreed that Sinn Féin would be admitted to the talks after six weeks had passed since the ceasefire was announced (they would rejoin the talks in September 1997). He also announced that the negotiations would cease on 1 May 1998, thus addressing Sinn Féin claims that the unionists would simply slow any progress to such an extent that the talks would amount to nothing. Blair and Bertie Ahern, the Taoiseach (1997–2008), also agreed that IRA decommissioning of arms would take place during the talks. In turn, Clinton endorsed these developments in a White House press statement on 19 July in support of the IRA's ceasefire announcement. On 13 October 1997, Blair became the first British prime minister to meet with the Sinn Féin leadership since 1921; the last time the unionists held talks with Sinn Féin was in 1920.[144] The significance of this development was not underestimated in the American coverage.[145]

Outside of Congress, Irish–Americans were sceptical. The AOH wrote to Clinton and Sandy Berger (NSA, 1997–2001) about the status of the MacBride Principles, the use of plastic bullets in Northern Ireland, the issue of visas for all elected officials, and extradition.[146] On this last subject, the AOH believed that Clinton's 'Pontius Pilate' approach to 'deportation cases' was 'hurtful to all . . . who have placed so much faith and trust in his good will and sincerity'.[147] Berger replied to the AOH on 27 October.[148] He noted that there had been 'historic progress' since his meeting with Joe Roche, the AOH National Chairman, in March 1997: the restoration of the IRA ceasefire in July, the admission of Sinn Féin to the talks in Belfast, and finally the agreement of all major parties on the procedures and structures for the forthcoming substantive discussions. Reassuring the AOH of the administration's engagement with the peace process, Berger wrote, 'We are in close touch with both governments and the main unionist and republican parties. I met with Gerry Adams last month, and had the opportunity recently to receive ministers from both Dublin and the Northern Ireland Office.' On MacBride and the IFI, Berger stated that the administration was not opposed to 'the MacBride language that is in the House authorization bill for the coming fiscal year'.[149] The remainder of 1997 saw the Clinton administration act further in order to ensure that the ceasefire held. Six convicted members of the IRA who were living in the US found their deportation proceedings cancelled. Likewise, three other Irish–Americans who faced expulsion for their IRA connections were also allowed to remain in the US. That year, even the IRA no longer found itself listed as a terrorist organisation by the State Department. So, in an attempt to balance their involvement, Clinton and Gore were quick to meet with David Trimble, offering reassurances of support and good cheer, while the UUP leader was meeting with Berger in the White House.[150]

Clinton's personal engagement continued. In his meeting with Blair at the White House in February 1998, the President explained: 'We will continue our contacts and dialogue with Sinn Fein [sic]. I also intend to keep seeing Trimble and the other key Unionist leaders when they come to town.'[151] Unfortunately, the records of Clinton's meetings with the Sinn Féin and unionist leaderships are unavailable. However, it is likely that those conversations referenced the *Propositions on Heads of Agreement*, published on 12 January 1998.[152] This document established that, ultimately, any resolution to the 'Troubles' would require an answer to the Northern

Ireland question that involved a change in the constitutional relationship between Britain and Ireland, a new Anglo-Irish Agreement, a Northern Ireland Assembly, and a British–Irish Council
that related the new Assembly to the North–South structures and
other relevant bodies. Although Sinn Féin accepted that the talks
would not lead to a united Ireland, it was clear that they still harboured long-term hopes for the constitutional settlement that they
had long sought. On 8 March 1998, Adams outlined Sinn Féin's
objectives for the peace process in *Ireland on Sunday*: police and
courts under new all-Ireland institutions; disbanding of the RUC;
withdrawal of the British Army; release of paramilitary prisoners; the Irish constitution continuing to have a territorial claim
to Northern Ireland; and the creation of cross-order bodies that
would be independent of the Northern Ireland Assembly.[153] As
promised, Clinton endeavoured 'to keep reassuring and pushing
all the parties into the framework George Mitchell was construct-
ing'.[154] The President utilised the Northern Ireland leaders' time in
the US to celebrate St Patrick's Day in order to meet them, including 'extended visits with Gerry Adams and David Trimble'.[155]
Despite the St Patrick's festivities, the administration's agenda
was serious. As *The Irish Times* reported on 14 March 1998, the
White House wanted Clinton to be viewed as the president who
brought peace to Northern Ireland.[156] On his meeting with Clinton and Madeleine Albright (Secretary of State, 1997–2001) in the
White House in March 1998, Adams recalled that the President
'knew that we were particularly irked that the unionists were still
refusing to talk to us' and could empathise, as he was encouraging
Trimble to talk to Adams 'and expressed some frustration that so
far he had not done so'.[157]

The INC was frustrated regarding the implementation of the
MacBride Principles, and McManus's 'partisan attacks' on the
issue ensured that he was not invited to the White House's St
Patrick's celebrations in 1998.[158] The significance of such exclusion cannot be underestimated. As Mo Mowlam recalled in her
memoir, 'The great jamboree for St. Patrick's Day in Washington
became all important under President Clinton, part of his determination to galvanize Irish American support for the peace process.'[159] By the time of McManus's poor relations with the White

House, 'it was the event-you-couldn't-afford-not-to-be-at for all the players in the N. Ireland peace process'.[160] Seeking to repair his relationship with the White House, McManus wrote to Berger:

> I want to say again how I deeply appreciate the good work you are doing for peace in Northern Ireland and how I admire the skill with which you are doing it . . . . Sandy, I know in the past there may have been some difference in our approach to the MacBride Principles. But since we are encouraging Unionists and Nationalists in Northern Ireland with fundamental disagreements to come to an honourable accommodation, then I'm sure we in the U.S. can live amicably with different emphases.[161]

Berger used the opportunity provided by McManus's letter to emphasise the Clinton administration's policy:

> Employment equality is an important issue for Northern Ireland, as it is here in the United States. The President continues to believe that positive change in Northern Ireland must come from inside, with support and encouragement from us. He welcomes the British government's recent proposals on employment, which demonstrated a strong commitment to equality and making a difference in people's lives; that is what the peace process is about.[162]

Very shortly after Berger's letter to McManus, major developments occurred in Northern Ireland – and the American President was personally involved.

## The 1998 Good Friday Agreement

The talks that led to the GFA began in September 1997 and ultimately ended with the signing of an agreement on 10 April 1998. Participants in the talks agreed to the Mitchell Principles, which demanded a commitment to non-violence and democracy. The key components of the 1998 GFA were devolution under a Northern Ireland Assembly (Strand One); the establishment of the North–South Council, which would develop cross-border cooperation (Strand Two); the Irish government's decision to amend its constitutional claim to Northern Ireland; policies on decommissioning;

the release of prisoners; and steps to ensure equality and effective policing in Northern Ireland. A new British–Irish Agreement superseded the Anglo-Irish Agreement (Strand Three). Thus, the GFA meant that there would be power-sharing in Northern Ireland between unionists and nationalists, who would in turn co-operate with the Irish government on any cross-border issues. Nationalists accepted that Northern Ireland was legitimate and would remain so until the majority of its residences consented otherwise and Sinn Féin was shown that they had a role in Northern Ireland.[163] Clinton described the agreement as 'a fine piece of work, calling for majority rule and minority rights'.[164]

On 7 April 1998, a 'Draft Paper for Discussion' had been presented to the party leaders by the independent chairmen of the talks: Mitchell, Chastelain and Holkeri.[165] The peace process had been internationalised, with the US clearly having taken a leading role. Talks continued through the night of 9 and 10 April, with Strand One a final point of disagreement – Adams knew that the Unionists would be the majority in the Assembly and therefore needed a concession from them on the release of prisoners in order to pacify Sinn Féin. It was at this point that Clinton's promise to intervene in the negotiations, if called upon by Blair, was called upon. According to the diary of Alastair Campbell (Downing Street Press Secretary, 1997–2000; Tony Blair's Director of Communications and Strategy, 2000–3), at 3.37am (UK time), Blair spoke with the President about the status of the negotiations. The Prime Minister briefed Clinton:

> We were close to a deal . . . . SF have an issue on prisoners, and on language. They want their prisoners out in a year. They want to put together a long list, which they just want to throw in at the last minute. They are playing silly buggers. They have suddenly come up with a new list of amendments days and days into the negotiations. He said he was worried they were getting nervous about doing a deal at all.[166]

Clinton wanted to participate in the process and asked Blair whether he could make a telephone call. Campbell wrote in his diary that Blair suggested the President speak to Bertie Ahern (the Taoiseach) 'and emphasise the big changes they have won there', although he believed that a deal on prisoners was unachievable 'unless SF [Sinn Féin] sign up to the whole agreement'. For Blair, Clinton's involvement 'was now putting the pressure on SF', although 'he still felt best to hold BC from SF for now'. Clinton's determination to help was clear to Blair: 'Bill said there is nothing more important to me right now than this. Call me whenever, even if it means waking me up.'[167] Almost an hour later, Clinton reverted to Blair, having 'made some calls and said it was time to move for it'. At 5.35 a.m., Blair agreed that Clinton should speak to Adams and would stress 'how difficult the prison issue was, unless they signed up to the whole deal'.[168] Ultimately, a deal was achieved and, writing in his memoirs, Blair attributed much credit to Clinton's role in the peace process. He recalled that the President

> was a total brick throughout, tracking the negotiation, staying up all night, calling anyone he needed to call, saying anything he needed to say and much more besides, and being supremely on the ball, and typically, with that instant knack of his, getting right to the political nub.[169]

Clinton described his involvement in his memoir similarly: 'I talked to Bertie Ahern, and to Tony Blair, David Trimble, and Gerry Adams twice, before going to bed at 2:30 a.m.' He was then woken again at 5 a.m. 'with a request to call Adams again to seal the deal'.[170] In their respective memoirs, Ahern and Adams both praised Clinton for his enthusiasm and ability to understand the nuances and personalities involved in the peace process.[171] Much credit must be given to Mitchell for his chairmanship of the talks. He imbued the process with confidence and the focus to achieve a compromise, all in the face of opposition from the Democratic Unionist Party (DUP) and the suspicions of the Ulster Unionists.[172] On Mitchell's role, Lake opined that he 'did the real hard negotiating, should have had a Nobel Peace Prize'.[173]

Clinton clearly made an important contribution to the GFA. There were some disagreements, however, between members of the Blair government and the Clinton administration. Steinberg told *The Sunday Times* on 8 February 1998 that Blair was sometimes too ready to make allowances for the Unionists, while some in 10

Downing Street believed that the White House never appreciated British concerns over republican terrorist activity and the importance of decommissioning.[174] Blair was left disappointed when Clinton did not visit Northern Ireland and Ireland to campaign for a 'yes' vote in the referendum on the GFA.[175] Upon the announcement of the GFA in the US, the White House press corps inevitably focused on the President's role in brokering the peace. In questions following the President's heartfelt praise for the peace process and its protagonists, Clinton addressed his role. On whether his administration had made any promises to ensure the agreement, Clinton explained,

> all I have tried to do is to help create the conditions in which peace could develop and then to do whatever I was asked to do or whatever seemed helpful to encourage and support the parties in the search for peace.[176]

Clinton was similarly modest when asked about the nocturnal phone calls that he made in the final hours of the negotiations:

> In terms of the give and take, you know, I made a lot of phone calls last night and up until this morning, actually until right before the last session. But I think the specifics are not all that important . . . . I just did what I thought would help. And I tried to do what I was asked to do.

Clinton was also offered an opportunity to revisit the Adams visa controversy when asked about whether he felt that the policy had been vindicated: 'I believe it was a positive thing to do. I believed it then, I believe it now.' However, the President again returned to his attempt to portray the US as a junior partner in this peace process:

> If anything that I or the United States was able to do was helpful, especially because of our historic ties to Great Britain and because of the enormous number of Irish–Americans we have and the feelings we have for the Irish and their troubles, then I am very grateful. But the credit for this belongs to the people who made the decisions.[177]

Given this example of successful peace talks, the press conference turned to the Middle East and the possibility of a Clinton-led resolution:

> Well, we got Bosnia and Haiti, and now, I hope, Ireland. And I'll just keep working on it. The Irish thing ought to give you hope for the Middle East because the lesson is: just don't ever stop.[178]

Clinton's modesty seemed effortless but his involvement was obvious. Nonetheless, the White House was well prepared to ensure that both credit and blame were assigned in a way that was favourable to the President. A few days before the GFA, it was resolved that should there be no agreement before the deadline; the President would 'need to publicly scold the leaders for failing to seize this moment in history while balancing the need to keep the process and hopes of the Irish people alive for the future', which could 'be done by a written statement in order to keep some distance between the White House and Stormont'.[179] The media planning for a successful conclusion to the talks included Clinton's statement; coverage and photographs of presidential telephone calls with Ahern, Blair and Mitchell; a ten-minute interview between the President and a 'key reporter on significance of agreement', such as a *New York Times* journalist; staff management of 'tic-toc stories with timeline on US and presidential involvement including any last minute phone calls the President was asked to make'; a presidential roundtable with Irish reporters so as 'to applaud accomplishments and prod population to accept the agreement in referendum'; and meetings with Mitchell, who would also offer briefings to the White House press corps. Key US foreign policy actors would make telephone calls to interested members of Congress and participants in the peace process. Steinberg was scheduled to make a conference call designed to 'ensure appropriate validation from the Irish–American community'.[180] The administration was determined to ensure that Northern Ireland was used to the President's advantage: a legacy from his time in office. Moreover, as Joe Carroll suggested in *The Irish Times*, Clinton's modesty was also political: the White House did not want to help unionists complain about external interference.[181]

This was also a factor in Clinton's decision not to visit Northern Ireland during the referendum.

The administration's interest in Northern Ireland did not end following the GFA. Upon the success of the peace talks, the NSC on 14 April 1998 identified 'two communications objectives' in the interim period between the referendum and implementation of the GFA: 'To line up broad-based, subtle U.S. support for the agreement, seeking to minimize our exposure to unionist opponents in Northern Ireland – our message should be non-partisan, future-focussed (benefits of peace and prosperity)' and 'to recognize the leaders who took courageous steps towards peace'.[182] The administration was keenly aware that 'opponents of the agreement, particularly unionists, will be quick to exploit any sign that we are interfering in the referendum process'. This second phase of the White House's action plan again included interaction between Clinton and the press, including 'several key Irish journalists to applaud accomplishments and prod population to accept the agreement in referendum', albeit with the caveat 'to be careful to avoid overexposure though'; the assembling of an economic package, such as an increase to the IFI; and positive contact with interested members of Congress, participants in Northern Ireland, and the Irish–American community. Clinton's meeting with Mowlam later that month was identified as an opportunity to reinforce Clinton's role:

> She has not had a meeting with the President up until now. This would afford an opportunity to acknowledge her contributions and profile the President's efforts (Mowlam is guaranteed to be effusive in her thanks for the President in press events during her visit).[183]

The White House was just as prepared for a successful resolution to the talks as they had been in co-ordinating the response to a failure to reach an agreement.

It was decided that Clinton would not visit Northern Ireland again until after the 22 May referendum.[184] This was a consensus opinion amongst British and Irish officials, and Adams and Trimble. Lyons advised Berger that, in his view, a visit by the President 'would only play to Paisley' and so the administration should 'defer to Trimble' and arranged a presidential visit if it was 'critical to his targeted outcome, i.e. 60+ percent favorable from the Unionist community'.[185] Clinton candidly confirmed this in his memoir: 'I didn't want to give Ian Paisley any ammunition to attack me as an outsider telling the Northern Irish what to do.'[186] Mowlam recalled that Clinton 'remained throughout ready to come at any time if we thought it would help'.[187] Despite the decision that Clinton should not visit Northern Ireland to campaign for a 'yes' vote in the referendum, he continued to support Blair. In a telephone conversion on 24 April 1998, he sought to buoy the Prime Minister:

> It will be a great victory . . . . You're better at campaigning than the rest of them and have a more sophisticated insight; you should just treat it like another election and do whatever is necessary to win the election.[188]

Concurrent with discussions about Clinton's role in the referendum, the administration's financial support for Northern Ireland was challenged by the realities of policy with a Republican Congress. On 1 May 1998, Lawrence E. Butler (Director for European Affairs, NSC, 1997–9) advised Steinberg that while staffers had 'pulled together a meaningful package of initiatives that will have a lasting impact on Northern Ireland', they had done so 'without having to spend a lot of money'.[189] Indeed, it was the case that, 'despite supportive noises from staff on the Hill, the budget people up there are likely to be hard-nosed about spending more on prosperous Ireland'. In order to further Clinton's achievements in Northern Ireland, Steinberg was briefed that he could 'point to a $100 million contribution over the past five years, and intention to maintain that level'.[190] Regardless, the administration would portray the GFA as a success for the Clinton administration. A CNN programme was due to air in the week before the 22 May referendum and Steinberg was to be part of it.[191] Butler briefed Steinberg that his objectives were to explain 'the positive role the President and the United States have played in Ireland . . . stressing our role in fostering economic development and providing neutral political encouragement for an end to violence and commitment to a purely political process'.[192]

The GFA included ambiguities, vetoes and safeguards, which reflected longstanding mutual suspicion and conflicting agendas. It was clear that, under the principle of consent, Northern Ireland remained part of the UK. Sinn Féin had therefore failed to change the core constitutional arrangements for Northern Ireland. Articles 2 and 3 of the Irish constitution were revised while the cross-border bodies were not independent of the Northern Ireland Assembly. The GFA was therefore a success that met the objectives of the SDLP and the Ulster Unionists. In return for the nationalists' acceptance of Northern Ireland's status in the UK, unionists accepted power-sharing in the assembly in cross-border arrangements. However, the most controversial issue for the unionists was the 'soft landing' for Sinn Féin. The IRA renounced violence but, in return, Sinn Féin achieved their aims on policing, decommissioning and the release of paramilitary prisoners. The British government was determined to afford Sinn Féin their 'soft landing' and, extraordinarily, decommissioning did not take place until 2005 – five years later than agreed in the GFA. What was immediately clear was the desire for peace in Northern Ireland: the 1998 referendum resulted in a 71 per cent majority in favour of the GFA in Northern Ireland, which was comprised of a large majority of nationalist support, coupled with a smaller majority of unionists. The first elections to the new Assembly resulted in the UUP becoming the largest party.[193]

The Clinton administration's approach to extradition frustrated Irish–Americans, particularly the case of Kevin Artt, Terry Kirby and Pol Brennan, who escaped from the Maze Prison to the US in 1983. In 1992 and 1993, the three men were arrested for holding fraudulent passports and the British government issued an extradition request. The District Court in California initially granted bail (although this was opposed, unsuccessfully, by the Justice Department). In August 1997, the District Court decided that the men would be extradited and, along with the Ninth Circuit, denied bail pending their appeal. The Justice Department opposed bail on the grounds that the three men posed a 'risk of flight' and undermined the administration's 'treaty obligations'.[194] The British government informed the administration that they still intended to extradite the three men and opposed bail. Some members of Congress wrote to

Clinton, trying to convince him to persuade the British to abandon their opposition to bail. In reply, Berger explained that the White House did not intervene in individual cases.[195] By not directly involving the President, the administration had greater flexibility should there be changing circumstances, such as agreements in the peace process or new facts in the case.[196] Nonetheless, the appeals of the three men against extradition were upheld on the basis that Northern Ireland's legal system was biased against them.[197]

The Clinton administration remained involved and consulted with all interested parties. On 29 May 1998, Adams met Clinton in the Oval Office. White House briefings show that Adams sought 'to confirm that U.S. support continues to be even-handed' in the context of his view that 'London is seeking to secure (diminishing) unionist support by setting new preconditions related to IRA decommissioning.'[198] On 17 June, Steinberg met with members of the FOI, including the group's chairman, James T. Walsh (R-NY). Steinberg was briefed to persuade them that the White House 'continued high level involvement in NI peace efforts'.[199] One factor was the renewed interest in the IFI, with Senators Robert Torricelli (D-NJ) and Al D'Amato (R-NY), along with FOI members Gilman and King, seeking an additional $4.75 million.[200]

The summer of 1998 saw renewed tensions with the advent of the annual Marching Season, particularly the Orange March in Drumcree. In 1998, just three months after GFA, Loyalists murdered three Catholic boys as they slept in their firebombed home on Sunday, 12 July (Jason, Mark and Richard Quinn, who were 8, 9, and 10 years old, respectively).[201] That atrocity, along with the combined difficulties of the Marching Season and the failure to agree terms on decommissioning, were on-going challenges to the peace process. There was another reminder of the importance of the peace process on 5 August 1998, when the Real IRA carried out a car bombing in Omagh in Northern Ireland. The bomb killed 29 people while 220 others were injured. The Omagh bombing, however, did not distract from the peace process and was greeted by outrage and disgust across the British Isles and around the world. The extent to which all parties were committed is demonstrated by Ahern's admission to Clinton that 'the IRA had warned the Real IRA that if they ever did anything like that again, the British police would be the least of their worries'.[202]

In August 1998, Adams was still concerned by the implementation of the GFA, and shared with Steinberg a memo he had prepared for Mowlam.[203] In his letter to the NSA, Adams explained how, in the months following the GFA, 'we communicated our deep disquiet and concern at the manner in which many of the mechanisms for change, agreed on Good Friday, have been constructed'.[204] Adams and Sinn Féin were concerned about the policing commission and Chris Patten's appointment as its chair (Independent Commission on Policing for Northern Ireland, 1998–9), and the sidelining of nationalist parties and Irish government opinion. For Adams, there was a 'range of concerns expressed by Sinn Féin in relation to the Human Rights Commission, the review of the justice system, the review of fair employment legislation and the prisoner release mechanisms', which had 'largely been discounted by the British Government'. He was also worried by the Northern Ireland Bill, 'which in key areas departs from the Agreement and in others fails to adequately provide for provisions of the Agreement'. Adams was scathing in his criticism of Trimble, arguing that he

> continues to proclaim his intention to obstruct, simultaneously tries to rewrite the Agreement, cherry-picks where this fails and seems to be under no pressure to adopt the type of positive and inclusive approach by which we could all start to assist each other against the critics of the Agreement.

He told Steinberg that the executive had to be established 'on the inclusive basis agreed on Good Friday', as did the North–South Ministerial Council, and with 'the release of prisoners and a speedy process of demilitarisation'.[205] Adams was sharing his frustrations with the White House and defending his own position; the Clinton administration, extending its peace-making efforts beyond the GFA, was a conduit for all parties.

The Marching Season also saw Clinton becoming the focus for members of the Protestant community in Northern Ireland. Following the events at Drumcree, the local Orange Order continued to be a presence in the area and was the cause of some disorder as they endeavoured to complete their march.[206] Perry Reid, the Grand Secretary of the County Tyrone Grand Lodge, wrote to Clinton on 3 September 1998. Reid asked the President 'to use all your good offices' to ensure that politicians and other protagonists in the peace process become 'aware of the real depth of feeling which our people are suffering at this time'.[207] In reply, Clinton requested that Reid 'reach out' to the other residents in his area: 'I am certain that you will find more in common that you might think, and that by dialogue you can reach a suitable outcome.'[208] This echoed his comment to Blair that the politicians were hampering the people's desire for peace. The President was viewed as someone who could influence British policy over individual cases. Following Mowlam's successful efforts to secure the release from prison in August 1998 of two British soldiers who were responsible for the death of Peter McBride, a Northern Irish Catholic, in 1992 (both of whom subsequently returned to the British Army), McBride's mother wrote to the President.[209] Mrs McBride argued that 'a hierarchy of victims in this conflict' meant that 'families who have lost loved ones through the actions of the British Army and the RUC are marginalised, ignored, blamed and deceived'.[210] As such, Mrs McBride asked Clinton to use his 'influence to ensure that the British Government treats all victims and all perpetrators equally'.[211] The President's response displayed his familiar empathy: 'I read your letter with understanding and appreciation for the pain and loss that only you can fully know . . . . A just peace is the greatest legacy to your son and all the other victims.'[212]

The quest for such a peace was problematised by the decommissioning impasse. Thus, much of the GFA continued without implementation, including the new Executive throughout 1998 and into the following year. Joseph Jamieson wrote to Clinton on 26 May 1999, on behalf of the Irish–American Labor Coalition. He urged the President 'to use again the positive influence of the American people and government to ensure that the Agreement is implemented as negotiated'.[213] In his response, the President was optimistic about the peace process.[214] In a handwritten aside, he added, 'We're working hard to save the peace – keep your fingers crossed.'[215] That same month, the five co-chairs of the ACCIA wrote to the President, concerned by the decommissioning stalemate.[216] Clinton wrote to each of them individually, assuring them that 'the peace process remains on track'.[217] Yet Clinton's persuasive abilities were contingent on the Northern Ireland parties' willingness to agree. For instance, during the abortive attempt to reach a settlement on decommissioning a year after the GFA, the President urged all sides to come to an agreement. On 30 June 1999, Blair and Campbell witnessed the impact that Clinton's call had on David Trimble: 'looking away from us, whispering and mumbling, humming like he did when was nervous, then turned to us, wiped his mobile on his sleeve and said "It's President Clinton"'.[218] Despite Trimble's embarrassed reaction, on this occasion, even the President could not guarantee a deal. The unionists had already negotiated the GFA with Sinn Féin, despite the IRA failing to decommission its arms. Trimble was unwilling to agree to Sinn Féin being admitted to the Northern Ireland Executive without decommissioning. Blair proposed that Sinn Féin participate in the Executive, but with the caveat that decommissioning should occur by May 2000. Trimble's refusal to accept Blair's compromise meant that decommissioning remained a threat to the GFA for another six years.[219]

The president's optimism, and active interest, was ultimately rewarded. On 2 December 1999, the institutions described in the GFA, including the National Executive, were finally established with powers devolved to Stormont. On 23 October 2001, nine months after Clinton had vacated the White House, the IRA commenced decommissioning. Almost four years later, on 26 September 2005, the IRA completed its decommissioning. Over the next three years, unionist paramilitary groups would also decommission its weapons. Despite subsequent setbacks and challenges, the GFA's success was arguably personified by Ian Paisley (leader of the Democratic Unionist Party, 1971–2008), who withdrew from the peace talks on the admittance of Sinn Féin and would campaign against the resulting agreement, but serve as Northern Ireland's First Minister (2007–8).[220]

## Conclusion

Anthony Lewis, writing in *The New York Times* three days after the GFA, identified the changing circumstances that enabled the peace process.[221] He explained that Ireland was a prosperous nation, which had ceased to be controlled by Catholicism. This eased the fears of Protestants. Republicans could no longer portray Britain in colonial terms, given that the British interest in Northern Ireland revolved around a sense of duty to its Protestant community. The American involvement – namely, the risk of Clinton issuing a visa to Adams – helped steer the IRA towards the peace process. The role of the US was enabled by changes amongst Irish–Americans, who were no longer dominated by mistrust towards Britain and a pro-republican solution to the 'Troubles'. Lewis concluded by noting the key change in Northern Ireland: the majority of the people wanted peace and accepted the need for compromise.[222] Mary McGrory, writing in *The Washington Post*, acknowledged the role of other protagonists, albeit reserving special praise for the President.[223]

The context of his immediate predecessors grants the opportunity to attempt a more nuanced understanding of the forty-second President's role in the signing of the GFA. Much like Nixon, Carter and Reagan, Clinton was a conduit between the interested parties and protagonists in the Northern Ireland. Much like his predecessors, Clinton was willing to help if the US government was invited to do so. Unlike his predecessors, he was in the right place at the right time: he could become directly involved in the process of answering the Northern Ireland question. The ending of the Cold War and the DSD meant that Clinton did not have to be worried about siding with one ally against another, or risking the 'special relationship' amidst concerns for Western security. Clinton was the right person at the right time: his detailed understanding of the issues, coupled with the knowledge of his NSC about Northern Ireland, meant that he was arguably the most prepared president since Nixon to offer a cogent and considered intervention. Perhaps Clinton's key attribute was his empathy. For instance, in July 1999, he remarked to Blair:

> [S]omebody ought to talk to Gerry [Adams] about what are their people going to do with their lives when this is over. I think it's a big problem. It plays on their psychology . . . . I think you really have to think about what we can do not only to guarantee their security and safety, but to give some meaning to their lives, some way that they can participate in the new Ireland. I may be wrong, but I think it's a huge problem for Gerry Adams, even if most are not aware of what the real problem is . . . .[224]

Clinton was clearly engaged in the human drama of the peace process. More broadly, Clinton's work on Northern Ireland was part of all three aspects of his presidency: domestic, foreign and electioneering. In domestic politics, he satisfied the Irish–American lobby and worked with relevant members of Congress to help secure Northern Ireland's future. The GFA helped attain one of Clinton's political legacies: the peacemaker. Likewise, Northern Ireland underlined Clinton's peace-making credentials in foreign policy and cemented his partnership with Blair. Irish–America was a key component of Clinton's electioneering strategy.

Clinton's work on Northern Ireland does lend credence to the importance of individuals in history. Nevertheless, broader structures and phenomena were just as important as individuals such as the President. In the post-Cold War epoch, internal national – and ethnic – conflicts became internationalised. Moreover, the peace process would not have happened unless the Northern Ireland parties wanted it to happen, regardless of any encouragement or demands from the Oval Office. The US government's view was consistent during the 'Troubles': it was ready to assist if invited to do so. The Clinton administration was invited by all participants to do just that and did so to great effect.

## Notes

1. John Dumbrell, 'Diplomacy in Northern Ireland: Successful pragmatic international engagement', in Mark White (ed.), *The Presidency of Bill Clinton: The Legacy of a New Domestic and Foreign Policy* (London: I. B. Tauris, 2012), 181.
2. Adrian Guelke, 'The United States, Irish Americans and the Northern Ireland peace process', *International Affairs*, 72:3 (July 1996), 535–6.
3. See Mark White, 'Introduction', in White (ed.), *The Presidency of Bill Clinton*, 5; Jason A. Edwards, *Navigating the Post-Cold War World: President Clinton's Foreign Policy Rhetoric* (Plymouth, MD: Lexington, 2008), xiii; John Dumbrell, *Clinton's Foreign Policy: Between the Bushes, 1992–2000* (Abingdon: Routledge, 2009). For Clinton's domestic policy, particularly with reference to his relationship with Speaker Newt Gingrich (R-GA, 1995–9) and the positioning of his

party as 'New Democrats', see, for instance, Steven M. Gillon, *The Pact: Bill Clinton, Newt Gingrich, and the Rivalry that Defined a Generation* (Oxford: Oxford University Press, 2008); and Kenneth S. Baer, *Reinventing Democrats: The Politics of Liberalism from Reagan to Clinton* (Lawrence: University Press of Kansas, 2000).

4. Wilson, *Irish America*, 293.
5. Timothy Lynch, *Turf War: The Clinton Administration and Northern Ireland* (Aldershot: Ashgate, 2004).
6. See Guelke, 'The United States, Irish Americans and the Northern Ireland peace process', 521–36; Eamonn O'Kane, 'The Republic of Ireland's policy towards Northern Ireland: The international dimension as a policy tool', *Irish Studies in International Affairs*, 13 (2002), 121–33; Feargal Cochrane, 'Irish-America, the end of the IRA's armed struggle and the utility of "soft power"', *Journal of Peace Research*, 44:2 (March 2007), 215–31; and Mary-Alice C. Clancy, *Peace Without Consensus: Power Sharing Politics in Northern Ireland* (Farnham: Ashgate, 2010), 171–88.
7. See, for instance, Michael Cox, 'Bringing in the "international": The IRA ceasefire and the end of the Cold War', *International Affairs*, 73:4 (October 1997), 671–93; Michael Cox, 'Northern Ireland: The war that came in from the cold', *Irish Studies in International Affairs*, 9 (1998), 73–84; Michael Cox, 'The war that came in from the cold: Clinton and the Irish question', *World Policy Journal*, 16:1 (Spring 1999), 59–67; and Paul Dixon, 'Performing the Northern Ireland peace process on the world stage', *Political Science Quarterly*, 121: 1 (Spring 2006), 61–91.
8. Wilson, *Irish America*, 293.
9. Andrew J. Wilson, 'From the Beltway to Belfast: The Clinton administration, Sinn Féin, and the Northern Ireland peace process', *New Hibernia Review*, 1:3 (Autumn 1997), 25.
10. Bill Clinton, *My Life* (London: Arrow Books, 2005), 401.
11. Ibid.
12. Miller Center, 'Interview with Anthony Lake (2002)', University of Virginia, 21 May 2002, http://millercenter.org/president/clinton/oralhistory/anthony-lake-2002, accessed 4 June 2015.
13. Ibid.
14. Conor O'Clery, 'British wary of Clinton statement: Bill Clinton's message to Irish voters has been well received by Irish–American group', *The Irish Times*, 28 October 1992, 11.
15. Clinton, *My Life*, 401.
16. Thompson, *American Policy*, 166–7.

17. Democratic Party platforms, 'Democratic Party platform of 1992', 13 July 1992. Online by Gerhard Peters and John T. Woolley, *The American Presidency Project*, http://www.presidency.ucsb.edu/ws/?pid=29610, accessed on 7 May 2015.

18. Republican Party platforms, 'Republican Party platform of 1992', 17 August 1992. Online by Gerhard Peters and John T. Woolley, *The American Presidency Project*, http://www.presidency.ucsb.edu/ws/?pid=25847, accessed on 7 May 2015.

19. William J. Clinton, 'Address accepting the presidential nomination at the Democratic National Convention in New York', 16 July 1992. Online by Gerhard Peters and John T. Woolley, *The American Presidency Project*, http://www.presidency.ucsb.edu/ws/?pid=25958; George Bush, 'Remarks accepting the presidential nomination at the Republican National Convention in Houston', 20 August 1992. Online by Gerhard Peters and John T. Woolley, *The American Presidency Project*, http://www.presidency.ucsb.edu/ws/?pid=21352. Both accessed 5 June 2015.

20. 'The first Clinton–Bush–Perot presidential debate', 11 October 1992, http://www.debates.org/index.php?page=october-11-1992-first-half-debate-transcript and http://www.debates.org/index.php?page=october-11-1992-second-half-debate-transcript; 'The second Bush–Clinton–Perot presidential debate', 15 October 1992, http://www.debates.org/index.php?page=october-15-1992-first-half-debate-transcriptandhttp://www.debates.org/index.php?page=october-15-1992-second-half-debate-transcript; and 'The third Clinton–Bush–Perot presidential debate', 19 October 1992, http://www.debates.org/index.php?page=october-19-1992-debate-transcript. All accessed 24 July 2015.

21. William J. Clinton, 'Inaugural address', 20 January 1993. Online by Gerhard Peters and John T. Woolley, *The American Presidency Project*, http://www.presidency.ucsb.edu/ws/?pid=46366, accessed 24 July 2015.

22. Wilson, 'From the Beltway to Belfast', 24–6.

23. Gordon Greig, 'Stop your interfering: Major plans warning to Clinton on Ulster', *Daily Mail*, 9 November 1992, 20.

24. Ibid.

25. Miller Center, 'Interview with Edward M. Kennedy (2/27/2006)', University of Virginia, 27 February 2006, http://millercenter.org/oralhistory/interview/edward_m_kennedy_2-27-2006, accessed 5 October 2015.

26. Interview with Mr Seán Donlon (former Irish ambassador to the US), 12 December 2014.

27. Ibid.
28. Thompson, *American Policy*, 165. This was ostensibly a low priority for Warren Christopher, the US Secretary of State (1993–7). The issue is not discussed in his memoir: Warren Christopher, *Chances of a Lifetime: A Memoir* (New York: Scribner, 2001). Neither was it discussed in Christopher's contribution to the Miller Center's Oral History Project on the Clinton administration, although he noted that it was 'an important achievement'; see Miller Center, 'Interview with Warren Christopher and Stroke Talbott', University of Virginia, 15–16 April 2002, http://millercenter.org/oralhistory/interview/warren-christopher-strobe-talbott, accessed 30 September 2015.
29. Andrew J. Wilson, 'From the Beltway to Belfast', 34. For an introduction to Anglo-American relations during the Clinton era, see, for instance, Dumbrell, *A Special Relationship*, 134–59.
30. Letter, Hamilton Fish, Thomas J. Marton, et al. to The Honorable William Jefferson Clinton, 22 February 1993, Clinton Presidential Records, NSC Records Management, [Major, Telcoms, Memcons], [9300727], [OA/ID 2204], National Security Council, Lake Subject Files 1993–1996, Box 1 of 8, William J. Clinton Library (hereafter Clinton Library).
31. Ibid.
32. Letter, Edward M. Kennedy, Christopher J. Dodd, John F. Kerry et al. to The President, 22 February 1993, Clinton Presidential Records, NSC Records Management, [Major, Telcoms, Memcons], [9300727], [OA/ID 2204], National Security Council, Lake Subject Files 1993–1996, Box 1 of 8, Clinton Library.
33. Miller Center, 'Interview with Anthony Lake (2002)', University of Virginia, 21 May 2002, http://millercenter.org/president/clinton/oralhistory/anthony-lake-2002, accessed 4 June 2015.
34. Ibid.
35. Thompson, *American Policy*, 169–72.
36. Miller Center, 'Interview with Niall O'Dowd', University of Virginia, 18 November 2010, http://millercenter.org/oralhistory/interview/niall_odowd, accessed 4 October 2015.
37. Raymond Seitz, *Over Here* (London: Weidenfeld & Nicolson, 1998), 286, 289.
38. William J. Clinton, 'Statement on the peace process in Northern Ireland', 30 October 1993. Online by Gerhard Peters and John T. Woolley, *The American Presidency Project*, http://www.presidency.ucsb.edu/ws/?pid=46046, accessed on 10 June 2015.
39. Ibid.

40. Bew, *Ireland*, 541.
41. Ibid.
42. Tim Pat Coogan, *The Troubles: Ireland's Ordeal and the Search for Peace* (New York: Palgrave, 2002), 439.
43. See, for instance, Editorial, 'Ulster Breakthrough', *The Washington Post*, Friday, 2 September 1994, A22; and William E. Schmidt, 'Day 1 of I.R.A.'s cease-fire: Hopes tinged by skepticism', *The New York Times*, Friday, 2 September 1993, A1.
44. William J. Clinton, 'Statement on the peace process in Northern Ireland', 15 December 1993. Online by Gerhard Peters and John T. Woolley, *The American Presidency Project*, http://www.presidency. ucsb.edu/ws/?pid=46244, accessed on 10 June 2015.
45. Ibid.
46. Conor O'Clery, 'Clinton feels the pressure to make efforts for Ireland', *The Irish Times*, 22 December 1993, 5.
47. Ibid.
48. Clinton, *My Life*, 563.
49. Ibid., 578.
50. Ibid.
51. Ibid., 579–80.
52. Ibid., 580.
53. Seitz, *Over Here*, 290.
54. Ibid.
55. Interview with Mr Donlon.
56. Seitz, *Over Here*, 287.
57. Ibid., 290.
58. Ibid.
59. Ibid.
60. John Major, *The Autobiography* (London: HarperCollins, 1999), 456.
61. Nancy Soderberg, 7 March 2000, quoted in Timothy J. Lynch, 'The Gerry Adams visa in Anglo-American relations', *Irish Studies in International Affairs*, 14 (2003), 35.
62. Lynch, 'The Gerry Adams visa', 35.
63. Clinton, *My Life*, 580.
64. Ibid., 581.
65. Major, *The Autobiography*, 456.
66. Interview with Mr Donlon.
67. Miller Center, 'Interview with Nancy Soderberg (2007)', University of Virginia, 10–11 May 2007, http://millercenter.org/president/ clinton/oralhistory/nancy-soderberg, accessed 4 June 2015.

68. Miller Center, 'Interview with Gerry Adams', University of Virginia, 11 November 2010, http://millercenter.org/oralhistory/interview/gerry_adams, accessed 30 September 2015.
69. Ibid.
70. Seitz, *Over Here*, 279.
71. Ibid., 280.
72. Ibid., 292.
73. Ibid., 289. (Kennedy was challenged by Mitt Romney for his Massachusetts US Senate seat in 1994.)
74. Lynch, 'The Gerry Adams visa', 43.
75. Ibid.
76. Steven Greenhouse, 'Clinton in bind over visa for I.R.A. wing leader', *The New York Times*, 27 January 1994, A7.
77. R. W. Apple, Jr, 'President overruled officials in granting a visa to Adams', *The New York Times*, 2 February 1994, A1.
78. Ibid.
79. O'Clery, *The Greening of the White House*, 150–7.
80. Ibid., 157.
81. Ibid., 160–1.
82. Miller Center, 'Interview with Anthony Lake (2002)', University of Virginia, 21 May 2002, http://millercenter.org/president/clinton/oralhistory/anthony-lake-2002, accessed 4 June 2015.
83. Conor O'Clery, 'UUP leader says Clinton meeting was very fruitful', *The Irish Times*, 2 November 1995, 5.
84. Bew, *Ireland*, 546.
85. Thompson, *American Policy*, 175–9.
86. Kevin Rafter, 'George Mitchell and the role of the peace talks chairman', *The Irish Review*, 38 (Spring 2008), 16.
87. Clinton, *My Life*, 648.
88. Ibid.
89. Thompson, *American Policy*, 181.
90. Speech by the President of USA to the People of Derry, 30 November 1995, accessed via University of Ulster, *CAIN Web Service: Conflict and Politics in Northern Ireland*, http://cain.ulst.ac.uk/events/peace/docs/pres2.htm, 28 April 2015 (hereafter just URL).
91. Ibid.
92. Major, *The Autobiography*, 484.
93. Clinton, *My Life*, 686.
94. Ibid., 687.
95. Conor O'Clery, 'White House impatience at slow pace of peace process hinted in replies', *The Irish Times*, 3 August 1995, 5.

96. Quoted in Conor O'Clery, 'Clinton carves out rule as world peace-maker', *The Irish Times*, 2 December 1995, 9.

97. Quoted in Martin Walker, 'US view: Re-elected are the peacemakers: White House ecstatic at O'Clinton's Irish triumph', *The Guardian*, 2 December 1995, 3.

98. R. W. Apple, Jr, 'Clinton's peace strategy; President hopes to do well with voters by doing good on the international stage', *The New York Times*, Saturday, 2 December 1995, 1.

99. Ibid.

100. Thompson, *American Policy*, 182.

101. George J. Mitchell, John de Chastelain and Harri Holkeri, *Report of the International Body on Arms Decommissioning*, 22 January 1996, accessed via http://cain.ulst.ac.uk/events/peace/docs/gm24196.htm, 18 April 2015.

102. Rafter, 'George Mitchell and the role of the peace talks chairman', 17.

103. Bew, *Ireland*, 547.

104. Thompson, *American Policy*, 184–5.

105. Clinton, *My Life*, 700.

106. Bew, *Ireland*, 547.

107. Anthony Lake, Briefing, Meeting with British Labour Party Leader Tony Blair, Date: April 12, 1996, Location: Oval Office, Time: 10:45–11:05 a.m., 'Points to be made for meeting with British Labour Party Leader Tony Blair', date unknown, in Declassified Records MDR 2009-0816-M United Kingdom, Adobe Acrobat Document, 'Declassified Documents concerning United Kingdom', *Clinton Digital Library*, http://clinton.presidentiallibraries.us/items/show/16210, accessed 4 April 2015.

108. Memorandum of Conversation, Meeting with British Labor [sic] Leader Tony Blair, April 12, 1996, 11:00–11:30am, The Oval Office, in Declassified Records MDR 2009-0816-M United Kingdom, Adobe Acrobat Document, 'Declassified Documents concerning United Kingdom', *Clinton Digital Library*, http://clinton.presidentiallibraries.us/items/show/16210, accessed 4 April 2015.

109. Ibid.

110. Ibid.

111. See Geoffrey Smith, *Reagan and Thatcher* (London: Bodley Head, 1990), 228.

112. William J. Clinton, 'Message to the House of Representatives returning without approval foreign relations legislation', 12 April 1996. Online by Gerhard Peters and John T. Woolley, *The American Presidency*

*Project*, http://www.presidency.ucsb.edu/ws/?pid=52671, accessed 6 November 2015.

113. Ibid.
114. H.R. 1561 – Foreign Relations Authorization Act, Fiscal Years 1996 and 1997, 104th Congress (1995–1996), accessed via https://www.congress.gov/bill/104th-congress/house-bill/1561, 7 May 2016.
115. Kevin McNamara, *The MacBride Principles: Irish America Strikes Back* (Liverpool: Liverpool University Press, 2009), 75–8.
116. Letter, Bill Clinton to James Lyons, U.S. Observer for the International Fund for Ireland, U.S. Department of States [Same one to Brian Atwood, Administrator, Agency for International Development], 24 August 1996, Clinton Presidential Records, National Security Council, European Affairs, Lawrence Butler, N. Ireland – Economic Initiatives – IFI [International Fund for Ireland] 1998 [1- [OA/ID 1574], National Security Council, Box 2 of 16, Clinton Library.
117. Ibid.
118. Arthur, *Special Relationships*, 133.
119. Republican Party platforms, 'Republican Party platform of 1996', 12 August 1996. Online by Gerhard Peters and John T. Woolley, *The American Presidency Project*, http://www.presidency.ucsb.edu/ws/?pid=25848, accessed 5 June 2015.
120. Robert Dole, 'Address accepting the presidential nomination at the Republican National Convention in San Diego', 15 August 1996. Online by Gerhard Peters and John T. Woolley, *The American Presidency Project*, http://www.presidency.ucsb.edu/ws/?pid=25960, accessed 5 June 2015.
121. Democratic Party platforms, 'Democratic Party platform of 1996', 26 August 1996. Online by Gerhard Peters and John T. Woolley, *The American Presidency Project*, http://www.presidency.ucsb.edu/ws/?pid=29611, accessed 5 June 2015.
122. Ibid.
123. Ibid.
124. William J. Clinton, 'Remarks accepting the presidential nomination at the Democratic National Convention in Chicago', 29 August 1996. Online by Gerhard Peters and John T. Woolley, *The American Presidency Project*, http://www.presidency.ucsb.edu/ws/?pid=53253, accessed 5 June 2015.
125. Ibid.
126. Wilson, 'From the Beltway to Belfast', 26–7.
127. Ibid., 27.
128. Ibid. For the 1996 presidential election, see, for instance, E. D. Dover, *Clinton's Incumbency and Television* (Westport, CT: Praeger,

1998); and Bob Woodwood, *The Choice: How Clinton Won* (New York: Simon & Schuster, 1996).

129. Miller Center, 'Interview with Anthony Lake (2002)', University of Virginia, 21 May 2002, http://millercenter.org/president/clinton/oralhistory/anthony-lake-2002, accessed 4 June 2015.

130. Anthony Seldon, *Blair* (London: Free Press, 2005), 349.

131. Ibid., 353.

132. Address by the Prime Minister Mr. Tony Blair at the Royal Agricultural Society Belfast, 16 May 1997, accessed via http://cain.ulst.ac.uk/events/peace/docs/tb16597.htm, 16 April 2015.

133. Ibid.

134. Seldon, *Blair*, 353.

135. Letter, Rep. Ben Gilman et al to President William Jefferson Clinton, 19 May 1997, Clinton Presidential Records, NSC Records Management, [Northern Ireland Peace . . .], 9703523 [OA/ID 1621], NSC Records Management, Box 15 of 16, Clinton Library.

136. Ibid.

137. Miller Center, 'Interview with James Steinberg (2008)', University of Virginia, 1 April 2008, http://millercenter.org/president/clinton/oralhistory/james-steinberg, accessed 4 June 2015. This complementary comparison of Blair and Clinton's personalities lends weight to the enquiry into personalities as a factor in the 'special relationship'. See, for instance, John Dumbrell, 'Personal diplomacy: Relations between prime ministers and presidents', in Dobson and Marsh (eds), *Anglo-American Relations*, 82–104.

138. Memorandum of Conversation, Private Meeting with Prime Minister Blair and British Cabinet, May 29, 1997, 11:40 a.m.–12 noon, The Cabinet Room, No. 10 Downing Street, in Declassified Records MDR 2009-0816-M United Kingdom, Adobe Acrobat Document, 'Declassified Documents concerning United Kingdom', *Clinton Digital Library*, http://clinton.presidentiallibraries.us/items/show/16210; Memorandum of Conversation, Restricted Meeting with British Prime Minister Tony Blair, May 29, 1997, 12:00–12:30 p.m., No. 10 Downing Street, London, in Declassified Records MDR 2009-0816-M United Kingdom, Adobe Acrobat Document, 'Declassified Documents concerning United Kingdom', *Clinton Digital Library*, both accessed 4 April 2015.

139. Memorandum of Conversation, Restricted Meeting with British Prime Minister Tony Blair, May 29, 1997, 12:00–12:30 p.m., No. 10 Downing Street, London, in Declassified Records MDR 2009-0816-M United Kingdom, Adobe Acrobat Document, 'Declassified Documents concerning United Kingdom', *Clinton Digital Library*,

http://clinton.presidentiallibraries.us/items/show/16210, accessed 4 April 2015.

140. Ibid.
141. Miller Center, 'Interview with Anthony Lake (2002)', University of Virginia, 21 May 2002, http://millercenter.org/president/clinton/ oralhistory/anthony-lake-2002, accessed 4 June 2015.
142. Letter, Bill Clinton to The Honorable Benjamin A. Gilman, Chairman, Committee on International Relations, House of Representatives, 2 July 1997, Clinton Presidential Records, NSC Records Management, [Northern Ireland Peace ...], 9703523 [OA/ID 1621], NSC Records Management, Box 15 of 16, Clinton Library.
143. Ibid.
144. Thompson, *American Policy*, 195–7.
145. See, for instance, AP, 'Britain's Blair on the hot seat after handshake with IRA ally', *St. Louis Post-Dispatch*, Tuesday, 14 October 1997, 08A; and Dan Blaz, 'Blair has historic meeting with leader of IRA ally', *The Washington Post*, Tuesday, 14 October 1997, A01.
146. Letter, Joe Roche, National Chairman, Political Education (Facilitator), Ancient Order of Hibernians, to President Clinton, 9 June 1997, and Letter, Joe Roche, National Chairman, Political Education (Facilitator), Ancient Order of Hibernians, to Mr Sandy Berger, National Security Adviser, 9 June 1997, Clinton Presidential Records, NSC Records Management, [Northern Ireland Peace ...], 9703523 [OA/ID 1621], NSC Records Management, Box 15 of 16, Clinton Library.
147. Letter, Joe Roche, National Chairman, Political Education (Facilitator), Ancient Order of Hibernians, to Mr Sandy Berger, National Security Adviser, 9 June 1997, Clinton Presidential Records, NSC Records Management, [Northern Ireland Peace ...], 9703523 [OA/ID 1621], NSC Records Management, Box 15 of 16, Clinton Library.
148. Letter, Samuel R. Berger, Assistant to the President for National Security Affairs, To Joe Roche, National Chairman, Political Education (Facilitator), Ancient Order of Hibernians in America, 27 October 1997, Clinton Presidential Records, NSC Records Management, [Northern Ireland Peace ...], 9703523 [OA/ID 1621], Clinton Presidential Records, NSC Records Management, Box 15 of 16, Clinton Library.
149. Ibid.
150. Thompson, *American Policy*, 197–8.
151. Memorandum of Conversation, Meeting with Tony Blair, Prime Minister of the United Kingdom, February, 5, 1998, 11:00 a.m. – Oval

Office, in Declassified Records MDR 2009-0816-M United Kingdom, Adobe Acrobat Document, 'Declassified Documents concerning United Kingdom', *Clinton Digital Library*, accessed 4 April 2015.

152. 'Propositions on Heads of Agreement', 12 January 1998, accessed via http://cain.ulst.ac.uk/events/peace/docs/hoa12198.htm, 18 April 2015.

153. Bew, *Ireland*, 548–9.

154. Clinton, *My Life*, 780.

155. Ibid.

156. Joe Carroll, 'Admission fee to White House party is progress on the North; Irish politicians, from North and South, will hobnob next week in Washington. But Bill Clinton wants to see a peace settlement and will be breathing down their necks', *The Irish Times*, 14 March 1998, 8.

157. Gerry Adams, *Hope and History: Making Peace in Ireland* (Kerry, Ireland: Brandon, 2004), 339.

158. Memorandum, Lawrence E. Butler through Donald K. Bandler to Samuel R. Berger, Subject: Letter to Father Sean McManus on Northern Ireland and MacBride Principles, 2 April 1998, Clinton Presidential Records, NSC Records Management, [Northern Ireland Peace . . .], 9802130 [OA/ID 2024], NSC Records Management, Box 16 of 16, Clinton Library.

159. Mo Mowlam, *Momentum: The Struggle for Peace, Politics and the People* (London: Hodder & Stoughton, 2002), 202.

160. Ibid.

161. Letter, Fr. Seán McManus (President, Irish National Caucus, Inc.), to The Honorable Samuel R. Berger (Assistant to the President for National Security Affairs), 18 March 1998, Clinton Presidential Records, NSC Records Management, [Northern Ireland Peace . . .], 9802130 [OA/ID 2024], NSC Records Management, Box 16 of 16, Clinton Library.

162. Letter, Samuel R. Berger (Assistant to the President for National Security Affairs) to The Reverend Sean McManus (President, Irish National Caucus), 6 April 1998, Clinton Presidential Records, NSC Records Management, [Northern Ireland Peace . . .], 9802130 [OA/ID 2024], NSC Records Management, Box 16 of 16, Clinton Library.

163. Seldon, *Blair*, 360.

164. Clinton, *My Life*, 784.

165. 'Draft Paper for Discussion' by Independent Chairmen of the Multi-Party Talks (6 April 1998), accessed via http://cain.ulst.ac.uk/events/peace/docs/gm060498draft.htm, 16 April 2015.

166. Alastair Campbell and Richard Stott (eds), *The Blair Years: Extracts from the Alastair Campbell Diaries* (London: Hutchinson, 2007), Friday, 10 April 1998, 296.
167. Ibid.
168. Ibid., 297.
169. Tony Blair, *A Journey* (London: Hutchinson, 2010), 173.
170. Clinton, *My Life*, 784.
171. Bertie Ahern, *The Autobiography* (London: Arrow Books, 2010), 234; and Adams, *Hope and History*, 205.
172. Rafter, 'George Mitchell and the role of the peace talks chairman', 20.
173. Miller Center, 'Interview with Anthony Lake (2002)', University of Virginia, 21 May 2002, http://millercenter.org/president/clinton/oralhistory/anthony-lake-2002, accessed 4 June 2015. (The 1998 Nobel Peace Prize was awarded to John Hume and David Trimble.)
174. Seldon, *Blair*, 361.
175. Ibid.
176. Remarks on the Northern Ireland Peace Process and an Exchange with Reporters, April 10, 1998, Administration of William J. Clinton, 1998/Apr. 10, *The Public Papers of the Presidents of the United States: William J. Clinton, Book 1 – January 1 to June 30, 1998* (Washington, DC: United States Government Printing Office, 1999), 550.
177. Ibid.
178. Ibid., 551.
179. Memorandum, Larry Butler and David Leavy to Sandy Berger and James Steinberg, Subject: Strategy for Northern Ireland Settlement Agreement, 7 April 1998, 'FOIA 2006-1759-F - Good Friday Agreement and the Northern Ireland Peace Process', *Clinton Digital Library*, http://clinton.presidentiallibraries.us/items/show/14597, accessed 11 June 2015.
180. Ibid.
181. Joe Carroll, 'Clinton saw need to play down vital role in NI: The White House played an active role behind the scenes but believed it would have most impact as a facilitator rather than as a mediator', *The Irish Times*, 11 April 1998, 62.
182. Memorandum, Lawrence E. Butler through Donald K. Bandler to James Steinberg, Subject: Northern Ireland Peace Roll-out: Phase II, 14 April 1998, 'FOIA 2006-1759-F – Good Friday Agreement and the Northern Ireland Peace Process', *Clinton Digital Library*, http://clinton.presidentiallibraries.us/items/show/14597, accessed 11 June 2015.
183. Ibid.

184. Memorandum, Jim Lyons to Sandy Berger, re: Northern Ireland, 27 April 1998, Clinton Presidential Records, National Security Council, European Affairs, Keirn Brown, Ireland-Coordinated Meeting/ US Initiatives [2], [OA/ID 2390], National Security Council, Box 1 of 16, Clinton Library.
185. Ibid.
186. Clinton, *My Life*, 587.
187. Mowlam, *Momentum*, 235.
188. Memorandum of Telephone Conservation, 'Telcon with British Prime Minister Tony Blair', 24 April 1998, accessed via National Security Council and Records Management Office, 'Declassified documents concerning Tony Blair', *Clinton Digital Library*, http://clinton.presidentiallibraries.us/items/show/48779, accessed 11 December 2015.
189. Memorandum, Jim Lyons to Sandy Berger, re: Northern Ireland, 27 April 1998, Clinton Presidential Records, National Security Council, European Affairs, Keirn Brown, Ireland-Coordinated Meeting/ US Initiatives [2], [OA/ID 2390], National Security Council, Box 1 of 16, Clinton Library.
190. Ibid.
191. Memorandum, Lawrence E. Butler through Donald K. Bandler to James Steinberg, May 8, 1998, Subject: Your interview with CNN, 3:00-3:30p.m., Monday, May 11, White House TV Studio, 459 OEOB, Clinton Presidential Records, National Security Council, European Affairs, Lawrence Butler, Northern Ireland, 1 May 1998 [4], [OA/ID 1574], 2006-1759-F, National Security Council, Box 3 of 16, Clinton Library.
192. Ibid.
193. Bew, *Ireland*, 549–50.
194. Memorandum, Mary B. Derosa through James E. Baker to Samuel R. Berger, March 9, 1998, Subject: Replies to Six Representatives, Senator Torricelli and Ron Dellums Concerning Bail for Irish Extraditees, Clinton Presidential Records, NSC Records Management, [Northern Ireland Peace . . .], 9800075 [OA/ID 2008], NSC Records Management, Box 15 of 16, Clinton Library.
195. Ibid.
196. Ibid. The Congressmen who wrote to Clinton were Rep. Benjamin A. Gilman, R-NY (Chair of the House Committee on International Relations), Rep. Richard E. Neal (D-MA), Rep. Edward A. Pease (R-IN), Rep. James T. Walsh (R-NY), Rep. Peter T. King (R-NY) and Rep. Tom Lantos (D-CA), along with Senator Robert Torricelli (D-NY) and former Rep. Ron Dellums (D-CA).

197. See, for instance, Jenny McCartney, 'It's not so far from Guantanamo Bay to the Maze', *The Telegraph* online, 13 July 2003, http://www.telegraph.co.uk/comment/personal-view/3593718/Its-not-so-far-from-Guantanamo-Bay-to-the-Maze.html, accessed 10 April 2015; BBC News, 'IRA men can challenge extradition', http://news.bbc.co.uk/1/hi/events/northern_ireland/latest_news/190327.stm, accessed 10 April 2015.

198. Schedule Proposal, Samuel Berger to: Stephanie Streett, Request: Meeting with Gerry Adams, Purpose: To reinforce support for Sinn Fein's [sic] engagement in making the April 10 Northern Ireland peace accord work, Date and Time: May 29, after 1 p.m., Clinton Presidential Records, National Security Council, European Affairs, Lawrence Butler, Northern Ireland, 1 May 1998 [4], [OA/ID 1574], National Security Council, Box 3 of 16, Clinton Library.

199. Memorandum, Lawrence E. Butler through Donald K. Bandler to James B. Steinberg, June 17, 1998, Subject: Your meeting with House Irish Caucus Members, H140, 1:30-2:00 p.m., Thursday, June 17, Clinton Presidential Records, National Security Council, European Affairs, Butler, Lawrence, Northern Ireland, 1 May 1998 [2], [OA/ID 1574], National Security Council, Box 2 of 16, Clinton Library.

200. Ibid.

201. 'Developments at Drumcree', accessed via http://cain.ulst.ac.uk/issues/parade/develop.htm, 13 May 2015.

202. Clinton, *My Life*, 808.

203. Memorandum, Lawrence E. Butler through Donald K. Bandler to James Steinberg, August 20, 1998, Subject: Gerry Adams' Letter and Memo on Peace Accord Implementation; Aspects of the President's visit, Clinton Presidential Records, NSC Records Management, [Northern Ireland Peace . . .], 9805807, [ON/ID 2055], NSC Records Management, Box 16 of 16, Clinton Library.

204. Letter, Gerry Adams to Jim Steinberg, 5 August 1998, Clinton Presidential Records, National Security Council, European Affairs, Lawrence Butler, Northern Ireland, October 1998 – [3], [OA/ID 1963], National Security Council, Box 3 of 16, Clinton Library.

205. Ibid.

206. Memorandum, Samuel Berger to the President, Subject: Letter from Northern Ireland Orange Order Lodge on Parades and Your Visit, Date unknown, Clinton Presidential Records, National Security Council, European Affairs, Lawrence Butler, Northern Ireland, 1 May 1998 [1], [OA/ID 1574], National Security Council, Box 2 of 16, Clinton Library.

207. Letter, Perry Reid, County Grand Secretary, County Tyrone Grand Orange Lodge, to President Clinton, 3 September 1998, Clinton Presidential Records, National Security Council, European Affairs, Lawrence Butler, Northern Ireland, 1 May 1998 [1], [OA/ID 1574], 2006-1759-F, National Security Council, Box 2 of 16, Clinton Library.

208. Letter, Bill Clinton to Perry Reid, Date unknown, Clinton Presidential Records, National Security Council, European Affairs, Lawrence Butler, Northern Ireland, 1 May 1998 [1], [OA/ID 1574], National Security Council, Box 2 of 16, Clinton Library.

209. Memorandum, Samuel Berger to the President, Subject: Letter to Jean McBride – Northern Ireland, date unknown, Clinton Presidential Records, National Security Council, European Affairs, Lawrence Butler, Northern Ireland, 1 May 1998 [1], [OA/ID 1574], [OA/ID 1574], National Security Council, Box 2 of 16, Clinton Library.

210. Letter, Jean McBride to President Clinton, 3.9.1998, Clinton Presidential Records, National Security Council, European Affairs, Lawrence Butler, Northern Ireland, 1 May 1998 [1], [OA/ID 1574], [OA/ID 1574], National Security Council, Box 2 of 16, Clinton Library.

211. Ibid.

212. Letter, Bill Clinton to Mrs. Jean McBride, date unknown, Clinton Presidential Records, National Security Council, European Affairs, Lawrence Butler, Northern Ireland, 1 May 1998 [1], [OA/ID 1574], [OA/ID 1574], National Security Council, Box 2 of 16, Clinton Library.

213. Letter, Joseph Jamieson, Director, Irish–American Labor Coalition, American Labor Committee for Human Rights in Northern Ireland, to President William Jefferson Clinton, 26 May 1999, Clinton Presidential Records, NSC Records Management, [Good Friday Agreement . . .], 9904101, [ONID 2732], NSC Records Management, Box 15 of 16, Clinton Library.

214. Letter, Bill Clinton to Joseph Jamison, 29 June 1999, Clinton Presidential Records, NSC Records Management, [Good Friday Agreement . . .], 9904101, [ONID 2732], Clinton Presidential Records, NSC Records Management, [Good Friday Agreement . . .], 9802977, [OS/ID 2032], NSC Records Management, Box 15 of 16, Clinton Library.

215. Ibid.

216. Letter, Benjamin A. Gilman, Co-Chair, Ad-Hoc Committee on Irish Affairs, Richard E. Neal, Co-Chair, Ad-Hoc Communities on

Irish Affairs, Peter T. King, Co-Chair, Ad-Hoc Committee on Irish Affairs, Joseph Crowley, Co-Chair, Ad-Hoc Communities on Irish Affairs, James T. Walsh, Chairman, Friends of Ireland, to The President, 18 May 1999, Clinton Presidential Records, NSC Records Management, [Good Friday Agreement . . .], 9904101, [ONID 2732], NSC Records Management, Box 15 of 16, Clinton Library.

217. (Identical) Letters, Bill Clinton to Benjamin A. Gilman, Co-Chair, Ad-Hoc Committee on Irish Affairs, Richard E. Neal, Co-Chair, Ad-Hoc Committee on Irish Affairs, Peter T. King, Co-Chair, Ad-Hoc Committee on Irish Affairs, Joseph Crowley, Co-Chair, Ad-Hoc Committee on Irish Affairs, James T. Walsh, Chairman, Friends of Ireland, 27 July 1999, Clinton Presidential Records, NSC Records Management, [Good Friday Agreement . . .], 9904101, [ONID 2732], NSC Records Management, Box 15 of 16, Clinton Library.

218. Campbell, *The Blair Years*, Wednesday, 30 June 1999, 413.

219. Colin McInnes, 'A farewell to arms? Decommissioning and the peace process', in Cox, Guelke and Stephen (eds), *Farewell*, 85–6, 89.

220. Rafter, 'George Mitchell and the role of the peace talks chairman', 20.

221. Anthony Lewis, 'Abroad at home: solving the insoluble', *The New York Times*, Monday, 13 April 1998, A27.

222. Ibid.

223. Mary McGrory, 'Irish ayes smile on Clinton', *The Washington Post*, Thursday, 16 April 1998, A03.

224. Memorandum of Telephone Conservation, Telcon with British Prime Minister Blair, 16 July 1999, accessed via National Security Council and Records Management Office, 'Declassified documents concerning Tony Blair', *Clinton Digital Library*, http://clinton.presidentiallibraries.us/items/show/48779, accessed 11 December 2015.

# Conclusion

---

> The very fact that someone internationally as powerful as the President of the United States was supporting our peace process obviously strengthened our process enormously. We've a great debt of gratitude to him.
>
> John Hume on Bill Clinton, 29 September 2005.[1]

This monograph has examined the extent and nature of interventions by successive US presidents in the Northern Ireland conflict. In doing so, it has sought to identify the reasons for, and consequences of, American involvement in both Anglo-Irish relations and the peace process in Northern Ireland. This concluding chapter contends that this involvement was shaped by three differing components of the presidency: electioneering, domestic politics and foreign policy. Yet these components are all influenced by a single factor: the power of the US presidency. A president's interest in an issue inevitably legitimises its being worthy of wider attention and endorses any position or policy advocated by a party that gains the support of the US government. Thus, the role of the individual in history, particularly when that individual is the American president, is significant in the saga that ended the 'Troubles'. Indeed, the interest and action of individual presidents must be examined in the context of wider political and social structures and interests.[2]

Regardless of their motivations, that US presidents became increasingly interested in Northern Ireland underlines the importance of those individuals in taking advantage of the broader political changes and evolution of protagonists' objectives in Northern Ireland. Although historians can never know for certain, it is unlikely that President George W. Bush (2001–9) would have had the same level of interest in the nuances of Northern Ireland required to engage actively with the peace process. Dumbrell surmises that, while the Bush administration readily identified itself with the peace process, given its success, American interest in Northern Ireland's affairs was downgraded due to the Bush administration's world-view, concern about terrorism after 9/11, belief that any need for serious American intervention had eased, and, again after 9/11, an unwillingness to intervene without the full approval of the British government.[3] Bertie Ahern recalled that the Bush administration lacked its predecessor's faith in the peace process.[4] He believed that Bush's 'natural instinct was to say that the Sinners [Sinn Féin] were terrorists who could never be changed. That was his view and we permanently were convincing him'. Accordingly, Ahern praised Senator Kennedy's involvement during the Bush years:

> There were a few occasions when George Bush did not take the advice of his own people and took Teddy's advice. When we wanted to get some things brought to attention, we went to Teddy to try and get them.[5]

Thus, another individual's importance to American support for the peace process came to the fore. Gerry Adams echoed this view-point, noting that although 'Bush continued to engage on Ireland . . . the style was different'.[6] While thirty-minute meetings scheduled with Clinton would last for two hours and the President was 'maybe more informed than the most senior officials' in the UK and Ireland, Adams recalled that, with Bush, 'you would see him for 15 minutes; but they continued the process'.[7]

The significance of Clinton's determination to wrestle control of American policy towards Northern Ireland away from the State Department in favour of the White House cannot be underestimated. O'Dowd recalled, 'We would never have had a hope with George Bush, either of them, to have that independence from the bureaucracy'.[8] Similarly, Trina Vargo, who served as Kennedy's Foreign Policy Adviser (1987–98), argued that if the 'peace process' had commenced under the Bush administration, American support would not have been as forthcoming:

The issue would have stayed in the State Department and . . . it would have never gotten off the ground. So it mattered that Clinton was there and that Tony [Blair] was there and Nancy [Soderberg] was there and the Kennedys [Ted Kennedy and Jean Kennedy Smith] were there – everybody.[9]

Regardless of obvious caveats that should be applied to any retrospective 'other-ing' of the Bush administration in relation to Clinton's contribution to Northern Ireland, the importance of a president's willingness to act on the issue is clear.

The interest of individual presidents must be contextualised by processes and events. The success of Clinton's intervention was the result of a combination of various factors: the interest and willingness of a US president, the internationalisation of the issue, a vision and policy shared between the British and Irish governments, the IRA ceasefire, and the preparedness of parties in Northern Ireland to secure a political settlement. Nonetheless, Clinton's policy towards Northern Ireland essentially echoed that of his predecessors during the 'Troubles': the US was willing to support any peace process if invited to do so and if it could be helpful. Clinton, like his predecessors, was willing to assist, except for the fact that it was Clinton who was afforded the opportunity to do so. The factors that influenced him were also present in the presidencies of his predecessors: domestic politics, electioneering and foreign affairs. Johnson, Nixon, Ford, Carter, Reagan and Bush were each lobbied by Irish–American groups and members of Congress to intervene in the conflict. The Ford–Carter election campaign marked the issue as a factor in American presidential campaigns. The British and Irish governments, again beginning with Nixon, briefed US presidents on developments: the Irish in order to secure American pressure on the British, and the British to seek continuity in de facto American neutrality. Nixon and Ford each adhered to advice, particularly from Kissinger, to remain detached from the issue. Carter's campaign comments would have remained unfulfilled without pressure from the Four Horsemen; his policies towards Northern Ireland reflected both Democratic Party politics and an understandable desire to win presidential elections. Reagan's interest in Northern Ireland was channelled through

Clark's hopes for American involvement, while other advisers saw the opportunity to use Northern Ireland as a means to bargain with O'Neill over Nicaragua. Ultimately, Reagan's contribution, ostensibly guided by Shultz, was a positive one. Bush's inaction towards Northern Ireland, unsurprising given other foreign policy interests, demonstrated that the issue would remain under the purview of the State Department in the absence of pressure or interest from the White House.

Clinton's contribution to the 'peace process' should therefore be viewed within a broader context. Developments in Northern Ireland ensured that he was able to act positively on campaign promises, domestic lobbying for action, and the acceptance by the British and Irish governments and Northern Irish protagonists that a US president could play a key role. As with his predecessors, Clinton's involvement in Northern Ireland was sought due to the power of the US presidency to legitimise a course of action. Just as, for instance, successive British governments feared that American involvement would undermine their position, Clinton's involvement legitimised the peace process. Clinton internationalised the Northern Ireland question and satisfied the requests of Irish–Americans, members of Congress, nationalists and republicans, and the British and Irish governments. However, he was undoubtedly motivated by the three components of the US presidency. Northern Ireland was a useful issue in the 1992 New York primary and was used to cultivate Catholic votes in the 1992 and 1996 general elections. It was a foreign policy success, an important component of Clinton's political legacy and the fostering of political support for his domestic agenda.

The role of US presidents in the Northern Ireland conflict was a factor in Anglo-American relations. Johnson, Nixon and Ford prioritised Anglo-American relations over Northern Ireland, focusing on other Anglo-American objectives during the Cold War. However, other presidents were willing to focus on their own objectives related to Northern Ireland, even over what they claimed to be a 'special relationship' with Britain. Carter downgraded Anglo-American relations in favour of his approach to Northern Ireland due to the electoral benefits and demands of domestic politics. Reagan certainly hoped to avoid problematising Thatcher's situation with regard to Northern Ireland, but was willing to allow Speaker O'Neill, for the benefit of his own policy priorities, to believe that he had pressured Thatcher to work constructively towards an agreement with the Irish government. Clinton effectively downgraded Anglo-American relations vis-à-vis Northern Ireland during the 1992 presidential election and in issuing a visa for Gerry Adams. The potential rewards for peace-making and domestic politics had replaced the common cause of Cold Warriors. The obvious power of the American president, however – coupled with common Anglo-American interests in foreign affairs and, for instance, other historical, sentimental and institutional ties – meant that Clinton's decision never risked a permanent schism with the UK.

There is undoubtedly further academic study required about the US and Northern Ireland. For instance, a more detailed account of congressional activity is needed. Nonetheless, this work has offered an otherwise untold account of US presidents and the Northern Ireland conflict. It has underlined the importance of individuals within a broader context. Northern Ireland was clearly a marginal issue for successive presidents, albeit gaining increasing significance based on the demands of Irish–Americans in presidential campaigns, the relationship between the White House and Congress, relations with the British and Irish governments, and developments in the province itself. Nixon acted as an inquisitive conduit between the British and Irish governments who recognised his potential influence over the matter. Carter was convinced to fulfil his campaign slogans by Democrats in Congress. Reagan's interest was part of a series of events that led to the Anglo-Irish Agreement. Clinton was interested and successfully identified an opportunity to apply his political aptitude. Northern Ireland was a marginal priority in US foreign policy, but it ultimately became a success story for the global role of the US presidency.

## Notes

1. Miller Center, 'Interview with John Hume', University of Virginia, 29 September 2005, http://millercenter.org/oralhistory/interview/john_hume, accessed 30 September 2015.

2. For the role of the 'individual' in history, see, for instance, Philip Pomper, 'Historians and individual agency', *History and Theory*, 35:3 (October 1996), 281–308.
3. John Dumbrell, 'The new American connection: President George W. Bush and Northern Ireland', in Michael Cox, Adrian Guelke and Fiona Stephen (eds), *A Farewell to Arms? Beyond the Good Friday Agreement*, 2nd edn (Manchester: Manchester University Press, 2006), 364.
4. Miller Center, 'Interview with Bertie Ahern', University of Virginia, 8 November 2010, http://millercenter.org/oralhistory/interview/bertie_ahern, accessed 30 September 2015.
5. Ibid.
6. Miller Center, 'Interview with Gerry Adams', University of Virginia, 11 November 2010, http://millercenter.org/oralhistory/interview/gerry_adams, accessed 30 September 2015.
7. Ibid.
8. Miller Center, 'Interview with Niall O'Dowd', University of Virginia, 18 November 2010, http://millercenter.org/oralhistory/interview/niall_odowd, accessed 30 September 2015.
9. Miller Center, 'Interview with Trina Vargo', University of Virginia, 7 November 2008, http://millercenter.org/oralhistory/interview/trina_vargo, accessed 30 September 2015.

# Select Bibliography

## Diaries and memoirs

Adams, Gerry, *Hope and History: Making Peace in Ireland* (Kerry, Ireland: Brandon, 2004).

Ahern, Bertie, *The Autobiography* (London: Arrow Books, 2010).

Blair, Tony, *A Journey* (London: Hutchinson, 2010).

Brzezinski, Zbigniew, *Power and Principle: Memoirs of the National Security Adviser 1977–81* (London: Weidenfeld & Nicolson, 1983).

Campbell, Alastair and Richard Stott (eds), *The Blair Years: Extracts from the Alastair Campbell Diaries* (London: Hutchinson, 2007).

Carter, Jimmy, *White House Diary* (New York: Farrar, Straus & Giroux, 2010).

—— *Keeping Faith: Memoirs of a President* (London: Collins, 1982).

Clinton, Bill, *My Life* (London: Arrow Books, 2005).

FitzGerald, Garret, *All in a Life: An Autobiography* (London: Macmillan, 1991).

Henderson, Nicholas, *Mandarin: The Diaries of Nicholas Henderson* (London: Weidenfeld & Nicolson, 1995).

Jordan, Hamilton, *Crisis: The Last Year of the Carter Presidency* (New York: G. P. Putman's Sons, 1982).

Kissinger, Henry, *The White House Years* (London: Weidenfeld & Nicolson, 1979).

Major, John, *The Autobiography* (London: HarperCollins, 1999).

Mondale, Walter F., *The Good Fight: A Life in Liberal Politics* (New York: Scribner, 2010).

Mowlam, Mo, *Momentum: The Struggle for Peace, Politics and the People* (London: Hodder & Stoughton, 2002).

Nixon, Richard, *The Memoirs of Richard Nixon* (London: Arrow Books, 1978).

O'Neill, Tip with William Novak, *Man of the House: The Life and Political Memoirs of Speaker Tip O'Neill* (New York: Random House, 1987).

Powell, Jody, *The Other Side of the Story* (New York: William Morrow & Company, 1984).

Reagan, Ronald, *The Reagan Diaries* ed. by Douglas Brinkley (New York: HarperCollins, 2007).

Seitz, Raymond, *Over Here* (London: Weidenfeld & Nicolson, 1998).

Shultz, George P., *Turmoil and Triumph: Diplomacy, Power, and the Victory of the American Ideal* (New York: Charles Scribner's Sons, 1993).

Thatcher, Margaret, *The Downing Street Years* (London: HarperCollins, 1993).

Turner, Stansfield, *Secrecy and Democracy: The CIA in Transition* (Boston: Houghton Mifflin, 1985).

Vance, Cyrus, *Hard Choices: Critical Years in America's Foreign Policy* (New York: Simon & Schuster, 1983).

## Oral histories with the author

Mr Seán Donlon, London, 12 December 2014.
The Lord Hurd of Westwell, London, 20 June 2012.
Mr Clark S. Judge, Washington, DC, 19 November 2012.
Mr Edwin Meese, Washington, DC, 19 November 2012.
The Lord Powell of Bayswater, London, 20 June 2012.

## Archives

National Archives of Ireland
National Archives of the United Kingdom
George H. Bush Presidential Library
Jimmy Carter Presidential Library
Bill Clinton Presidential Library
Gerald R. Ford Presidential Library
Lyndon B. Johnson Presidential Library
Richard M. Nixon Presidential Library
Thomas P. O'Neill Papers, Burns Library, Boston College
Ronald Reagan Presidential Library

## Websites

The American Presidency Project (http://www.presidency.ucsb.edu/)

Clinton Digital Library (http://clinton.presidentiallibraries.us/)

Commission on Presidential Debates (http://www.debates.org/)

Conflict and Politics in Northern Ireland (CAIN Web Service), University of Ulster (http://cain.ulst.ac.uk/index.html)

Gerald R. Ford Library Digital Collections (http://www.fordlibrarymuseum.gov/)

Foreign Relations of the United States (https://history.state.gov/historical-documents)

John F. Kennedy Presidential Library Digital Collections (http://www.jfklibrary.org/Research/Search-Our-Collections/Browse-Digital-Collections.aspx)

The Margaret Thatcher Foundation (http://www.margaretthatcher.org)

Miller Center (http://millercenter.org/)

Public Papers of President Ronald W. Reagan, Ronald Reagan Presidential Library (http://www.reagan.utexas.edu/archives/speeches/publicpapers.html#.VjS7e2ThD-Y)

The Reagan Files (http://www.thereaganfiles.com/)

The White House (https://www.whitehouse.gov/)

# Index

EU representative:
Easy Access System Europe
Mustamäe tee 50, 10621 Tallinn, Estonia
Gpsr.requests@easproject.com